THE INDIAN ECONOMY

WORLD ECONOMIES

A series of concise modern economic histories of the world's most important national economies. Each book explains how a country's economy works, why it has the shape it has, and what distinct challenges it faces. Alongside discussion of familiar indicators of economic growth, the coverage extends to well-being, inequality and corruption, to provide a fresh and more rounded understanding of the wealth of nations.

PUBLISHED

Matthew Gray
THE ECONOMY OF THE GULF STATES

Matthew McCartney
THE INDIAN ECONOMY

Vera Zamagni
THE ITALIAN ECONOMY

The Indian Economy

Matthew McCartney

agenda
publishing

To Bhargavi whose research takes her behind sand-bags –
a true inspiration

First edition published in 2019 by Agenda Publishing

Agenda Publishing Limited
The Core
Bath Lane
Newcastle Helix
Newcastle upon Tyne
NE4 5TF

www.agendapub.com

ISBN 978-1-78821-008-9 (hardcover)
ISBN 978-1-78821-009-6 (paperback)

British Library Cataloguing-in-Publication Data
A catalogue record for this book is available from the British Library

Typeset by Patty Rennie
Printed and bound in the UK by TJ International

Contents

Acknowledgements

To Bhargavi who has become my very own *Time Out* London guide and thanks to all those evenings relaxing after penning insufficient words. To Ashwin of course in the hope that his frequent laments about "oh EU" return to the more familiar "Aie ooh". To Daryl and Stavi and congratulations on the recent demographic productivity. To Marko and Dubi and those productivity retarding bottles of Slivovitz.

To the principal, scholars and students of Aitchison School and to Professors Chaudhry at the Lahore School of Economics where many of the revisions to this book were made. To Imdad and Sara for generous food deliveries that slowed post-lunch afternoon progress. To Ayesha and Ali who orchestrated evening food and music soirees that had a similar impact on morning-after productivity. For Ranjana and the miracle of providing toast and marmite in both India and Pakistan.

To Andrew Lockett at Agenda who originally commissioned this book and made voluminous useful suggestions throughout. Also to the anonymous reviewer who made wonderfully detailed comments and made particular request for more mention of automobiles and West Bengal.

MATTHEW McCARTNEY
Oxford

Tables and Figures

Map of India showing major cities and rivers

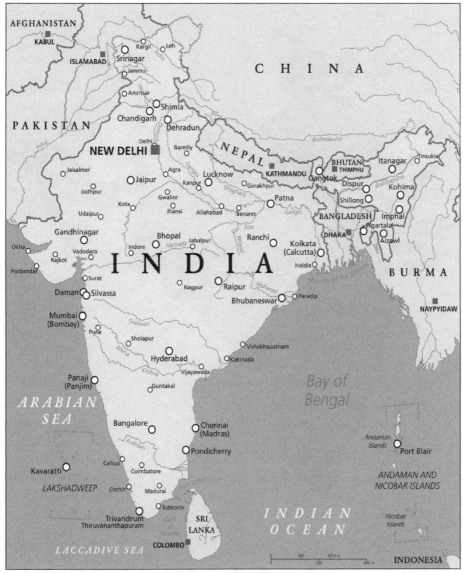

India administrative regions

Source: Pavel Cherepianyi/Alamy

1

Introducing the Indian economy, 1947–2017

It seems obvious to begin a book about contemporary India in 1947, the moment the British Indian Empire became just India (and Pakistan). But it does need justification. Some scholars have emphasized 1947 as being more about continuity. Gradual political change, such as the 1909 Morley-Minto Reforms and 1935 Government of India Act had slowly increased both the number of Indians able to vote and the participation of Indians in political office. After 1937 Indian politicians formed governments to rule at state level while the British political presence was increasingly being squeezed out of day-to-day local politics and became ever more isolated at the highest levels of government. During the Second World War the British Indian Army expanded rapidly through the recruitment of Indian soldiers and senior officers. While almost entirely British in the 1930s only around half the officers of the elite Indian Civil Service (ICS) were British by 1946. As this book shows later rapid growth of Indian owned business, particularly in consumer goods but also in banking, shipping and iron and steel had also reduced the predominant economic role of Britain in India by 1947.

But 1947 is crucial.

The year marked much more than just a change in personnel at the top of government. The British colonial government was very much in power until independence. In 1939 Britain declared war on behalf of India without local consultation and mobilized the entire country for soldiers and supplies. In 1942 the mass anti-British Quit India Movement was crushed and its leadership easily rounded up and imprisoned. Independence in 1947 marked a real change in political power relations. The year also saw a real change in the foundation of political power from a very restricted voting franchise to democracy based on a universal franchise, which rejected property, gender and education qualifications. The British had long rejected universal franchise. The final legislatures elected under British rule in 1946 had rested on an electorate of 30 million people, or less than 10 per cent of the population. Independence was also scarred by the horrors of partition which saw British rule across the sub-continent being replaced by two independent nations, India and Pakistan (then comprising West and East Pakistan, the latter becoming independent Bangladesh in 1971). Partition caused the largest mass migration (14 million people) in human history and during the few months around independence perhaps one million people lost their lives. We cannot understand the heavy expenditure on the military, the ongoing conflict between India and Pakistan, nuclear threats in recent decades and occasions of actual warfare, the problems experienced by the 172 million Muslims in India or the near absence of trade between these two countries without reference to Partition. It is often forgotten that British India was not ruled as a single entity but was an amalgam of chunks under direct British rule and 562 states that were ruled by hereditary princes and governed under close supervision of the British government. This all changed with independence. By 1950 all of the princely states except Sikkim had chosen to accede to one of the newly independent states of India or Pakistan, or else had been invaded and annexed, most notably with the invasion of the state of Hyderabad in 1948. The Portuguese colony of Goa was only integrated into India by force of arms in 1961. This book also makes the case that economic policy-making and the pattern of economic growth underwent a dramatic shift after independence. The state shifted to a much more interventionist and pro-industry economic strategy after 1951. Big private business released the Bombay Plan in 1944 acknowledging their acceptance of independence and as a manifesto for more government efforts to promote economic development. Looking at data on economic growth for the entirety of the twentieth century, Hatekar and Dongre (2005) argue that the most significant break (increase) in growth rates occurred alongside this shift in policy-making, around 1952.

THE CONSTRAINTS AND OPPORTUNITIES FOR ECONOMIC GROWTH

This chapter examines the economic constraints and opportunities that existed for the new Indian state, ruling elite and wider population in 1947. It engages with the debate about whether an objective observer in 1947 should have been optimistic or pessimistic about the likely prospects of the Indian economy after 1947. This reflects very well the longstanding British narrative that India would fail without the support of colonial rule and the promise of the nationalist movement that colonialism was a drag on the Indian economy. A related question is whether the economic growth of the Indian economy in the 70 years since independence has been better or worse than we would have reasonably anticipated in 1947. This chimes with the common practice in India on major post-independence birthdays, such as the fiftieth and sixtieth, to reflect on achievements since 1947.

Table 1.1 below shows limited but important economic and social data for 1947 and 2017. Can we draw from them any conclusions about whether India has experienced successful economic growth and development over the 70-year period?

One way of judging the "economic success" of independence would be to look at average growth rates before and after independence. Such a comparison would give us a very clear conclusion. Between 1900 and 1946, the average annual economic growth rate of British India was about 1 per cent, or zero per cent in per capita terms. Between 1951 and 2017, GDP annual growth averaged about 5 per cent, or around 3 per cent in per capita terms (Hatekar & Dongre 2005). Although the term "miracle" would be an exaggeration, this before and after comparison can be used to label independence as an "economic success". The problem with such a comparison is that economic growth was much easier to come by after 1947. The first half of the twentieth century encompassed the two world wars and the Great Depression of the 1930s when world trade and world agricultural export prices collapsed. This had serious implications for an economy such as India, which was so heavily dependent on agricultural and raw material exports. The world economy and with it, world trade boomed after 1947. So was India a success or was she just lucky?

Table 1.1　1947 and 2017: two snapshots

	1947	2017
GDP per capita	$50	$2,134
Main exports	Tea, cotton textiles, jute manufactures, hides and skins, spices and tobacco, cashew kernels, black pepper, tea, coal, mica, manganese ore, raw and tanned hides and skins, vegetable oils, raw cotton, and raw wool	Pearls, precious and semi-precious stones and jewellery, mineral fuels, oils and waxes and bituminous substances, vehicles, parts and accessories, nuclear reactors, boilers, machinery and mechanical appliances, pharmaceutical products, and organic chemicals (all goods) and software services, followed by business, travel, transportation (all services)
Life expectancy	32 years	68.8 years
Literacy	12%	74%

Source: various government reports

Another method would be to compare India with similar developing countries and to judge India a success after 1947 if in economic terms India outperformed them. Scholars have conducted such an exercise between India and variously South Korea, China, Pakistan, Ghana and other developing countries. Figure 1.1 shows that Ghana and South Korea had broadly equivalent levels of GDP per capita in 1960 and then probably a bit higher than India. Ghana experienced an economic disaster, with years of negative growth until the mid-1980s, which saw its GDP per capita drop by about 30 per cent. Steady economic growth then resumed and by 2017 GDP per capita in Ghana was around $1,800, slightly below India. Figure 1.2 by contrast shows how decades of rapid economic growth in South Korea transformed its GDP per capita from levels broadly equivalent to India in 1960 to more than ten times that in India by 2017. This relentless expansion was only briefly interrupted by short recessions in 1997 and 2008. So India can be judged a success by comparison to some developing countries (such as Ghana) and a failure relative to others (such as South Korea). Not surprisingly, many scholars remain suspicious of efforts to compare and make judgements among countries with such different histories, geographies, and cultures.

Figure 1.1 Ghana per capita GDP (2010 constant prices, US$)

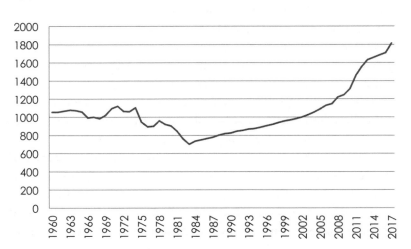

Source: World Bank Development Indicators 2018.

Figure 1.2 South Korea per capita GDP (2010 constant prices, US$)

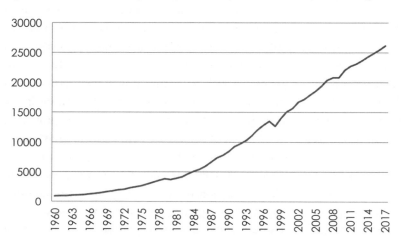

Source: World Bank Development Indicators, 2018.

A third way to judge success is to learn from the discussion of post-1948 China in Bramall (2009) who declares the "potential-outcome framework" to be the "best" way to approach such a question. The criterion for this method is straightforward. If India experienced faster economic growth (outcome) in the post-independence period than we could reasonably have expected in 1950 (potential) we can judge it to be a success. The big problem is what determines economic "potential"?

This chapter focuses on five deep determinants of economic potential that have been identified as significant, both generally in the study of economic growth and specifically for the case of post-independence India. These are the role of the state, geography, institutions, culture and economic structure. The aim of the rest of this chapter is not to evaluate the relative strength of these various deep determinants of economic growth, rather to present and discuss the relevance of five well-supported theories in relation to the experience of India, post-independence, and to then make a judgement about the success of the Indian economy between 1947 and 2017.

THE ROLE OF THE STATE

Theorists of the "developmental state" have focused on what allows a state to intervene successfully to promote economic growth. In doing so they have typically drawn upon the rapid growth stories of countries in Asia. They have argued, for example, that the state in South Korea pushed investment into industry, and within industry promoted the pace of technological advance and compelled firms to export rather than sell to the domestic market (Chang 1993; Rodrik 1995). Variously a state with a growth oriented leadership, a meritocratic bureaucracy free of political interference, and autonomy from domestic and foreign interests are three of the necessary features of a developmental state (Grabowski 1994; Leftwich 2000; Huff *et al.* 2001). We will now explore these features of a developmental state and gauge the extent to which they were present in India in 1947. Another important features of the developmental state, the ability to dominate or co-opt civil society, is discussed later.

Leadership

Economic growth is often driven by a strong leader with a growth-oriented vision. Such leaders have included Lee Kuan Yew in Singapore and President Park in South Korea. Leading the Indian nationalist movement were some of the greatest political figures of the twentieth century. When Mohandes Karamchand Gandhi (The Mahatma) was assassinated in 1948 the charisma of his leadership fell to Jawaharlal Nehru. Nehru survived at the helm of the Congress Party and as prime minister for 17 years, until his death in 1964. Nehru provided continuity in leadership: "Throughout the 1950s Nehru enjoyed unlimited, indeed, virtually unchallenged power over the Indian republic. He was the darling of India's people, the hero of his party, the unrivalled leader of his government" (Wolpert 1996: 457). One of the facets of Nehru's strong leadership was in his ability to support the growth of strong layers of leadership at every level of the party. By the 1960s such state-level leaders included Kumaraswami Kamaraj in Madras, Sanjiva Reddy in Andhra Pradesh, Siddavanahalli

7

Nijalingappa in Mysore, Atulya Ghosh in West Bengal and Sadashiv Kanoji Patil in Maharashtra. The difference between Nehru and other "developmental state" leaders like Lee Kuan Yew and Park was that Nehru did not have a single-minded commitment to economic growth. Nehru had parallel commitments to socialism, equality, balanced regional economic development, and achieving economic independence that in various ways undermined any drive to maximize economic growth. India after 1947 for example remained committed to trying to achieve a measure of regional equity in industrialization, rather than maximizing industrial growth by directing resources to those regions with easy access to raw materials or ports and consequently the best prospects for industrialization.

Meritocratic and non-political bureaucracy

A key feature of developmental states is "bureaucratic power". The ability of the state to promote long-term growth is shaped by the creation of a "powerful, professional, competent, insulated, career based bureaucracy" independent of the vagaries of short-term politics and able to formulate and implement economic goals through long-term planning. Such a bureaucracy is characterized by promotion on merit, good salaries in comparison with private sector alternatives, usually life-time tenure in office, clear sanctions for corruption, and is often dominated by a planning agency standing outside and above individual ministries – often known as a "pilot agency" (Chibber 1999; Leftwich 2000; Wu 2004; Doner *et al.* 2005). Often the developmental bureaucracy is bound together through an esprit de corps built from a common and shared training process, in France this was through recruitment from the *Grandes Ecoles* (Loriaux 1999), Korea from the Korean Military Academy (Cotton 1991) and in Japan from the Tokyo Law School (Leftwich 1994).

India in 1947 had a bureaucracy that was meritocratic and elitist but not one that was oriented to promoting economic growth. Over the nineteenth century, British colonialism had established something like a modern civil service. Landmarks in this effort included the shift to an exam-based system for recruitment in 1853 and the establishment of the

Indian Civil Service (ICS) in 1892. This effort created a highly professional service based on a competitive exam and an internal merit system that largely eradicated nepotism and patronage (Rothermund 1993; Roy 2002; Kohli 2004). The ICS was regarded by many as the best civil service of any developing country in the 1940s, and "could stand comparison with any analogous body of senior administrators anywhere in the world" (Hanson 1966: 268). By 1951 it was an elitist, meritocratic, professional institution of bureaucratic power. It was corporate and autonomous, with a shared elite or educational background and well-structured path of promotion (Herring 1999). Recruitment into the top echelons was through competitive examination (with an acceptance rate in recent years of 0.01%) and subsequent training was done on a batch basis through dedicated staff colleges first in Delhi and later in Mussourie. This shared training experience created an esprit de corps that remained with ICS members throughout their careers. The new Constitution of independent India protected civil servants from arbitrary dismissal or reduction in rank (Chakrabarty 2006). The ICS continued functioning on the British model for the first few decades after independence and provided a check on the populist or corrupt inclinations of politicians. Even now, badly governed states such as Bihar were well served (Appu 2005).

In practice the ICS was unable to translate its potential into promoting rapid economic growth. The colonial state had done much to, in the words of Leftwich (2000:126), "concentrate sufficient power, autonomy and capacity at the centre to shape, pursue and encourage the achievement of explicit development objectives". The political reality below the summit of the 1,000 officers of the ICS was considerably more fragmented. British colonialism was based on securing agreements with influential members of traditional ruling classes to secure order and only secondarily to raise tax revenue (remember those 562 princely states noted earlier) (Kohli 2004). This limited the ability of the state and elite bureaucracy to penetrate society and subordinate it to growth-oriented goals (Evans 1995). The limited penetration was reflected in the very low level of tax collection which never exceeded more than 10 per cent of GDP during the colonial era. As well as a limited downward reach the colonial state was not growth-oriented. The limited developmental inclinations of the colonial state can be seen in patterns of government expenditure. Expenditure on development functions such as irrigation (0.1% of GDP in 1879–80) and education (2% in 1900–01) were minimal (Habib 2006: 146). During the colonial era there was no industrial policy, no department charged with promoting new industrial technologies and there were few public subsidies to promote industrial growth (Kohli 2004). (Critics, however, have accused the Indian colonial government of effectively running an industrial policy to benefit manufacturing firms based in Britain by assuring them of easy access to Indian markets and to cheap Indian raw materials (Habib 2006).) Independent India inherited a civil service with limited downward reach and one attuned to maintaining law and order but not promoting rapid economic growth and industrialization.

Autonomy from domestic and foreign interests

Developmental states tended to consolidate state power and autonomy before national or foreign businesses and other groups became influential. This enabled developmental states to promote economic growth and industrialization without compromise to either domestic or foreign interests with different agendas (Leftwich 1995; Evans 1995). This section shows that the Indian state used the moment of independence to strengthen its own power over national business and other groups with mixed success and over foreign business with striking success.

The Indian state strengthened itself at independence. The independence of the princely states and the political role of the princes ended and they were amalgamated into India. Where negotiations failed, military force was used. The large states of Kashmir and Hyderabad were incorporated by military force and the communist uprising in Telengana was brutally suppressed. The strength of the state was strengthened through the Preventative Detention Act in 1950 and subsequently through the Defence of India Act, the Terrorist and Disruptive Activities Act, and the Maintenance of Internal Security Act.

The Indian state in the 1950s was relatively autonomous of certain key interest groups. Agricultural groups had interests such as high food prices that hindered rapid industrialization (Byres 1981) but this influence was muted until the mid-1960s (see Chapter 4) (Bardhan 1984). The government took steps to weaken then aggressive unions in 1947. Unions were given various legislative benefits (such as holidays and inflation-protected pay for their members) in return for facing restrictions on the right to strike and joining the newly established all-India Indian National Trade Union Congress (INTUC). The INTUC was affiliated to and dominated by the ruling Congress Party. Strikes dropped off after 1947 and labour ceased to be a threat to business. The Indian state was less successful in achieving domination over domestic business which was able to have a significant influence over early industrial policy. Through lobbying and going on an investment strike the domestic business class ensured that legislation creating "a Planning Commission and the Industries Bill – were both in their final design, fashioned to accommodate business demands as much as possible" (Chibber 2003: 146). The Planning Commission was weakened to the extent that it was not given direct control over the annual budget, allocation of investment licences, or allocation of foreign exchange control, which was retained by different ministries (*ibid*.:179). Recall the importance of such "pilot agencies" to the economic success stories of other countries as discussed above.

By contrast the autonomy of the Indian state after independence was greatly enhanced vis-à-vis foreign capital. At independence 75 per cent of foreign capital was held by private British corporations and foreign capital dominated sectors such as tea, coal, shipping and foreign trade (Kidron 1965: 4). There were some signs of change in the years leading up to 1947. British business started leaving (capital flight), especially during the 1942 Quit India campaign, and there was a corresponding Indianization of ownership and control (Mukherjee 2007: 18). The extent of this decline can easily be exaggerated. Large and well-established expatriate firms such as Bird and Heilgers, Andrew Yule & Co, Begg Sutherland & Co, Finlay James & Co and Parry retained dominance in traditional sectors and even expanded in the 1940s into new sectors such as sugar and concrete (Tripathi & Jumani 2007). The big change was only after 1947, when the fortunes of foreign capital were undermined by a determined state-directed drive for self-sufficiency. In some sectors the state entered to produce on its own account (oil, tinplate, electrical equipment, drugs and shipping) and in others by encouraging Indian-owned firms to enter or increase market share (matches, soap, vanaspati, industrial gases, rubber tyres) (Kidron 1965). Where foreign capital entered India it now only did so under joint ventures with Indian firms. Of the 324 foreign investments given consent between April 1956 and December 1964 only 5 per cent of them envisaged full foreign ownership. At the same time previously giant foreign-owned firms such as Union Carbide, Goodyear, Hindustan Lever, Philips India, and Dunlop increased the share of local ownership and firms like Tata grew by taking over British owned firms completely (Kidron 1965: 246; Tripathi & Jumani 2007).

After 1947 India was increasingly isolated from foreign capital. Between 1956 and the late-1960s foreign aid averaged only 3.2 per cent of GDP, then fell to 1 per cent of GDP in the 1970s. By the 1970s India was unusual for a developing country in that outgoing exceeded inward FDI. By the 1970s India had achieved near complete self-sufficiency in crucial sectors such as capital goods. By 1976 domestic banks accounted for more than 90 per cent of total deposits (Vanaik 1990). "The Indian state has played a decisive role in constructing the most self-reliant and insulated capitalist economy in the third world [...] There is no major capitalist country in the third world which has a more powerful state than India's or an indigenous bourgeoisie with more autonomy from foreign capital" (Vanaik 1990: 8, 11).

GEOGRAPHY

The "geography" hypothesis argues that the geographical endowments of a country are the most important influence on long-term growth and development. Those mechanisms through which geography can influence economic growth discussed here are proximity to, or ownership of, natural resources, human health, agricultural productivity and transport costs. A map showing GDP per capita of every country in the world in 1995 reveals two clear geographical correlates of economic development. Firstly, tropical countries (those nearer the equator) are poor. Of the top 30 countries ranked by 1995 PPP-adjusted GDP per capita only two are tropical (small) Hong Kong and Singapore. Secondly, nearly all landlocked countries are poor except for a few in Western and Central Europe. Those exceptions like Austria have easy access to large European markets such as Germany and are accessible to the coast through efficient land and river routes. Gallup and Sachs (1999) use data from 150 countries for the period 1960 to 1990 and find four geographic variables – the prevalence of malaria, transport costs, the proportion of the population near the coastline, and endowment of hydrocarbons per capita – explain more than two-thirds of differences in per capita incomes between countries.

India is a tropical and monsoon-based economy and offers good evidence to support the geography hypothesis. The early work on geography used single countries as data points so that India was labelled "coastal". This ignores the size and diversity of India and that large portions of the land area were located far from the coast. In India six of the eight richest states are coastal and over the 1990s slow-growing states were mostly landlocked (Kurian 2000). Nordhaus (2006) overcame the crudity of this early work by dividing the world into almost 20,000 data points, rather than just 150 country observations. This approach allowed him to use more finely-tuned geographic data (including climate, location, distance from markets or seacoasts, and soils) which are collected on a geographic basis rather than being based on political boundaries. Nordhaus confirmed that both climate and coastal location are linked to economic growth, not just in India but in other countries as well.

A particular problem for India as shown by Figure 1.3 is that much of its population lives in landlocked parts of the country. Historically the most fertile and wealthy part of India was along the Ganges in the north-centre of the country (and Indus Valley in what is now Pakistan).

This made economic sense in past centuries when wealth was created by farming. After 1947 the ability to engage in international trade to facilitate a shift from agriculture to processing raw materials and manufacturing for export became more important drivers of growth. Patterns of population density that had been a historical virtue became a constraint on modern economic growth. By comparison for historical reasons of its own, population density in China is greatest along the coastal regions of the country. This ensured that the bulk of the population were readily able to participate in the rapid growth China experienced as it opened up to global trade and investment after the late-1970s.

Figure 1.3   Population density in India (2001 census)

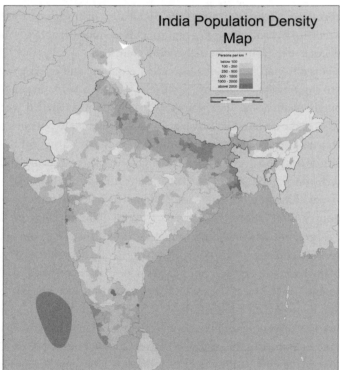

If people are in the wrong place they can either migrate to areas of better geography, or interventions such as improved transport are implemented to ensure that economic growth can spread more easily to where the population is located. As was shown in Figure 1.3 hundreds of millions of people in India remain stuck in the Gangetic heartland, in some of the poorest states such as Madhya Pradesh, Rajasthan and Bihar. There is no indication of mass migration to the more rapidly growing coastal states such as Gujarat or Maharashtra. India has long experienced relatively low levels of migration going back to at least the nineteenth century (Collins 1999) and this pattern continued into the period after independence (Cashin & Sahay 1996). A representative sample of rural Indian households found that the likelihood of male migration actually declined between 1982 and 1999 despite growing wage inequality between states and urban–rural areas (Munshi & Rosenzweig 2005). The most common reason for migration in contemporary India is that of young women moving short distances when getting married (World Bank 2009: 163). In the hyper-mobile United States, by contrast, every decade a quarter of the population changes its state of residence (*ibid.*: 46). This immobility in India has been ascribed to various reasons, including government welfare programmes, such as employment guarantee or subsidized food that are targeted to particular locations meaning that migration will end access; the compulsion to marry within one's own local caste network; kinship and caste based informal insurance networks that would be undermined by migration; and the enormous linguistic, religious and caste diversity of India (relative to for example China, where over the 1980s and 1990s perhaps 100 million people moved from inland to coastal regions). Migration in India is also associated with political constraints. The influential Shiv Sena party in Mumbai for example have a dedicated programme to keep the city a preserve of the locally born. A more recent estimate analysing railway traffic data suggests that the census estimates are a serious underestimate. The new estimate indicates an annual average flow of work-related migration of close to 9 million people, more than double the census estimates and not far off work-related migration in China (Subramanian 2018: 50).

Geography and natural resources

There is strong empirical evidence of a close relationship between natural resources and economic growth. Growth rates between the 1970s and 1990s were much lower in developing countries exporting natural resources rather than manufactured products (Isham *et al.* 2005). A particularly notorious example of a country that seemed cursed by its abundant natural resources is that of Nigeria. In the 25 years up to 2000, Nigeria earned some $250 billion in oil export revenues. During this same period per capita income declined by 15 per cent and the number of people living on less than $1 per day increased from 19 to 84 million. This discussion has little relevance for India. In 1947 only 30 per cent of its exports were agricultural goods (49% were manufactures). This pattern is very similar today with chemicals, pharmaceuticals, iron and steel, precious and semi-precious stones and other manufactured and processed goods forming the main exports. India does export oil but this is mainly imported crude oil that has been refined in India; for its own consumption India has long been import-dependent.

Human health

Cholera, for example, may impact on health (and so growth) but it is also a disease of poverty. Poor sanitation increases the prevalence of cholera. Other diseases are products of a tropical climate so can be labelled diseases of geography. The most discussed health issue related to geography is the prevalence of malaria. The symptoms of malaria are bouts of fever, headaches, fatigue, nausea, and anaemia and severe forms may result in death. Survivors of malaria may be left with long-term mental impairments such as speech disorders and epilepsy. Malaria is linked to iron deficiency anaemia which in turn may lead to reduced educational performance among school-age children or low birth weights among pregnant women. In the early 2000s there were an estimated 200–500 million cases per year globally, all almost entirely concentrated in the tropics, and around 1 million deaths per year, 90 per cent of which occurred in Sub-Saharan Africa (Sachs *et al.* 2004). Other diseases of geography (not poverty) include dengue, yellow fever, or schistosomias which are endemic in tropical regions and nearly absent elsewhere.

There is good evidence that malaria impacts economic growth. Between 1965 and 1990 countries with a substantial amount of malaria experienced slower economic growth (Gallup & Sachs 1999). In the late 1990s the average per capita income of countries with intensive malaria was $1,526 and those without $8,268 (Gallup & Sachs 2000). The mechanism was probably the diversion of resources away from investment and education towards expenditure on health care. In the early 2000s evidence from Malawi indicated that expenditure on malaria treatment was over 25 per cent of household incomes among very low-income households. For Rwanda it was estimated that nearly 20 per cent of the Ministry of Health budget went on treating malaria. In Kenya primary school students were estimated to have on average four episodes of malaria per year and to miss on average five days of school per episode (Chima *et al.* 2003).

Malaria was a potential constraint on growth in India at independence but was successfully tackled. In 1947 India suffered an estimated 75 million annual cases of malaria and 800,000 deaths (Cutler *et al.* 2010: 74–5). There were relatively successful efforts to eliminate malaria in India in the 1950s through the use of Dichlorodiphenyltrichloroethane (DDT) spraying in human dwellings and cattle sheds during the peak months for mosquitos. The number of malaria cases declined to 100,000 cases per year by 1965. Data on the causes of death indicate that the number of malaria deaths dropped by 91.2 per cent in Uttar Pradesh and 98.3 per cent in West Bengal between 1952 and 1963. Cutler *et al.* (2010) found evidence that this decline had a positive impact on the Indian economy as households were able to increase participation in the labour force as a consequence of a reduced burden of illness, which reduced medical expenses and also boosted household earnings. In 2006 there were an estimated 10.6 million cases of malaria in India and 15,000 deaths. These large numbers reflect high population density rather than the widespread prevalence of malaria. The estimated incidence of malaria in South Asia in 2006 was 5–49 per 1000 population while it was over 200 in much of Sub-Saharan Africa (WHO 2008).

Agricultural output

Tropical climates are more prone to both drought and flooding (Bloom *et al.* 1998). What rain does fall is subject to high rates of moisture loss due to high temperatures (Sachs *et al.* 2004). Heat and abundant rain mean tropical soils are low in nutrients as organic matter decomposes rapidly and are also subject to severe erosion. In tropical climates generally temperatures tend to remain high during the year and even at night so plant losses of net photosynthesis (energy) are high. Overall tropical agriculture suffers a productivity penalty of between 30–50 per cent compared to temperate zone agriculture (Gallup & Sachs 1999). Cotton, for example, is grown in both temperate and tropical environments but yields are much lower in the tropical regions (Bloom *et al.* 1998).

India in 1947 inherited a stagnant agricultural sector. The annual growth rate of agricultural output never exceeded 1 per cent in any decade between 1900 and 1950. With population growth this implied falling output per person over 50 years. To sustain even this meagre growth required using ever more land to compensate for the steady decline in the already low yields (productivity) of land in the key crops of rice and wheat (Kurosaki 1999: 161, 164). The vulnerability of the population was demonstrated by the massive Bengal Famine in 1942–3 in which 3–4 million people died. There is little evidence, however, that the productivity of agriculture in 1947 was mainly determined by geography. In India there was a long history of public policy successfully overcoming geographical constraints on agriculture. Between 1885 and 1947 canal irrigated area in the previously barren wastelands of the Punjab in north-west India increased from under 3 million to 14 million acres. This led to rapid increases in the cultivated area, output, marketed output and both domestic and international trade. The region was transformed into a hub of international trade in wheat, cotton and oilseed (Ali 2003). The latent potential of agriculture in India in 1947 can also be seen in the relative success of the Green

Revolution in the mid-1960s. Here the Indian government used subsidies and price guarantees to push farmers (again mainly in the north-west of India) to increase their use of newly developed high yield variety (HYV) seeds, irrigated water, chemical fertilisers and pesticides. The production of rice and wheat, for so long stagnant, grew steadily after independence, between 2 and 4 per cent each year and with the Green Revolution the output of rice alone increased annually by nearly 6 per cent in the 1960s (Kurosaki 1999: 164).

Location and transport costs

Transport costs impose additional costs on exporters. Transport costs are positively related to the distance of the country from core areas of the world economy and to the accessibility of the country to sea-based trade. Half of the world's trade takes place among countries located within 3,000 km radius of each other (Gallup & Sachs 1999). Transport costs are particularly important in those sectors that grow via importing inputs for domestic assembly and eventual re-export, such as in textiles and electronics. Mauritius, Hong Kong, Singapore and Taiwan experienced sustained economic growth by escaping their tropical geographical burden through export-led growth in textiles and electronics (Woods 2004). As this chapter will show later, India made good progress in shifting towards manufacturing from the 1920s through to the 1960s but progress stalled thereafter.

There are significant market failures in the construction of transport links, especially those that cross international borders. Improving the railway line in landlocked Uganda, for example, would have little effect unless there was similar improvement of the rail line as it passes through Kenya on the way to the port in Mombasa. But why should Kenya take into consideration those external benefits to its investment for Uganda? (Naude 2007). This is where India had an advantage in being one country. Between 1860 and 1920 the number of railway track miles increased from 838 to 37,029 (Hurd 1975; Habib 2006: 42). In 1947 India already had an integrated national transport system that linked up major metropolitan areas and interior regions to coastal ports. The motivation of railway building was not British benevolence but to ensure (after 1857) that troops could move quickly from ports to the interior, between urban areas and to the borders with Afghanistan to meet a supposed Russian threat. Overcoming the problems of geography was an unintended consequence. The railway system was nationalized after independence and the government made great efforts to strengthen its cohesion as a national system, for example standardizing the railway gauge across the whole country.

In the 1860s the prices of grains in some districts were eight to ten times higher than prices in other districts. In India, railway construction prompted falls in transportation costs of about 80 per cent per mile, which made trade in bulk goods possible. By 1910 almost 30 per cent of the wheat crop and 14 per cent of the rice crop was transported at distance by rail (Hurd 1975). Railways helped reduce variations in prices between regions and contributed to the growth of a national market in agricultural produce (Mukherjee 1980; Studer 2008; Donaldson 2010). The 1,200-mile journey across north India from Calcutta to Ahmedabad originally could take up to three months, mainly by river. After the introduction of the railways the journey could be done over several days (Derbyshire 1987). Better physical transport was not the only factor in creating a national market. Having established their military dominance by c.1800 the British then slowly united India politically and economically. By 1858 the subcontinent was politically unified under a single and uncontested central power, had a universal legal system, a single weight system, a single currency, a single official language and was free of any internal customs barriers (Studer 2008).

INSTITUTIONS

Douglas North who won the Nobel Prize in economics for his work on institutions described institutions as "the humanly devised constraints that structure human interaction. Institutions can be formal (e.g., rules, laws, constitutions) or informal (e.g., norms of behaviour, conventions, self-imposed codes of conduct). Together, they define the incentive structure of societies and specifically economies" (1994: 359). The Indian constitution for example sets formal rules about the circumstances under which a prime minister is elected to office and the laws that parliament cannot change, such as the fundamental rights to private property and liberty. The most widely studied institution is an aspect of the legal system, that of property rights. Property rights can exist over land or buildings (a title deed), over a business (share certificates), over images and trademarks (copyrights) or even over ideas and production processes (patents). North and others have argued that there are four principal mechanisms through which property rights impact on economic growth. Firstly, reducing the costs of undertaking an exchange so making markets work more cheaply and efficiently. These are "transaction costs" and include comparing prices between competing sellers, checking the quality of the good being sold and the time taken to get a refund in case the good purchased is defective. The exchange is protected by the legal system so that a buyer cannot refuse to pay once the exchange has been completed. Secondly, to undertake long-term investment in physical capital a business or farm needs equivalent long-term secure ownership of the factory or land, that it won't be grabbed by a well-connected politician or that profit taxes won't be raised by the government to "confiscate" higher profits if the investment is successful. To undertake the research and development (R & D) costs that can run into hundreds of millions of pounds to develop a new drug or treatment, a pharmaceutical company will need assurance that their drug will be protected by copyrights and not duplicated by other firms. Without well protected property rights resources may be allocated to short-term and less productive investments such as money-lending and property speculation that can be easily shifted and hidden or sent overseas in the form of "capital flight". Empirical work has found that the risk of investing in Sub-Saharan Africa due to weak property rights has led to 40 per cent of the region's wealth being held overseas (Collier 2007). Thirdly, by defining and registering property rights it will be easier to reallocate those property rights over time to the most productive user through a market mechanism. A registry of household ownership, for example, will make it easier to locate owners, undertake a purchase and re-register the new owner. Fourthly, when a large proportion of inputs (e.g. fertiliser, seeds, irrigation water) and outputs (wheat, rice) are sold through the market, assets and resources must be used productively/efficiently to make a sufficient profit otherwise they will be lost or sold to more efficient users (Khan 2010). Together these impacts on investment, reallocation and productivity gains support the view of North and others that institutions, and specifically property rights, are *the* "underlying determinant of the long-run performance of economies" (North 1990: 107), consequently, "the heart of development policy must be the creation of policies that will create and enforce efficient property rights" (North 1995: 25).

These findings, however, have been contested. The big historical puzzle is China. Well-protected private property rights in the fourteenth century did not lead to modern economic growth and industrialization; and the absence of well-protected private property rights after 1976 has not hindered decades of rapid economic growth.

The history of British rule in India has been read as a series of ultimately failed interventions to create property rights to promote productive agriculture while at the same time attempting to maintain stability. These two objectives (investment and stability) were ultimately incompatible and led to the creation of conflicting sets of rights, more contradictory than extractive or settler. The Permanent Settlement of 1793 gave landlords (known as *zamindars*) rights to collect tax revenue for the British government from lands under their control. This right was held in perpetuity and could be sold or inherited but required a fixed monthly payment to the state (Khan 2010). One intention of this reform was to boost agricultural growth by strengthening property rights. This effort led to massive changes in landownership as landlords lost land when defaulting to creditors or after failing to pay taxes to the British state. By 1880 in the Punjab, for example, considerable amounts of land were being taken over by moneylenders in lieu of mortgage defaults. This undermined the landowning groups that the British had traditionally relied on for political support, tax revenue, and military recruitment. In consequence the British intervened through law to prevent this transfer of land. The 1900 Punjab Alienation of Land Act forbade the passing of land from agricultural to non-agricultural castes (Ali 2003). After the 1857 rebellion the colonial state tried to avert further threat to its rule by passing legislation to protect tenants and strengthen their rights to avoid future discontent and instability. Such legislation included the Rent Act of 1859 and Tenancy Act of 1885. These acts strengthened the rights of the small landlords who were the tenants of the larger *zamindars* (Khan 2010). Ultimately, the British "attempted through the Permanent Settlement of 1793, however unsuccessfully, to create property rights that it hoped would create taxpaying productive gentry farmers. The experiment failed not because it was a cynical attempt to maximize extraction but because the colonial power did not want to risk the political costs of forcing adjustment" (Khan 2010: 10). In 1947 India was faced with the legacy of this mass of intervention and legislation which left India with a bewildering, complex and overlapping variety of property rights. Post-1947 a single piece of property could be simultaneously subject to claims based on formal ownership, informal purchase, tenancy, inheritance, sub-letting, and actual occupancy. This complex set of rights turned land acquisition by business or farmers into a nightmarish political task after 1947 (Sarkar 2007; Mohanty 2007). This hindered the transition of a small-scale agricultural economy to one based on the amalgamation of plots for large-scale mechanized agriculture and the transfer of land from agriculture to urban-industrialization (Khan 2010).

To overcome problems of land transfer governments have typically utilized compulsory acquisition laws. India established powers of compulsory acquisition in the Land Acquisition Act of 1894. This act enables the state to make compulsory purchases of private assets for public purposes with compensation linked to market prices. This law was reincarnated as the 2005 Special Economic Zone (SEZ) Act that set a framework for state governments to acquire land for industrial estates. By 2008 404 SEZs had been approved covering more than 50,000 acres. Many SEZs were held up by conflict regarding land reacquisition through direct political protest and lengthy legal cases. These included the Salim Group's petrochemical SEZ in Nandigram, West Bengal, the Reliance Group multipurpose SEZ near Mumbai, and the $12 billion POSCO steel SEZ in Orissa (Levien 2011).

In response to these protests the central government tried to reform the legal framework regarding land acquisition. The result was the Land Acquisition and Resettlement Bill of 2013 which finally replaced the 1894 law. In an effort to reduce conflict related to land acquisition the Bill promised significant increases in compensation for those affected. Such compensation could include offering land and housing in return for the acquired land. The proposed law also placed several restrictions on state acquisition of fertile agricultural land and tightened the definition of public purpose to include infrastructure, irrigation, and industry but to exclude luxury housing which had previously been included. Procedural safeguards were introduced including social impact assessment, adequate notification and gaining the consent of at least 80 per cent of the affected community. The Bill was finally passed into law in 2014. The new government under Prime Minister Modi later that year made several efforts to waterdown the law to ease supposed burdens on business. These efforts have so far stalled owing to Modi's lack of control over the Rajya Sabha (the second chamber of the national parliament) (Ghatak & Ghosh 2011; D'Costa & Chakraborty 2017).

CULTURE

Before examining the impact of culture, we need to define and measure it. Culture according to one definition is "those customary beliefs and values that ethnic, religious, and social groups transmit fairly unchanged from generation to generation" (Guiso *et al.* 2006: 23). This definition is limited by focusing only on prior beliefs and values, and ignores those that are acquired later in life. A second problem is the notion that values, religious or otherwise remain unchanged. The main religions have evolved over centuries and can be interpreted in various contradictory ways that are either good or bad for economic development. Hinduism, which some 80 per cent of India's population follow in some form, contains many strands that have been extracted and combined in a variety of ways over the centuries to rationalize economic behaviours, ranging from profit-seeking to renouncing wealth in favour of spiritual motivations. Hinduism both values those who renounce worldly wealth, but also prominent is Lakshmi, the Goddess of wealth and prosperity (Morris 1967). Not surprisingly then Chang (2007) argues that no culture or religion is uniquely good or bad for economic development. The real question then is why a religion such as Islam (followed by about 13 per cent of India's population) has been utilized at certain periods in its history to promote economic growth by, for example, encouraging learning from non-Muslims and at other times to freeze society and so avoid the contaminating effects of innovation and free debate.

Any definition of culture that emphasizes beliefs that are acquired is inevitably going to be difficult to disentangle from the effects of economic growth. What can easily be regarded as a cultural norm of laziness, argues Chang, is often a product of the wider economic environment. Many people in developing countries are underemployed in inherently low-productivity occupations such as selling commodities by the side of the road (See Chapter 6). "Modern" attitudes to work develop as a result of the rise of modern corporate organizations, the driving of work by the pace of machines and the close scientific measurement of output and productivity. For Marx, culture would change in response to such underlying economic changes. A Marxist may argue, for example, that the rise of small-scale individualistic competitive capitalism out of feudal agriculture would create the conditions and need for a religion like Protestantism (about 2.5% of India's population are various denominations of Christianity) which stresses the importance of the individual and would provide a divinely inspired cultural support for the emerging economic order.

Cultural traits that have been argued to be of relevance to promoting economic growth have included ethnicity, trust and entrepreneurship (Weil 2005: Chp 14) and are here examined in relation to India.

Ethnicity

To repeat an over-used expression. India is very diverse. According to the 2001 Indian census, the population was then just over 1 billion people; by religion 80 per cent of these were Hindu, 13.4 per cent Muslim, about 2.5 per cent Christian, 2 per cent Sikh and small proportions of many other religions, including Buddhists and Jains. Hinduism (and in practice the other religions) are divided by caste, at the bottom of which remains the 166 million members of the Scheduled Castes (SCs) (16%) and outside the fold of traditional Hinduism the 84 million members of the Scheduled Tribes (STs) (6%) who are divided into 60 major groups and hundreds of smaller groups. The largest language group is Hindi which had more than 420 million first tongue speakers (41%), many other languages had more than 50 million speakers including Bengali (8%), Telugu (7%), Marathi (7%), Tamil (6%) and Urdu (5%), and by some estimates there are almost 800 other languages. India is a federal political system. The geographical spread of these language groups, as discussed later in this section, has often provided the basis for political mobilization and the resulting creation of new states after 1947. The chief minister of a state has significant constitutional powers that many have argued have grown in salience over time. The two biggest states in 2001 were Uttar Pradesh (166 million people) and Maharashtra (100 million) but others had a population of between 50–80 million people including Gujarat, Karnataka, Madhya Pradesh, Tamil Nadu, Bihar, West Bengal and Rajasthan.

How does this diversity matter for economic development?

A well-established and widely cited finding is that the degree of ethnic-linguistic diversity has a negative relationship with the rate of economic growth. The mechanism works through a more diverse society being less able to agree upon and mobilize taxes to pay for public goods that benefit other ethnic and linguistic groups. Representatives of ethnic-language interest groups are more likely to value only the benefits of a public good that accrue to their own group and not the benefits for other groups. Whichever group is temporarily in power has an incentive to choose to redistribute existing wealth to its own supporters even at the cost of economic growth for the whole economy. Measures of ethnic and linguistic diversity in Sub-Saharan Africa are correlated with measures of poor policy, such as inadequate infrastructure, basic education and financial development (Easterly & Levine 1997). The provision of certain goods such as education, roads and sewers are negatively related to measures of ethnic fragmentation (and racism) in US cities (Alesina *et al.* 1999).

The problem of ethnic-linguistic divisions is likely to become particularly significant when the size of one group gets so large relative to the others that some groups risk permanent democratic exclusion. Bates (2000) finds evidence that as the largest ethnic group reaches 50 per cent or more then other groups confront the possibility of permanent political exclusion. This situation has been perceived to exist in Malaysia, Belgium, Northern Ireland, Canada, Zimbabwe and Rwanda and here majority voting has been perceived by minorities to lead to their permanent exclusion and they have responded with protest that has in some become violent. Most countries are characterized instead by many fragmented cultural groups. In the case of fragmentation ethnic-linguistic politics will likely have only a more muted effect. In a fragmented society the political system may continue to try and build a minimum winning coalition which captures all the benefits of public expenditure for its own members. No such coalition can persist as any group which assembles 51+ per cent support can always be supplanted by another alliance, so majorities keep forming and breaking up. This debate has particular contemporary relevance for India. Many have accused the post-2014 Modi government in India of seeking to unite Hindus against the minority Muslims in a religious-political majoritarianism. The consequences, in accordance with this empirical literature, could be long-term heighted conflict. Others are more optimistic and suggest the profound ethnic, linguistic, religious and regional differences of India will militate against the formation of any permanent majority and lead to new alliances being continually formed in the quest for political power. The winning party (the BJP under Modi) in 2014 only won 31 per cent of the vote on a 66 per cent turnout, suggesting India is a long way from being locked into some form of exclusionary majoritarianism.

These empirical studies do not consider how political parties interact with social diversity. A political party may become the voice of a particular ethnic and religious group and mobilize on the basis of its supposed grievance. This can intensify the link between diversity and conflict. In India at independence the main political party, the Indian National Congress performed a very different role. The Congress was formed in 1885 and first existed as a loyalist body who gently petitioned the colonial government for political and administrative reforms. In the 1920s, the Congress, now under the leadership of Gandhi, became a mass movement against colonial rule, contested elections, and by 1935 was the ruling party in many states of India. The elite mobilization of the late nineteenth century had given way to mass mobilization that included the peasantry, the middle classes and newly emerging industrialists, by the 1940s also the trade unions, and by the 1960s farmer organizations.

What is crucial for the impact of diversity on conflict and governance is how these new groups enter politics and whether they do so identifying with established political norms and organizations. In a more institutionalized political system there are mechanisms that either slow down the entry of new groups into politics, or through a process of political socialization induce changes in the attitudes and behaviour of the political leaders of the new groups. In a well-institutionalized political system the most important positions of leadership can normally only be achieved by those who have served an apprenticeship in less important positions. The institutions impose political socialization as the price of political participation and provide a basis for stability (Huntingdon 1968). By the time of independence Congress had been a mass organization for more than 20 years. The provincial party was organized into 21 units in conformity with major linguistic boundaries. There was a concerted effort to decentralize the party and build upwards from local-level branches. Members of Parliament were mainly those that had risen up through the party ranks and who had been involved with the independence movement for decades. When elections to the Constituent Assembly occurred in July 1946 the leaders of the Congress took care to broaden minority representation to include Muslims, Sikhs, Parsis, Anglo-Indians, Indian Christians, STs and SCs, and women. In three years of constitutional deliberations (1947–9) the Congress-led Constituent Assembly leadership generally made decisions by first seeking consensus within itself and then seeking to bring rank and file into line through persuasion. "When disagreements over constitutional provisions occurred, either within the leadership or within party rank and file, notably democratic procedures – persuasion, accommodation, consensus, and ultimately submission to party vote – were used to create compromise." (Tudor 2013: 165). These democratic principles were forged over pre-independence decades by an urban, educated middle-class elite needing to co-opt other groups to build and sustain a prolonged and ultimately successful broad-based anti-colonial movement.

The broad alliance constructed before independence continued after 1947 and Congress continued to be an inclusive party that, as Brown writes

> functioned as an integrating mechanism by virtue of its ideological openness, welcoming many shades of opinions within its ranks to the extent that it was not only the dominant party within the polity but almost within itself an ideological party system [...] Congress, by its social openness and flexibility at state level, put down roots in every part of India, welcoming into its ranks virtually all those with a stake in public life who saw it as a vehicle for influence and power. Its chameleon-like adaptability to local social configurations of power was reflected and confirmed by its choice of candidates to fight elections for particular seats (Brown 2003: 221).

In the general literature, language was found to be a crucial marker of diversity that undermined economic performance. How independent India managed to cope with the politics of language shows how the Congress system was able to diffuse the potentially negative consequences of ethnic-linguistic diversity. At independence the inherited state boundaries of India were based on the historical vagaries of how Britain had colonized India, absorbed new geographical chunks into the empire and created new or changed old states in doing so. After the 1857 uprising, for example, states with rulers that had backed the colonial government were allowed to expand at the expense of those who had participated in the rebellion. At independence this left large minority language groups stranded in different states. Language in India has a crucial material aspect (Chandra *et al.* 2008: Chp 8). Proficiency in a language officially recognized by a state government was needed for those aspiring to public employment. This was crucial as some two-thirds of formal sector workers were employed by the state. Proficiency was also needed for entry into higher education. By the early-1960s, language had become a means by which large numbers were (indirectly) being excluded from the benefits of development and motivated a growing opposition movement. In 1960 Assamese was adopted as the official language of Assam. This was intended to limit access to state educational and employment opportunities for the non-Assamese. The sole official language of Bihar was Hindi while according to the 1961 census only 44.3 per cent of the population declared it as their mother tongue. The central state sought to avoid direct conflict and approached the problem with clear guidelines, based on arbitration and mediation with local leaders. The informal mechanisms of the Congress party organization and its decentralized reach proved crucial in this process. The party centre promoted and supported strong state leaders to facilitate mutual compromise on language issues. In 1955 the States Reorganisation Committee published its report and the southern states were reorganized in a manner that brought their boundaries into closer conformity with traditional linguistic regions. Somewhat later in 1960 Bombay province was split into Maharashtra and Gujarat. In 1966 Punjab was reorganized into two states, one primarily Sikh (the new Punjab) and the other Hindu (Haryana). The political heat was removed from the language movement. A number of parties agitating around the Tamil language in the south, for example, were dissolved and their leadership incorporated into the Congress party at senior levels (Frankel 1969:

454). Congress then retained political power in all these new states in the 1962 elections.

Things did change after the mid-1960s. After 1967 there was a decline in the capacity to govern, the evidence for which was manifest in a weakened ability to promote development and accommodate diverse interests (Kohli 1990). This was marked by a rise in activism outside formal political channels and the disintegration of political institutions, especially the Congress. Political leaders lost the capacity to influence those below them in the social hierarchy. The ultimate cause of this crisis of governance, argues Kohli, was a series of political changes. The spread of democratic values, he argues, hastened the decline of authority and deinstitutionalized the role of national leaders. Modern political mobilization among low-caste groups began with the anti-Brahmin Self Respect Movement in the south of India in the 1920s, and by the 1990s, low-caste groups had become central parts of political mobilization, although by then often outside the Congress in their own political parties (Weiner 2001). The rise in the political assertion and rise to political power of the lower castes has been called the "Silent Revolution" (Jaffrelot 2003). New groups have been mobilized by political entrepreneurs for electoral purposes in order to gain access to state resources. Weak political institutions encouraged undisciplined political competition and politicized all types of social division including caste and class ethnicity (Kohli 1990: ix).

Trust

Much economic activity takes place with reference to the future. Goods and services or credit may be provided in exchange for future payment secured through an employment or lending contract. Investment decisions rely on assurances by governments that they will not raise taxes to confiscate profits should the investment prove successful. Such activities are accomplished at lower cost in an environment of trust. When individuals can rely on trust they do not need to utilize the services of lawyers to write expensive contracts nor does the state need to utilize so many resources in enforcing contracts through the police and judicial system (Knack & Keefer 1997). It is hard to ascribe trust to culture. Trust could be an inherited cultural variable, or a characteristic acquired through repeated interaction, or people may simply behave as if they are trustworthy because they fear legal or personal retaliation. One influential argument is that group membership may build trust by facilitating repeated interaction and familiarity between individuals. One may be less likely to cheat someone in business if one is going to be meeting at the same cricket club next week. This is what has been called "social capital" (Putnam 1993). But, it may also be that more trusting and cooperative individuals are more inclined to join clubs (Knack & Keefer 1997).

There is a debate both about how trust (or social capital) benefits members or insiders and to what extent and in what way it impacts on outsiders. Trust between some may imply social exclusion for others (Harriss & Renzio 1997). In India interacting with fellow caste members, through dining, kinship networks and in the workplace can provide high observability of behaviour. The involvement and gossip of relatives ensures that the group is well informed about any anti-social behaviour such as cheating on contracts. This interaction stimulates relations of trust. Caste groups can enforce informal contracts among members without resort to the legal system and can provide group-level insurance based on a network of reciprocal obligations. Young members can acquire information by learning skills and acquiring networks of contacts from more senior caste fellows.

A widespread feature of the Indian economy from pre-independence and beyond is that of the family business rooted in a culture based on strong family ties. In 2015 15 of the top 20 business houses in India were family owned. A family business may be better able to trade over long distances through well-placed family members when communications and contract enforcement are hard. As with the example of caste above, a family business may facilitate the exchange of skills and sharing of contacts among members through relations of trust. Families may be better placed to pool capital in countries where there are poorly functioning banking systems. An important advantage of a family firm is that fewer resources need to be spent on monitoring the effort of labour. Family-based firms may offer a longer-term perspective to management due to a wish to protect and pass on an inheritance. Family firms may also have wider kinship networks that have been established by sending family members into politics and the civil service. Such connections can provide firms with preferential access to public resources such as subsidized credit and government policy-makers (Bertrand & Schoar 2006). A good example from India of how family facilitated the rise of business are Marwari firms in the late nineteenth century. The Marwaris are an ethno-linguistic group that originated from a small region in north-west India and spread throughout the north, east and central regions of India. A young Marwari starting in business would find through community links free hostels where he could stay, a certification of his creditworthiness from a guaranteed broker if he wished to start trading in textiles, and social centres where he could pick up and transmit commercial gossip. The migration across India during the late nineteenth century of 300,000 Marwari businessmen and their commercial success is testament to the influence of community-based networks of trust (Timberg 1971).

The preponderance of family in business can also have negative consequences. Business decisions may be based on the constraints of family rather than being an optimal response to market incentives. Profit for example may be sacrificed to preserve other values such as appointing a relative rather than the best qualified manager. Firm expansion may then be restricted by the number of family-managers available. Non-managerial employees may find opportunities for promotion are blocked, encouraging less effort, with the most dynamic seeking promotion elsewhere. Poorly performing family members are less likely to be sacked (Bertrand & Schoar 2006). The World Values Survey contains questions about the importance of family life, respect to parents, duty or independence of parents, and whether independence or obedience are the most important qualities in children. Data from 1980 to 2000 shows that countries where family is regarded as more important have lower levels of per capita GDP, smaller firms, and fewer publicly traded firms (Bertrand & Schoar 2006).

Overall the trust engendered by family businesses was probably an advantage to India in 1947 when it was still a predominantly agrarian economy in the early stages of industrialization. Then family business facilitated the establishment and subsequent growth of new industrial firms. It was only later when the continued expansion and modernization of such businesses required professional expertise in management, the use of modern technology, and the need to build up trading networks beyond the family that family dominance of business became a hindrance on economic growth. Even in 1947 there was a dark side to such closed networks of trust. Caste membership can hinder relations of trust between caste groups and it can facilitate exploitation as individuals may be deprived of the option to leave the hereditary occupation of a caste for a more lucrative occupation. Higher caste groups can use their own caste membership to prevent the entry of lower castes into those more lucrative occupations. In fieldwork Harriss-White (2003) finds that trade associations are often derived from caste associations. Those controlling the local commanding heights of the economy (jewellery, gold, rice, wholesale food, silk, lorries, buses, cinema) utilize such caste-trade associations in setting wages, fixing the length of the working day, the extent and frequency of holidays, the terms of employment for women and children, and managing labour disputes; they also fix rates in markets for raw materials, credit, even state-allocated licences, the payment of bribes to government officials, and allocate spatial trading monopolies between members. Much of this social capital is used to control, exploit and exclude outsiders.

Entrepreneurship

Lal argues India has prominent cultural prohibitions against entrepreneurship, "because of the ancient animus against trade and commerce and longstanding Brahminical attitudes against the market" (1998: 35). Earlier, Max Weber (1864–1920) had argued that Hinduism undermined economic progress in India through the restrictions imposed by the rigid social institution of caste (Morris 1967). Weber argued that Hinduism gave each caste group a specific role, Brahmins religious functions, Kshatriyas fighting and governing, Vaisyas commerce and Sudras agriculture and production. Hinduism, argued Weber, prevented tasks being performed by those best able to undertake them. The hierarchy of caste also favours those (Brahmins and Kshatriya) whose functions are not concerned with direct production activities or the accumulation of wealth. This means that social aspiration may then be about distancing oneself from trade, industry and entrepreneurship. The emphasis on the importance of reincarnation, karma and dharma may have placed an emphasis on passive acceptance rather than improving the human condition through innovation or hard work. Despite the religious diversity of India, Weber argued that Hinduism had spread its influence into other religions: Islam, Christianity and Sikhism all, for example, preserved the caste system (Morris 1967).

There is little evidence that caste hindered entrepreneurship, which was more obviously influenced by economic incentives. Although India's population had doubled to 400 million over the 50 years to 1947, this did not imply that entrepreneurs faced a large domestic market and so the lure of large profits. Low per capita incomes (around $50 per person) and expensive transport costs meant the level of effective market demand was actually very low (Morris 1979). Costs of production were also much higher than the low wages of Indian workers in 1947 may have suggested. All machinery had to be imported at high cost and skilled labour such as technical staff was scarce and again often had to be imported on high expatriate salaries. Before c.1900 Indian entrepreneurs were constrained by the lack of credit to confine themselves to small-scale investment over short gestation periods that offered quick returns. The establishment of stock exchanges in 1875 in Bombay (the first in an Asian country) and Calcutta in 1908 made little impact. Although the first European bank was launched in 1770, by 1900 there were still only four private banks in the entire country. These banks focused mainly on facilitating trade and exchange and were actually prohibited from granting any loan for a period longer than three months (Tripathi & Jumani 2007). The colonial state had no project to change these constraints through mass education, investment in infrastructure (other than railways and some regional irrigation networks) and promoting the banking system to provide cheap credit for business (Morris 1979).

When economic incentives improved, Indian entrepreneurship responded. The spread of the railway system after the mid-nineteenth century reduced trade costs and helped create all-India markets in grain, oilseeds, sugar and cotton. This led farmers to respond by changing patterns of regional cropping specialization. Cotton cultivation came to an end in the damp regions of Uttar Pradesh and central, northern and eastern Oudh, and became concentrated in the Middle Doab where yields were highest and where the plant could be sown early as part of the double cropping mix. The United Provinces saw a 30–50 per cent increase in sugarcane acreage between 1860 and 1895 and sold the output to markets across India (Derbyshire 1987: 529). Farmers and traders facilitated the emergence of international trade in agricultural commodities and, after 1876, 10 per cent of the wheat crop was being exported to Europe (Derbyshire 1987). Indian entrepreneurial responses were also evident in the modern sector. The first jute and cotton mills were started by Indians in the 1850s. By 1914 the Indian cotton textile industry was the fourth largest in the world and almost entirely Indian-financed and managed (Morris 1967). The most outstanding example of the entrepreneurial dynamic present among indigenous business groups was Jamsetji Tata (1842–1905). Tata transformed his family firm from trading to manufacturing and showed a willingness to take risks to invest in new technology. He opened a series of mills in the 1870s and 1880s using new training and new technology. Tata was the first to introduce ring spindles (then the pioneering cotton textile technology) into his mills and did so before British firms in Manchester (Misra 2000). In 1906 the Tatas failed to get finance from London to support a shift into steel production and appealed instead to Indians. The money was raised in a few weeks and the Tata Iron and Steel Company (TISCO) was successfully registered in 1907 as the first steel firm in India (Tripathi & Jumani 2007). TISCO managed to expand output, despite shrinking domestic demand during the Depression of the

1930s, to 1 million tonnes in 1939, by which time it controlled 75 per cent of the domestic market (Rothermund 1993). TISCO did pioneering laboratory research from the late-1930s and developed new products such as machine tools, service helmets, parachute harnesses, razor blades and corosion resistant extra strong steel which provided all-metal coaches for Indian railways (Tripathi & Jumani 2007). The transition from traditional mercantile to modern industrial activities was emulated by other Indian entrepreneurs such as the Birla family, Ramkrishna Dalmia, Sahu Jain, Shri Ram and J. K. Kasturbhai (Misra 2000).

ECONOMIC STRUCTURE

Economists known as "structuralists" argue that the structural features of the economy (the relative shares in GDP of agriculture, manufacturing and services) do not just passively change with economic growth over time but are also and more importantly a key driver of economic growth. The key result is that a more industrialized economy has greater potential for long-term economic growth than a predominantly agrarian economy. Structuralists identify two important external constraints on developing countries to highlight the importance of manufacturing. The first constraint works through the terms of trade. The Argentine economist Raúl Prebisch, in a hugely influential article in 1950, divided the world into a core (exporters of manufactures) and periphery (exporters of agricultural goods). He argued that as manufacturing productivity increased, domestic wages are likely to be rigid in core countries as they are protected by tight labour markets and trade unions, which would prevent export prices falling. Productivity gains would benefit core countries in the form of higher wages and profits. In periphery countries productivity gains would reduce costs of production. In an environment of competitive markets, a surplus of labour and flexible wages, this would lead to lower export prices, which would again benefit core countries. The dynamic is that all the gains from trade are transferred to consumers and producers in core countries.

The second key constraint, argued Prebisch, operated through the balance of payments. Due to the low income elasticity of demand for agricultural goods, periphery countries are likely to experience a slow growth of demand and export revenue for primary export products over time. Technical innovations (such as fibre optics replacing copper in telephone communication or artificial rubber replacing natural rubber) may even generate absolute declines in the demand for some raw materials. At the same time, periphery countries tend to be heavily dependent on imports of capital goods and inputs for industry and modern inputs such as fertiliser and machinery for agriculture. Periphery countries also tend to import luxury-branded consumer goods for which there is a high income elasticity of demand. Together these factors will lead to long-term balance of payments problems for periphery countries, leading to debt and slow growth. Recent evidence shows that for much of the modern period the terms of trade of primary commodities relative to manufactured goods has been declining (Sapsford & Balasubramanyam 1999), that primary commodity prices are more volatile, and economic growth is lower for countries relying on commodity exports, a phenomenon known as the "resource curse" (Ross 1999; Collier 2007).

The Cambridge economist Nicholas Kaldor (1967) formalized many of the arguments and empirical evidence of the structuralists to make an influential case for the "superiority of manufacturing". The relationship between the rate of growth of manufacturing and that of GDP is captured in Kaldor's first law, which states that the faster the rate of growth of manufacturing in the economy, the faster will be its growth of GDP. Dasgupta and Singh (2006) find just such a positive relation using 48 countries and also for 29 Indian states in the 1990s. Other evidence shows that rapidly growing countries are those with large manufacturing sectors. After 1965, rapid economic growth in East Asia was associated with industrialization. Slower economic growth or stagnation in Sub-Saharan Africa, South Asia and the Middle East and North Africa was associated with a manufacturing share stuck at around 15 per cent of GDP (Rodrik 2006). Kaldor's second law is that the rate of growth of the manufacturing sector leads to faster growth of productivity in the whole economy due to dynamic economies of scale. Dynamic economies of scale occur when the average costs of production per unit of output decline as the volume of output increases. This is enabled by producers gaining experience and learning-by-doing and so being able to utilize technology more effectively, improve methods of management, and workers becoming more adept in production. Higher output levels also allow more specialization by firms and workers in the process of production, such as using production lines which are likely to lower average costs per unit of output. Dasgupta and Singh (2005) find that productivity growth by country and also across Indian states varies positively with the expansion of the manufacturing sector. While in general, there is no systematic tendency for countries that start with lower productivity (measured as GDP per worker) to grow more rapidly, the outcome changes for those countries that start with a strong base in manufacturing. Those countries beginning with lower levels of labour productivity in industry experience more rapid growth in labour productivity. This effect is found to be independent of geography, policies, or any other country-level influences (so is unconditional) (Rodrik 2013).

As discussed in Chapter 1 India did make a shift into modern industry after the 1850s with the establishment of cotton and jute mills (Rothermund 1993; Mukherjee 2007). After a hiatus in the 1860s there was renewed expansion in the 1870s and by 1892 Bombay had 28 mills with 445,462 spindles and Ahmedabad had 11 mills with 289,416 spindles (Tripathi & Jumani 2007). From c.1875 virtually all regions of India experienced the rise of machine-based factories. In the western and eastern parts of the country, cotton, jute, coal, and tea dominated the emerging industrial firms. Companies in the south were largely concentrated in sugar manufacturing, navigation and shipping. The period also saw the emergence of paper mills, breweries, flour mills, cotton and jute presses, engineering, timber mills, coffee plantations, and railway companies (Tripathi & Jumani 2007). The twentieth century saw rapid import substitution in most of the major consumer goods industries, certain intermediate and capital goods industries such as textiles, sugar, matches, soap, cement, paper, glass, sulphuric acid, and other basic chemicals, magnesium chloride, tinplate, and iron and steel (Mukherjee 2007: 15). The Associated Chambers of Commerce (ASSOCHAM) founded in 1921 was the first pressure group ever formed in India that claimed to represent the whole of Indian business, native and European. The Federation of Indian Chambers of Commerce came into being in 1927. By 1911, of 129 spinning, weaving and other cotton mills owned by companies in Bombay 92 had only Indian directors. By 1947, around 73 per cent of the domestic market was controlled by indigenous enterprise (Mukherjee 2007; Tripathi & Jumani 2007).

These successes mostly amounted to a growing Indian presence in a small industrial sector rather than the sustained industrialization of the whole Indian economy. The share of industry in national income increased from 11.1 per cent in 1900–10, to 16.4 per cent in 1940–6. Large-scale industry (mainly cotton and jute mills) employed 2–3 per cent of India's industrial workers around 1900 and around 10 per cent by 1947 (Roy 2002). The failure of industrial growth to lead to GDP growth à la-Kaldor can be seen by the fact that India's real national annual income grew by only 1 per cent between 1868 and 1914 and per capita income by even less (Roy 2002). India was still predominantly an agrarian economy at independence: in 1950/51 agriculture comprised 57 per cent of GDP, industry 15 per cent (of which manufacturing was 9 per cent) and services 28 per cent (Panagariya 2008: 13).

CONCLUSION

We opened this section by asking whether 5 per cent annual growth in the seven decades after 1947 was a success or otherwise? At best the Indian state in 1947 was only partially developmental; the state was led by a powerful leadership but one motivated by mixed goals some of which forced them to compromise on efforts to boost economic growth and industrialization. India did have an elitist and meritocratic civil service but one without the power to transform the economy to promote rapid economic growth and industrialization. India's state did manage to achieve greater freedoms against foreign business but was unable to compel domestic business to follow its economic goals. India is a coastal economy and parts of the country have long proved adept at engaging with and profiting from international trade, such as the city of Mumbai or the state of Gujarat. Large portions of the population remain relatively isolated in landlocked north-central India and unable to migrate to coastal areas. Large (if not sufficient) investments in telecommunications, airways, road and railway-related infrastructure have helped overcome some of the constraints of distance. The impact of geography on disease (especially malaria) and agricultural productivity have been mitigated by public interventions in health care and the Green Revolution respectively. India has faced enduring problems related to protecting property rights and in allowing productive firms and farms to acquire land in order to expand production. By language, caste, religion, and region India is vast and diverse. While diversity elsewhere has been associated with debilitating conflict and chaotic and unstable political efforts to either manage, or plunder and benefit from that diversity, India in 1947 was fortunately endowed with the organization of the Congress Party and an unmatched leadership that were able to co-opt, diffuse and enforce compromise and so overcome the worst economic implications of diversity. In 1947 Indian capitalism was a diverse, dynamic and entrepreneurial entity waiting for various of the worst shackles associated with a tired colonialism to be removed. Networks of trust across kinship and caste groups had proved adept at facilitating the transition from agriculture to early industrialization. The ability of such networks to exclude outsiders would likely ensure that the benefits of economic expansion were retained by insiders, but in 1947, they were unlikely to prove an overall hindrance to economic growth. In 1947 India remained a very poor and backward economy with low levels of GDP per capita and a surprisingly small domestic market. But, India had experienced several decades of rapid industrialization and the momentum for further expansion lay with a dynamic indigenous capitalist class. Further industrial growth awaited the drive from an independent state as to its future direction. The debate is not clear-cut.

India had some significant constraints on economic growth in 1947. But, if anything, running through the opportunities that existed in 1947 the balance of the argument above does seem to be optimistic. We should perhaps think of the 5 per cent growth (no more than Pakistan for example) as disappointing and consider that only in the 2000s did India start realizing its economic potential in outcomes related to economic and industrial growth, export success and improvements regarding poverty and education.

2

The Indian economic story since 1947

This chapter presents a snapshot of the Indian economy in 2017, and discusses some of the key influences on the economy (the constitution, the federal system and the central bank). The chapter then offers an unfolding narrative to reveal the origins of the 2017 snapshot, considering variously inflation, trade, agriculture, remittances and episodes of economic growth since 1947.

THE INDIAN ECONOMY IN 2017

In 2017 in terms of total GDP, India is the world's seventh-largest economy, similar in size to either France or Italy. By 2050 it is forecast to be the world's second largest, having overtaken the United States and remaining only behind China. According to the 2011 Census India had a population of 1.21 billion, which is likely to have increased to 1.34 billion people by 2017, and by around 2024 it should overtake China (1.39 billion in 2017). In 2017 India had a GDP per capita of around $2,000 which put it at the bottom of the middle-income countries in the world. In PPP (purchasing power partity) terms (which adjusts for cost of living) India's per capita GDP was $7,170 in 2017 which put it 126th in the world. In 2017 the Indian economy had experienced several years of 7 per cent annual growth, which was among the world's fastest, and after nearly forty years of lagging behind China was just about faster. This rate was forecast to continue into the near future. This growth has been led by the service sector where India has become the world's largest base for technology startups, with more than 1,400 founded in 2016 alone.

Recent economic growth looks to be sustainable. India's domestic debt was around 70 per cent of GDP and foreign debt around 21 per cent of GDP, both had been stable or slowly declining over the years up to 2017. The inflation rate was around 4 per cent and had been steadily declining over the previous few years. India's export growth had been slowly declining over the years immediately before 2017, but the country had seen its oil import bill cut by almost $80 billion due to lower oil prices, which allowed the overall balance of payments to show some improvement. Import and export growth revived in 2017–18, with both growing by more than 20 per cent. In 2017–18 India imported $160 billion of goods and services more than it exported, a surplus on invisible inflows of $110 billion left a current account deficit of around $50 billion (about 2 per cent of GDP). Capital inflows of almost $90 billion in that same year (such as remittance income and FDI) left the external accounts healthy and allowed India to add some $43 billion to its foreign exchange reserves which in 2017 reached $420 billion.

Although the investment rate in India had fallen from highs of around 39 per cent of GDP in 2011–12, it still amounted to 32 per cent of GDP by 2017 and was almost entirely funded by domestic savings at 30+ per cent of GDP. In the three years to 2017, India received more than $200 billion in FDI, with most of it going into services, computer software and hardware, telecommunications, construction, trading and automobiles. India has improved its ranking in the World Bank's Doing Business Report by 30 places over its 2017 ranking and is ranked 100 among 190 countries in the 2018 edition.

In many ways it is wrong to think of "the" Indian economy. India has a vibrant federal system which could be said to comprise many Indian economies. India has a parliamentary system, where like the British system the leader of the largest party in parliament becomes prime minister, in recent years, usually in coalition with other political parties. The president has powers much like the British monarch and is the formal and ceremonial head of the Indian state. The Indian constitution is federal and compromises a central government and a government in each state. The president (under advice from the prime minister) can dismiss a state government if the governance of a state cannot be conducted in accordance with the constitution. Under so-called president's rule, the state will then be ruled directly from the centre. The Union List in the constitution describes those powers that the central government in New Delhi can legislate on. These consist of around 100 areas and include, defence, nuclear energy, foreign affairs, railways, shipping, airways, post, telephones, currency, foreign trade, inter-state trade, banking, insurance, control of industries, mining, mineral and oil resources, elections, income tax, custom duties and export duties, excise duties and corporation tax. There are around 60 areas reserved for state legislation including those vital for economic and human development, such as maintaining law and order, police forces, healthcare, transport, land policies, electricity in the state, and village administration. The centre is responsible for adjudicating in any conflict between states. The Concurrent List on which *both* the centre and states can legislate on includes around 50 items such as marriage and divorce, transfer of property other than agricultural land, education, contracts, bankruptcy and insolvency, adulteration of foodstuffs, drugs and poisons, economic and social planning, trade unions, labour welfare, electricity, newspapers, books and printing, and stamp duties.

Traditionally the balance of power has been with the central government (Weiner 1999). The most buoyant sources of tax revenue lie with the central government, including income and corporation tax. Many of the most important development functions such as health and education are the responsibility of state governments. This implies that the states are continually dependent on resource transfers and any political conditions attached to them from the centre. The constitution gives ultimate authority in the case of centre–state or inter-state disagreements to the centre. President's rule, whereby the centre dismisses a state government and assumes direct administration of a state has been used more than 120 times since 1950. Until recent decades this tool was often used by the central government to dismiss state governments run by opposition parties. For much of the post-independence period the government at the centre and many of the state governments were run by a single political party, the Indian National Congress, which gave significant all-India authority to the party leader. During the early decades after independence more than 50 per cent of national investment was conducted by the state and guided carefully by the central planning commission. The central government also implemented a licensing regime which meant central permission was required to establish a new, or expand an old, private-sector business. State governments were compelled to compete amongst themselves for central preferment in the allocation of investment projects like airports or steel mills.

Economic liberalization since 1991 has shifted the balance between centre and states. A greater share of investment is now carried out by the private sector so states now compete amongst themselves to attract private investment, often FDI projects, without reference to the centre. The abolition of the licensing system means private-sector business can make decisions according to market incentives rather than by the dictates of central regulations. State control over the allocation of land, power and other infrastructure often becomes the most important interface between business and the government. The decline of the Congress Party since the late-1980s means that any national party is typically heavily dependent on the favour of numerous small regional parties to acquire a national majority. Regional parties often have the power to make or break national governments and use that power to extract benefits for their state, such as extra public investment or central ministerial seats for their politicians. By the mid-1990s, central ministries such as industry, finance and commerce were being held by MPs from regional parties. State governments and often their chief ministers have set the pace with policy reform. The communist government of West Bengal announced a new industrial policy in 1994 that sought to welcome foreign investment and technology. Chandrababu

Naidu, as chief minister of Andhra Pradesh took power in 1995 and sought to make his state particularly welcome to foreign and domestic investment, especially in IT related services (Sinha 2007). Often, international organizations deal directly with state governments and bypass the central government in New Delhi. The World Bank was closely involved in reform of the power sector in Odisha, for example, and supported this in 1996 with a loan of $350 million direct to the state government (Sinha 2007).

There has also been a progressive decentralization of the private business sector. In the 1960s, most private investment in India was controlled by foreign corporations or traditional business communities from Gujarat or by Marwari or Parsi groups. These business houses tended to be based in Mumbai or Calcutta, and to have close relations with the Congress Party and the central government in New Delhi. The Green Revolution and cooperative sugar mill sector facilitated the rise of a new agrarian class of prosperous farmers in states such as Haryana, Punjab, western Uttar Pradesh, Gujarat, Maharashtra, Andhra Pradesh, Haryana, Karnataka and Tamil Nadu. By the 1980s this class had expanded out of agriculture into textiles, cement, sugar, chemicals, fertilisers, pharmaceuticals, electronics, steel, and engineering to form the first generation of new business groups. These newly emerging and regionally based groups built links with regional political parties and were often hostile to perceived discrimination by the central government (Basu 2000).

Since 1991 the richer states in India experienced faster economic growth than the poorer states leading to a widening of inter-state inequality. Capital and labour flows do not help in reducing inter-state inequalities: richer states get more foreign and domestic investment. By 2000, the five richest states held 55 per cent of the total capital stock and the five poorest states only 15 per cent. Labour does migrate to richer states to take advantage of higher wages but this process is very limited (Purfield 2006).

The Reserve Bank of India

India's central bank, the Reserve Bank of India (RBI) has a mandate to keep inflation between 2 and 6 per cent in a manner that is consistent with economic growth. The policy interventions of the RBI are determined by a Monetary Policy Committee (MPC) which meets regularly. The meetings of the MPC are transparent and its minutes are published. The RBI also issues and designs the Indian currency, the rupee, issues licences for opening of banks, and authorizes foreign banks to enter or expand into the domestic financial market. The RBI acts as the "lender of last resort" to banks that are solvent but which face temporary liquidity problems. The RBI reviews reporting and accounting standards to ensure the financial viability of the banking system and pays close attention to emerging global best practice. State-owned banks in India have regularly suffered from the problem of non-performing loans: loans granted to business or agriculture that cannot be repaid because either the investment has failed, or else the money was never intended for productive investment and lent instead to politically well-connected individuals. The volume of non-performing loans is estimated to have reached 15 per cent of total loans by 2018 (Joshi 2018); the problem had been long known, but the RBI had failed to act early enough (Subramanian 2018: xxvii). The new global regulations known as the "Basel III Capital Regulations", which force banks to raise their minimum capital requirements, are intended to be phased in for Indian banks by 2019. In other ways the RBI is different from central banks in developed countries and actively intervenes to support wider government development objectives. The RBI helps ensure credit flow to priority sectors such as small enterprises and promotes the new goal of financial inclusion (opening bank accounts and using non-cash transactions) among the poorest via the government's programme, "Pradhan Mantri Jan Dhan Yojana" (PMJDY).

The years after independence were marked by a fixed exchange rate regime whereby the rupee was tied to the UK pound. After the early 1970s, India shifted to a system of flexible/managed exchange rates with the rupee value monitored in relation to a basket of international currencies. From the 1990s, the exchange rate has become more influenced by market conditions with the RBI serving to smooth adjustments through buying and selling foreign currencies. For much of the post-independence period the financial and foreign exchange systems were tightly regulated and the RBI was responsible for managing those regulations. Liberalization after 1991 saw the RBI remove much of the framework of licensing, quantitative restrictions and other discretionary controls. The RBI issues licences to banks and other institutions to act as authorized dealers in the foreign exchange market. The RBI permits FDI into most sectors in India with only a few remaining restrictions. Foreign institutional investors are allowed to purchase shares on the stock market and to invest in Government of India debt. Indian firms can invest overseas in their own subsidiaries or purchase foreign corporations. Residents of India are permitted to remit currency overseas up to a fixed amount for any permissible purposes.

Figure 2.1 Inflation, consumer prices (annual %), 1960–2016

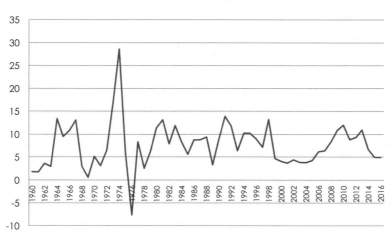

Source: World Development Indicators 2018.

The macroeconomic picture

Figure 2.1 shows one measure of economic stability, the rate of inflation. Partly because of the successful operation of the RBI, India has never suffered any serious problem with inflation as have other developing countries. India is often noted as being particularly inflation-sensitive, with large sections of the population living on near fixed incomes whom object vociferously through their democratic muscle to rapidly rising prices.

The surges in inflation in the mid-1960s, the early 1970s, and late 1970s, shown in Figure 2.1, were all driven by external shocks. Poor harvests in all three drove up the price of foodgrains, higher oil prices in the second two, and increased government expenditure associated with military conflict (the 1962 war with China and the wars with Pakistan in 1965 and 1971) in the case of the first two. In the first two inflationary interludes the government showed impressive speed, agility and expertise in its policy response to rising inflation: in 1965–7 the government cut back on public investment to reduce demand and imported millions of tonnes of foodgrains to moderate the rise in food prices. In the early 1970s the government responded with tough restrictions on bank lending and repressive measures against strike activity and wage claims. In both cases inflation fell rapidly. The rise in inflation between 1979 and 1981 occurred for similar reasons (drought and oil price rises) but the government response was very different. Unlike the earlier two inflation episodes, on this occasion the government had built up large stocks of foodgrains which were released onto the market and helped moderate upward pressure on foodgrain prices. Also in contrast to earlier years the government did not cut expenditure, but instead expanded both current expenditure and investment (partly funded by a $3.5 billion loan from the IMF) to maintain economic growth. Some of this went into a successful effort to boost domestic oil production which led for a few years to domestic self-sufficiency and to improve infrastructure. Much of it, however, went into politically popular current expenditures such as subsidies on food and fertiliser and transfers to loss-making state-owned enterprises. Rather than declining as in previous inflationary episodes the government budget deficit actually increased and remained high. Inflation fell from the peaks of the early 1980s but remained at relatively high levels throughout the 1980s. Inflation rose again to 10+ per cent in 1990–1 as India entered an election year ruled by a weak coalition government anxious to spend and so boost their popularity (Joshi & Little 1994). The last surge in inflation after 2008 was linked to the policy response to the Global Financial Crisis in 2008. The government budget deficit increased sharply after 2008 as the crisis impacted on both revenues and as the government boosted spending to maintain demand. Much of that extra spending went on subsidies to kerosene, diesel and other fuels, to moderate rising (and unpopular) international oil prices. This boosted consumption and imports rather than adding to productive capacity as extra infrastructure spending would have done. The government also acted to reduce interest rates and pushed the state-owned banking system to maintain lending. The economy experienced some slowdown, but to around 5 per cent of GDP and avoided the recessions that occurred elsewhere. The expansion continued too long and contributed to subsequent inflation and current account pressures, such that by 2012–13 the current account deficit had widened to 4 per cent of GDP (Mohan & Kapur 2015).

India was successful in reducing its demand for imports of consumer and industrial goods in the 1950s and paid little attention to exports. Exports remained flat in the early 1960s and the government had gradually tightened controls on imports to avoid unsustainable trade deficits. The resulting lack of imported spare parts and inputs for industry hindered industrial growth. The droughts of the mid-1960s reduced agricultural imports and necessitated emergency imports. The government responded with a massive devaluation in 1966 as well as efforts (noted above) to reduce domestic consumption. The balance of payments position improved noticeably from 1967 to 1970 but worsened again in late 1973 due to another drought and also to the rise in the international oil price which added almost $1 billion to India's import bill. The deflationary policy package in response reduced import demand sharply and combined with rapid export growth spurred by the depreciating value of the rupee and an increase in remittance income from abroad (from $97 million in 1972/3 to $470 million in 1975/6) greatly strengthened the balance of payments (Joshi & Little 1994). There were trade surpluses in the late 1970s and foreign exchange reserves increased. The balance of payments turned adverse again after 1979 due to a drought and a further rise in international oil prices. The choice of an expansionary adjustment sustained import demand and the trade balance worsened by more than $5 billion between 1979 and 1981, most of which was due to higher oil prices. India had little international debt and substantial foreign exchange reserves and so found financing the current account deficit easy through foreign borrowing. Export growth was rapid after the mid-1980s aided by a recovery of the world economy and the depreciation of the Indian rupee. The government made some efforts to promote exports after the mid-1980s – giving exporters preferential tax, credit and interest rates – and export growth occurred in various sectors including leather manufactures, gems and jewellery, chemicals, and engineering goods. Imports continued to grow ahead of exports, sucked in by a growing Indian economy and booming consumer demand that could turn to imports because of the gradual liberalization of trade that was now occurring. The result was that external debt increased from around $20 billion in 1980–1 to $64.4 billion in 1989–90. By 1990 more than 25 per cent of export revenue was required every year to service external debt (Joshi & Little 1994).

India's exports significantly lagged behind the growth of world trade in the 1950s and 1960s and although more successful in the 1970s and 1980s at best only kept up with world trade growth. India's share of world exports dropped from around 2.5 per cent at independence to around 0.5 per cent in 1990. Indian exports of $12 billion in 1990 were one-quarter of those from China or Singapore and one-sixth those from South Korea or Taiwan (Lall 1999). Trade was only a marginal activity relative to the aggregate economy. The share of trade in 1990 (exports + imports as a share of GDP) at 13 per cent was very low by international standards and had shown no increase over the 1980s (Veeramani 2007: 2420; Panagariya 2008: 91).

After liberalization in 1991, between 1993 and 1997 both merchandise and service exports grew by 13–14 per cent per annum. For the first time since independence India's export growth was faster than the rate of growth of world exports. There was some concern at the time that export growth until 2005 was confined to areas of existing specialization so that the structure of exports was showing remarkable persistence. These sectors included garments, textiles, jewellery, food items, chemicals, leather and rubber products, textiles, non-metallic mineral manufactures, and iron and steel (Ghemawat & Patibandla 1999; Veeramani 2007). There was a concern that India was stuck in either low-technology or resource-based exports that offered little scope for technological upgrading nor opportunities for rapid demand growth in the global economy (Lall 1999). There were also concerns when China joined the World Trade Organisation (WTO). The greater freedom for China to trade, it was feared, would flood India's domestic market with cheap manufactured goods and drive India's exports out of third markets. China did tend to export many of the same labour-intensive manufactured goods such as textiles, garments, leather goods, and light machinery as India, and the United States was then the largest export destination for both countries (Cerra *et al.* 2005).

In practice these fears were unfounded and India enjoyed even more striking export success from the early 2000s onwards. Total exports as a share of GDP increased from 10 per cent in 1995 to 25 per cent in 2013. Indian goods and services exports as a share of world goods and services exports tripled in the 20 years to 2013 to 1.7 and 3 per cent respectively. The share of service exports in total exports increased to more than 32 per cent by 2013, which is now larger than many middle- and high-income countries. Within manufacturing there has been a clear shift away from those traditional exports towards medium-high-technology manufacturing products, such as engineering goods, machinery, automobile components, mining equipment and cosmetics. Even in high-technology sectors India's is exporting veterinary and pharmaceutical products, television, telecommunication transistors, aircraft components, X-ray equipment and electronic R & D in elecro-medical, power and automotive industry products (Anand *et al.* 2015). Over time the importance of sophisticated technology-oriented business exporting services has increased. In particular computer services account for almost 70 per cent of total service exports. Finance, travel, sea transport (freight) and several business services such as legal, accounting, management, public relations, architecture, engineering, and technical services account for the remaining chunk of India's service export basket. India has also diversified its markets. The share of exports to the United States and the European Union fell from 45 per cent in 2000 to around 29 per cent in 2013. East Asia and the Middle East have emerged as the top two destinations (Anand *et al.* 2015).

In the 40 years before independence both food production and population increased by around 12 per cent allowing no increase in consumption per capita. In 1947 only around 15 per cent of cultivated land was under irrigation. Paddy (rice) yields were half those in China, and India had suffered from a massive famine (3–4 million dead) in Bengal in 1942–3. Early efforts after independence to boost production focused on giving more ownership rights to those working the land to strengthen incentives for small farmers to raise output, and also cooperative agriculture to encourage small farmers to pool land and other assets to farm on a larger and more efficient scale. There was also an emphasis on large irrigation projects with four major river valley projects under construction by the mid-1950s (Varshney 1994). In the 1950s, annual agricultural output growth was around 4 per cent, which was a dramatic improvement over the colonial period. Growth seemed to run out of steam by the early 1960s, with total food production stagnant between 1960 and 1962 and declining during two consecutive droughts between 1965 and 1967. Between 1964 and 1967 there was a fundamental change in agricultural strategy to one using price incentives and technical change. The government thereafter intervened to maintain prices at reasonable levels to provide an incentive for farmers to boost production. To this end the Agricultural Prices Commission (APC) and Food Corporation of India (FCI) were created to procure output from farmers at pre-announced prices. Some of these foodgrains were then sold to consumers at subsidized prices as an anti-poverty programme (see Chapter 5). By the mid-1980s the government had accumulated a stockpile of 30 million tonnes of foodgrains. The release of these stocks onto the market during the 1987 drought allowed the economy to continue growing without interruption. The new technology came in a package of recently developed high yield variety (HYV) seeds, fertilisers, pesticides, and controlled/irrigated water backed up by the establishment of an agricultural research service. The area planted with new seeds (mainly in the north-west of India in Punjab and Haryana) expanded rapidly. Between 1966 and 1971 $2.8 billion was allocated to imported fertilisers, seeds and pesticides (Varshney 1994). Between the mid-1960s and early 1990s trend output growth of 2.9 per cent per annum was slightly lower than the 1950s, but now based on productivity (yield) growth rather than as before using ever more land.

The nationalization of the banking system in 1969 permitted the government to channel cheap credit to farmers through state banks, which enabled small farmers to more easily purchase the new inputs associated with the Green Revolution. This policy went into reversal after 1991 as interest rates were liberalized, credit allocated to more profitable market segments and the policy to spread banking into rural areas was halted. Farmers became more dependent on high-cost informal sources of credit. At the same time, in efforts to reduce the budget deficit the government cut back sharply on public investment in infrastructure. Efforts to control subsidies on seed, fertiliser, and irrigation led to the costs of cultivation rising sharply over the 1990s and 2000s. Prices dropped below costs of production for key crops such as cotton, sugarcane and paddy (Narayanamoorthy 2007). The opening of international trade in agricultural products exposed Indian farmers to the greater volatility of international prices of food and non-food crops and some crop prices fell dramatically to match lower global prices (Ramachandran & Rawal 2009). Annual agricultural output growth in India slowed from 3.45 per cent in the 1980s to less than 2 per cent in the 1990s (Vakulabharanam & Motiram 2011: 103).

The increasing numbers of farmer suicides in Andhra Pradesh, Karnataka, Kerala, Punjab and Maharashtra during the 1990s has received a lot of attention. The total number of farmer suicides in Maharashtra increased from 1,083 in 1995 to 4,147 in 2004 (Mishra 2006). Suicides were associated with a shift to more valuable cash crops such as cotton, which offered higher average profits but also exposed farmers to volatile international prices and to the greater need to borrow (usually from high-cost money-lenders) to purchase inputs such as seed and fertiliser. In 2004–5, the cost of production for cotton in Maharashtra was above market prices. Suicides can lead to the cancellation of debt contracts so allow a family to keep land that has been pledged as collateral on a loan. Survey evidence among 111 cases of suicide in districts in Maharashtra found that debt was the most common explanatory factor and many of those had been harassed for payment. The debt was perceived to risk a family experiencing a fall in economic and social status through the loss or sale of assets, particularly land. The debt was often a consequence of crop failure due to a delay in rainfall (Mishra 2006). There is a difficulty in demonstrating a clear link between liberalization and the rise in farmer suicides which has only occurred in specific regions of a handful of the states. Some rich states (Punjab and Haryana) and poorer states (Rajasthan, Orissa and Bihar) have seen no trend decline or rise in male farmer suicide rates. While studies do show more debt among suicides, they also tend to show that there are many other causes such as alcohol and gambling addiction, chronic illness, family problems and property disputes (Panagariya 2008).

Figure 2.2 shows that remittances (money sent home by nationals working abroad) has never played a crucial role in the Indian economy, especially when compared to other countries in South Asia. In Sri Lanka, Bangladesh and Pakistan remittance inflows peaked at around 10 per cent of GDP. There are some exceptions within India. The state of Kerala has exported many of its teachers and medical professionals to the Gulf countries and elsewhere and up to a quarter of consumption in the state is funded by remittances (Harilal & Joseph 2003). In India as a whole remittances peaked in 2007 at 4 per cent of GDP. The following section shows that the high rates of investment during the 2000s were mainly funded through domestic savings. Remittances did, however, make a contribution along with FDI in financing India's enduring trade deficit.

Figure 2.2 Personal remittances, received (% of GDP), 1975–2017

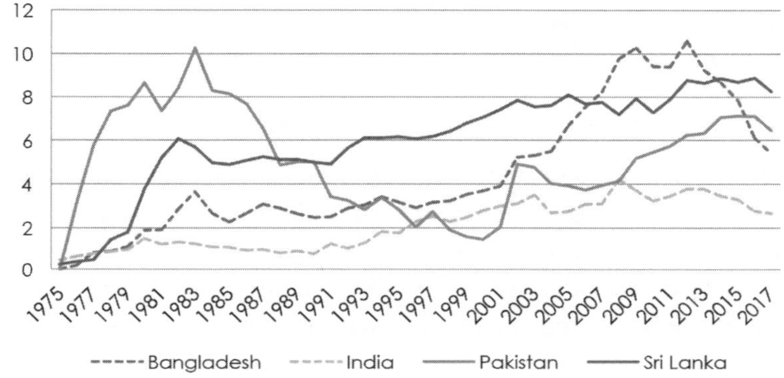

Source: World Development Indicators: 2018.

Economic growth

We can think about economic growth in India since independence in terms of a recent empirical finding about patterns of growth. Modern research has shown that the dominant feature of economic growth in developing countryies is not rapid or slow growth clubs, or perennial failures, or sustained take-offs into long-term growth success, but instead short to medium episodes of growth and stagnation. One study is that of Hausmann *et al* (2004) who define an "episode of growth" as an increase in per capita growth of 2 per cent or more sustained for at least eight years, and post-acceleration growth of at least 3.5 per cent. They identify more than 80 such episodes between 1957 and 1992. These episodes are widespread across time and space. More than half of their 110 country sample had at least one such acceleration, Asia had 21, Africa 18, Latin America 17, and the Middle East and North Africa 10. Other scholars have refined the definitions of episodes of growth and stagnation but have confirmed this central thesis (Jones & Olken 2008; Cuberes & Jerzmanowski 2009; Jong-a-Pin & De Haan 2011; Berg *et al.* 2011). This evidence demonstrates that the big problem for developing countries is not in initiating an episode of rapid economic growth – many countries have managed that. The key problem is rather in sustaining economic growth. India is no exception and has had at least three episodes of growth and one episode of stagnation since independence.

STATE-LED INDUSTRIALIZATION, 1950–65

The Nehru-Mahalanobis model was named after its two main protagonists and guided the developmental policies of the Indian state after 1947. The model was interventionist, it emphasized the importance of long-term planning by the state, of state investment in building up a heavy industrial base in the public sector, and the close regulation of the private sector in the name of national needs and priorities. This growth was oriented to the domestic economy through an emphasis on import substitution justified in terms of an aspiration to achieve self-sufficiency in industrial production rather than export promotion and was supported by a suspicion of foreign direct investment (FDI). The Nehru-Mahalanobis plan was an abrupt break with the laissez-faire of the colonial era, but was in keeping with the broad thrust of elite thinking in post-Independence India. These elites perceived free trade and FDI as the means by which India had been exploited by the British so saw a crucial need to build up an independent industrial base (Kaviraj 1988; Chatterjee 1997).

Looking back many scholars have criticized this choice of development strategy. Bhagwati (1993) argued that it heralded too much state intervention at the expense of the market and led to inefficiencies and low productivity. Other scholars have argued that while in principle the state-led industrialization model was sound – for example, it was similar to that pursued in 1950s South Korea to enormous success – the Indian state was too weak to make a success of it. Herring argues that India lacked the state capacity to implement planning from the outset due to a "state committed to planning yet too democratic, soft and embedded, to govern the market" (1999: 3). Chibber (2003) agrees and argues that the developmental autonomy of the Indian state was undermined in the late-1940s and early-1950s by opposition from the capitalist class against state controls. Bardhan argued that it was not just about big industrialists, but that also rich farmers and professionals were able to influence the state. He argued that these three, what he called "dominant proprietary classes" used their political influence to acquire subsidies from the government. These included higher wages and employment of public-sector workers, subsidized irrigation water and electricity for farmers, and cheap loans to big business. By the late 1980s subsidies were estimated to have reached 15 per cent of Indian GDP (Mundle & Govinda Rao 1991). Bardhan argued that the "Indian public economy has thus become an elaborate network of patronage and subsidies" (1984: 65). This increase in subsidies was at the inevitable expense of the public investment that was needed to drive economic growth and the result Bardhan argues was economic stagnation.

An alternative view emphasizes instead the economic success of the Indian economy after 1950 in making a decisive break with long-term colonial stagnation. Economic growth between 1900 and 1950 had barely kept up with population growth, implying that per capita incomes were no higher in 1950 than 50 or even 100 years before. By contrast annual economic growth averaged around 4 per cent during the 15 years after 1950, well ahead of the 2 per cent annual growth of population. There was an increase in economic growth in c.1950 statistically more significant than at any other moment in India across the entire twentieth century (Hatekar & Dongre 2005; Nayyar 2006; Balakrishnan & Parameswaran 2007). There were few signs of growth fatigue during the years up to the mid-1960s; if anything, industrial growth was showing signs of accelerating over time. Productivity growth (TFP) was relatively rapid between 1950 and 1965 and it was only after the mid-1960s that it slowed sharply (Sivasubramonian 2000: 286; Virmani 2004b: 23).

There is a lot of evidence for growth-promoting state interventions after 1950. The state was successful in mobilizing resources for the industrialization efforts. The share of national income raised in taxation almost doubled, from 7 per cent at the beginning of the 1950s to nearly 15 per cent by the mid-1960s (Bhagwati & Srinivasan 1975: 8). Tax mobilization was combined with a strict control of public spending. Government spending as a share of GDP was no more than about 6 per cent until 1960 when it increased, reaching around 8.5 per cent by 1965. Defence spending remained low, at around 1.8 per cent of GDP. Subsidies were controlled during the 1950s (Bardhan was correct only from the mid-1960s onwards) and losses from running the government irrigation system were reduced (Chakravarty 1987: 127). Deficit financing in India remained below 1 per cent of GDP from 1950 to the mid-1960s, except briefly in the crisis year of 1957–8 (Government of India 2015: 40). More tax revenue and controlled public spending led to an increase in public savings from (using three-year moving averages) 1.9 per cent of GDP in 1951–2 to 3.5 per cent in 1964–5 (Bardhan 1984: 99). This prudent management of public finances facilitated a big increase in public investment. Growth was state-led. Between 1951 and 1964 the growth of public investment (7.9%) was considerably faster than that of private investment (3.5%) (Virmani 2004a: 15) and public investment increased from 3.3 per cent in 1951 to 8.3 per cent in 1965 accounting for almost all the increase in total investment (Bardhan 1984: 97). The level of total investment increased (with fluctuations) from a range of 10–12 per cent of GDP in the early-1950s to nearly 17 per cent by the mid-1960s. The share of total central government expenditure accounted for by investment more than doubled from 25.56 per cent in 1950/1 to around 50 per cent from the late-1950s to the 1960s (Rudolph & Rudolph 1987: 231).

Between the early-1950s and the mid-1960s the evolution of the production structure responded in accordance with the aims of the government. This shows that the government was successfully able to implement licensing, fiscal policy and its own allocation of investment to achieve its economic goals. Economic growth was creating resources that were channelled into tax revenue or savings and used to expand public investment rather than private consumption. State investment to expand capacity has never been sufficient to ensure economic growth. The global history of such development efforts is littered with low-productivity white elephant projects operating at minimal capacity and making substantial losses. This problem was avoided in the post-independence decades and the emerging pattern of growth in India was a balanced one. Table 2.1 shows that capacity utilization rates remained high until the mid-1960s.

Table 2.1 Capacity utilization rates (%), 1960–65 to 1971–75

Industry Group	1960–65	1966–70	1971–75
Basic goods	86.0	82.0	77.4
Capital goods	85.9	66.4	60.2
Intermediate goods	89.3	81.9	79.7
Consumer goods	86.6	82.2	80.1

Source: Ahluwalia 1985: 109.

The relative growth of the public sector was not at the expense of growth in the private sector. Public investment was focused in basic, long-gestation, high-risk sectors and in infrastructure which generated profitable investment opportunities for the private sector. The private sector responded by increasing directly productive investment. There was a three-fold increase in private corporate investment between 1953–4 and 1955–6 and capital issues by the private sector trebled between 1953 and 1954 (Kidron 1965). The share of machinery investment by the private sector increased from 3.1 per cent of GDP in 1960–1 to 5 per cent in 1964–5. By contrast investment in inventories and construction (less directly productive) by the private sector declined sharply (Desai 1981: 279). The accumulation of machines rather than houses has been found to be a key determinant of economic growth. There is good evidence for a wide set of cross-country data that shows a positive association between output per worker and investment in machinery and equipment that is especially true for developing countries (De Long & Summers 1991).

Over the 1950s the Indian state made rapid progress in diversifying the structure of industry and achieving domestic self-reliance. By the early-

1960s the industrial structure had shifted from one dominated by textiles and sugar to one with substantial capacity in iron and steel, non-ferrous metals, machine building, coal and heavy chemicals (Chandra *et al.* 2008: 450–1). Annual industrial production grew by an average of 9 per cent between 1961 and 1965, in capital goods by nearly 20 per cent and in consumer goods by only 5 per cent (Rangarajan 1982: 292). More than half of total industrial growth was accounted for by capital and intermediate goods and less than 5 per cent by consumer durables (Chaudhuri 2002). Table 2.2 shows that the growth of output in cotton textiles was outpaced by rapid growth of chemicals, iron and steel and especially machinery.

Table 2.2   Index of industrial production (1950/51 = 100)

Group	1955/56	1960/61
General index	139	194
Cotton textiles	128	133
Iron and steel	122	238
Machinery (all types)	192	503
Chemicals	179	288

Source: Third Five-Year Plan (1961) Ch 3: 5.

As they were constructed, early industrial units rapidly reached capacity levels of production, indicating that the technical engineering skills necessary to produce were quickly acquired. Production of steel ingots at the Bhilai plant (in the state of Chhattisgarh) rose from 40.2 per cent of (estimated) capacity in 1960/1 to 111.8 per cent in 1964/5. At the Durgapur plant (in the state of West Bengal) these figures were 16.8 per cent and 100.6 per cent respectively. There were successful efforts to indigenize manufacture of equipment within the country and to absorb know-how and technology for the future design of steel plants and for the design and manufacture of equipment. The further expansion of capacity at plants in Bhilai and Rourkela (in the state of Odisha) relied on local equipment design and construction facilities. The design and engineering organization gradually built up in the Rourkela plant later became an independent organization under Hindustan Steel Plants (later SAIL) to serve the entire industry. The import content declined significantly at the expansion stage of these plants. There were similar stories of efficient domestic replication of early technology acquisition in machine tools (Mascarenhas 1982), oil refining (Mehrotra 1990) and motor vehicles (Narayana *et al.* 1992). While industry successfully acquired the capacity to expand on the basis of replicated technology it continued to lack the capacity to innovate and change that technology.

INDUSTRIAL STAGNATION, 1965–80

After 15 years of rapid economic growth the Indian industrial sector lurched into relative stagnation after the mid-1960s. Stagnation was located in industry and specifically in heavy industry. Slower growth was recorded in sectors such as chemicals and chemical products, basic metals, and electrical machinery. Petroleum products was an exception, where growth surged. In more labour-intensive sectors, such as textiles and food, growth was slow and steady (Bardhan 1984: 94–5). The slowdown was a surprise to contemporary observers. Industrial production had been expanding by 9 per cent per annum between 1961 and 1965 (Rangarajan 1982: 292), which represented one of the best interludes of industrial growth in India over the entire twentieth century. This stagnation was not just a statistical phenomenon; what made it important was that stagnation occurred relative to the continued priority given to industry by the planning system, macroeconomic policy, and also the continuing aspirations of the leadership to build an industrial base in India. From the 1960s onwards planning documents continued to target annual industrial growth of 12 per cent and kept doing so even as reality diverged.

Various explanations have been put forward to explain this stagnation. These have related to patterns of income distribution, agriculture–industry linkages, state–business relations, the policy framework as constraint, import substitution and public investment. These are examined in turn.

Income distribution. The conventional discussion relating growth and income distribution asks whether economic growth leads to more or less income inequality. Famously Simon Kuznets (1955) suggested the relationship was an inverted U-shape, inequality first worsens then later narrows with rising levels of average income in a country. More recently Thomas Piketty (2014) has suggested the declining inequality leg of the inverted U was a historical anomaly and much of the world is trending back to historical norms of significant inequality. The novelty of the industrial stagnation debate in India was to reverse this line of causation and to argue that inequality could influence the rate of economic growth. This link could work through two mechanisms. Firstly, increasing inequality in the distribution of income, it was argued, diverted demand from mass consumption goods to luxury production. The production of simple-technology, mass consumption goods in India is labour-intensive and stimulates production linkages with the local economy. By contrast luxury production was import intensive or produced by technology- and capital-intensive methods of production that generated little employment and so little consumption demand out of wages in India (Nayyar 1978). Secondly, rising income inequality may stimulate savings by the rich at the expense of consumption by the poor and so reduce aggregate demand (Chakravarty 1979).

The evidence on income and expenditure inequality and economic growth is mixed for India after 1965. The lack of demand seems apparent and is evidenced by the excess of national savings over national investment in the 1970s and also in the fact that during the 1970s India was piling up foreign exchange and foodgrain reserves despite high levels of poverty and hunger (Chakravarty 1979). However, the evidence is not completely convincing, output growth in the consumer goods industries actually increased in the years after 1965, which is not something we would expect if rising inequality was choking off consumption demand for basic consumer goods.

Agriculture–industry linkages. The key mechanisms by which agriculture can influence industrial growth include the supply of food and labour to the industrial sector, providing raw material inputs for agrobased industries (such as cotton and jute textiles, sugar, vegetable oils and tobacco), generating final incomes that provide a demand for industrial outputs, and more indirectly, as a source of savings and tax revenue to pay for industrial investment. The combination of a growing population (rising food demand) and a slowdown in agricultural output growth would put upward pressure on food prices. As the quantity of food consumed will be relatively independent of price, an increase in food prices would force poor farmers and agricultural workers to spend less on manufactured consumer goods (Vaidyanathan 1977; Rangarajan 1982). Higher food prices may also force industrialists to concede wage increases to workers so that both raw material and wage costs increase at the expense of profits, investment and industrial growth (Mitra 2005). Wider empirical evidence shows that agricultural output growth was sustained after 1967–8 (Balakrishnan & Parameswaran 2007) and that the patterns in the relative price of agricultural products fluctuated rather than showing a clear trend linked to slowing industrial growth over time (Desai 1981).

State–business relations. Scholars have argued that the vigorous state-led developmentalism of the 1950s withered after the mid-1960s. Shetty focused on "the impact of the absence of sustained developmental efforts" which, he argued, by the mid-1960s was evident "in the generation of apparent surpluses of foodgrains and foreign exchange reserves on a sizeable scale in the midst of rising malnutrition, poverty and unemployment on the one hand, and persistent sluggishness in domestic investment on the other" (1978: 132). There is certainly evidence during the 1970s that India had accumulated large unused stockpiles of key investment goods including steel, coal, and cement, and that in 1976/7 the domestic investment (14 per cent of GDP) could not even absorb the "meagre" level of savings (16% of GDP). Shetty further argues that there was an "atmosphere of permissiveness in the deployment of industrial control mechanisms instituted earlier in direct investment according to plan priorities"

(1978:141). While the availability of basic wage goods (such as soap, cotton yarn and textiles) was increasing slowly, there were "disproportionate" increases in the production of luxury goods (such as polystyrene and polyester fibre). Shetty argues that the cause of these maladies (echoing some of the arguments related to income distribution) was a "downgrading of the planning process" whereby a "significant proportion of the total public outlays was frittered away in non-developmental expenditure" and "simultaneously, the rigours of industrial controls – price and distribution controls, industrial licensing, capital issue controls etc – were drastically reduced" (1978: 174). The private sector was being provided ample funds from public-sector financial institutions, but these funds were not being used to boost investment or employment growth in the private sector. The relaxation of industrial controls, argues Shetty, led to a situation of "pumping in resources without a sound policy regarding their direction". Laxity in the regulation of the private sector allowed inappropriate production and investment by large industrial houses and a gradual shift of investment in favour of commodities with a low social priority. Chandrasekhar (1988) noted that large business houses were acquiring licences to produce, but not implementing them in order to preserve shortages of consumer and industrial goods and so higher profits for themselves.

The case studies of IT, pharmaceuticals and the space programme reveal some examples of successful state developmental interventions missed by this aggregate picture of pessimism. The average annual growth rates of software exports from India in the 1970s was approximately 50 per cent, rising to 58 per cent in the 1980s. D'Costa (2003; 2011) and Saraswati (2013) argue that the Indian IT industry is less a product of liberalization in the 1990s than of interventionist policies during the 1960s and 1970s. The military defeat against China in 1962 and consequences of the US arms embargo after war with Pakistan in 1965 highlighted the national importance of electronics and IT in the eyes of the Indian state. The response was the Bhabha Report which argued the case for domestic self-sufficiency. The Electronics Corporation of India Limited (ECIL) was established as a state-owned enterprise under the government

Department of Electronics (DoE) to be India's national champion in the production of telecommunications equipment. By the 1970s, the Indian industry so created was characterized by fragmented and small-scale producers doing little more than assembling imported kits. To boost exports, the DoE established the Software Export Scheme in 1974. In return for a commitment to export software services, the state provided 100 per cent loans on computer purchases to all firms that signed up. Within two years the scheme had established an export-oriented software services industry in India. Tata Consultancy Services (TCS) was the first firm to join the scheme after being established in 1968 and within two years was exporting software to the United States. India tended to import computer kits that did not come bundled with software and this led to rising local demand for skills in writing software. Between 1981 and 1986 revenues to Indian software industry through domestic software services provision increased 30-fold and revenue from software exports increased seven-fold (Saraswati 2012, 2013).

Between 1996 and 2006 annual sales of pharmaceutical firms increased by 9 per cent, employment in the industry rose to 500,000 people and on sales of €10 billion, India achieved a 2 per cent share of world markets. Again, it was the state between the mid-1950s and the 1970s that had a leadership role in the pharmaceutical sector. The government introduced high tariffs on imported medicines and demanded that foreign pharmaceutical companies reduce shares in their Indian subsidiaries to 40 per cent. The government set up five public-sector companies including Hindustan Antibiotics Ltd (HAL) and Indian Drugs and Pharmaceuticals Ltd (IDPL) and also public-sector research laboratories such as the Indian Institute of Chemical Laboratory (IICL) and National Chemical Laboratory (NCL). These organizations played a crucial role in building up technical competence in the industry and made efforts to both adapt and assimilate foreign technologies by making drugs developed in government laboratories available to other firms. Several IDPL staff founded their own successful private firms including Dr Reddy, Ranbaxy and Cipla. A key legislative reform was the 1970 Patents Act which recognized only process patents in pharmaceuticals. If Indian companies could invent new processes, they were liberated to manufacture previously patented drugs. The domestic pharmaceutical industry that emerged made India self-reliant in the production of drugs to meet demands from the domestic market. Drug prices dropped from one of the highest to one of the lowest in the world. The time lag for the introduction of a new drug in India after its global launch declined from 15 to 5 years (Perlitz 2008; Joseph 2011).

On 5 November 2013 India launched its Mars Mission rocket which entered the Mars orbit on 24 September 2014. India was the fourth country to reach Mars and the first in Asia. In February 2017 an Indian rocket launched 104 satellites on a single mission. These efforts date back to state-led initiatives in the 1960s and 1970s. The Indian Space Research Organisation (ISRO) based in Bangalore was formed in 1969. Its first satellite was launched by the USSR in 1975 and by 1980 India was launching its own satellites. ISRO spent $74 million on the Mars mission. A moon mission, estimated to cost $125 million was planned soon after. The Mars mission launched by the US National Aeronautical Space Administration (NASA) cost $671 million. Some have criticized the space programme, arguing that the money would be better spent on providing basic needs for the poor. The programme has, however, improved India's ability to forecast the weather and connect remote areas through satellite communications. A recent satellite launch cost India $5 million and with an expected life span of 10 years the annual operating cost is very low. This offers India good opportunities to break into the $6 billion global satellite launch industry of which France, Russia and the US currently hold 75 per cent. The global satellite market including building, launching and sustaining communications may be worth up to $120 billion a year.

The policy framework as constraint. Both private- and public-sector industries were subject to extensive government intervention after independence. The Industrial Licensing Act of 1951 mandated that firms acquire a license to establish a new undertaking, for expanding capacity, using new technology, to import, to exit an industry, or to manufacture a new product. Policy-making was characterized by administrative delays.

Overburdened ministries allocated licences using simple rules of thumb, such as allocation on the basis of already installed capacity, rather than making the time-consuming effort to evaluate which firms would be able to produce most efficiently. The uncertainties and delays associated with licence allocation discouraged long-term planning by industry. From 1967 onwards some areas of industrial production were reserved exclusively for the (often inefficient) small-scale sector and by 1977 the list comprised 180 items. The Monopoly and Restrictive Trade Practices Act (MRTP) passed in 1969 intended to reduce the market power of large companies, but in practice did little more than add an extra layer of licensing and reg-ulation. Foreign trade was strictly regulated through the use of tariffs and elaborate quotas. Trade protection was granted to all domestic produc-tion regardless of cost on the basis of indigenous availability (Bhagwati & Desai 1970; Bhagwati & Srinivasan 1975; Ahluwalia 1985). Scholars have connected such interventions with resulting inefficiencies and slower eco-nomic growth. Stagnation was a problem with the productivity of resource utilization, specifically the "effect of inadequacies in the policy design and framework showed itself in stagnant growth rates" (Bhagwati 1993: 40). The principle problem with this argument is how to reconcile the rapid economic growth up to the mid-1960s and industrial stagnation thereaf-ter with a policy framework in place throughout

Import substitution. There are two crucial parts to the argument linking import substitution to industrial stagnation. Firstly, that import substitution accounted for 23 per cent of total industrial growth between 1950/1 and 1965/6. By the mid-1960s Chandrasekhar (1988) argued that opportunities for further import substitution were exhausted. A second argument suggests that the inefficiency of import substitution was acting as a drag to further industrial growth by the mid-1960s. In the 1950s and 1960s protection against competition from imports was granted to any industry setting up production capacity in India regardless of the relative costs of foreign and domestic production. The size of the domestic Indian market was often not big enough to allow economies of scale. Together these policies are argued to have reduced the productivity of industrial production and raised the costs of any industrial firm using iron and steel, chemicals or any other inputs in their own production process. The net result was to slow industrial growth and undermine export potential (Ahluwalia 1985). The evidence linking the growth deceleration after the mid-1960s with the end of opportunities for further import substitution is not convincing. Even by 1978/9 the volume of imports as a percentage of availability was still high in various industries including paper and paper products, petroleum products, basic metals, non-electrical and electrical machinery and non-metallic mineral products (Bardhan 1984: 96). This implies there was still scope for continued growth based on import substitution. The argument also ignores other sources of economic growth such as domestic consumer or government demand.

Public investment. Public investment in India has long been crucial in creating capacity in sectors like railways, power, and fuel. Public investment reached a peak of 8.3 per cent of GDP in 1965 and was cut in response to rising inflation to a low of 6.3 per cent of GDP in 1970. The slowdown in public investment was borne disproportionately by infrastructure which grew by 17 per cent per annum between 1960 and 1965 and by only 2 per cent annually over the next ten years. This had a significant effect on heavy industrial growth as by the mid-1960s public investment provided a near-monopoly source of demand for the output of heavy industry (Ahluwalia 1985: 78–9). For example, by the mid-1960s the government was the sole purchaser of the output of railway equipment. The share of public investment going to railways fell sharply from 23.1 per cent in 1964 to 6 per cent a decade later (Virmani 2004a). Table 2.1 showed that reduced infrastructure investment after the mid-1960s led directly to a sharp decline in capacity utilization in the capital goods industry after the mid-1960s (Ahluwalia 1985: 109).

As well as a decline in the volume of public investment there were also inefficiencies that covered the entire public investment programme from project formulation, to implementation and to operational stages. Inefficiencies in the management of the state-owned railway system included poor performance on net tonne kilometres moved per wagon per day, net tonne kilometre moved per tonne of wagon capacity, engine utilization, and engine speed among others. The minimum time overrun for the construction of hydroelectric power was two years and the maximum nine years. Cost overruns were typically over 100 per cent (Ahluwalia 1985).

GROWTH WITHOUT LIBERALIZATION AND LIBERALIZATION WITHOUT GROWTH, 1980s AND 1990s

There is widespread agreement that economic growth in India increased from its post-independence annual average of around 3.5 per cent to 5 per cent per annum after *c*.1979. The growth acceleration was driven by both the public and private sectors (Nagaraj 1991) and manufacturing and services (Wallack 2003; Balakrishnan & Parameswaran 2007, 2919). There was also a more notable break with a long-term disappointing productivity performance which turned from negative to sharply positive in these years (Ahluwalia 1985).

Although frequently discussed as the year marking a significant shift towards economic liberalization few scholars have identified 1991 as ushering in a statistically significant increase in growth rates. Nagaraj (2000a) finds that economic growth continued at its trend growth rate of 5.7 per cent per annum for the ten years before and after 1991. There was even a statistically significant slow-down in the secondary sector after 1991/2. Kaur (2007) is one exception who finds that there was a statistically significant but only slight increase in economic growth from 5.3 per cent between 1980–81 and 1991–2 to 5.9 per cent between 1992–3 and 2003–04. As with the post-1965 stagnation debate, there are a range of explanations that have been put forward to explain the post-1980 acceleration.

Agriculture–industry linkages. Agriculture showed a better performance in the 1980s (4.75%) over the 1970s (1.4%) and 1990s (3.08%). Even this sharp acceleration underestimates the wider impact of agricultural growth as the agricultural sector was becoming better integrated with the rest of the Indian economy. One indication of this is that there was a sharp increase in the purchase of inputs used in agricultural production from the industrial sector from the 1970s (Thamarajakshi 1990).

There is little research for more recent years on the link between this growth of agriculture and the growth of other economic sectors. The debate after the 1990s has focused more narrowly on the "crisis of agriculture" seen in terms of the falling growth rate of agricultural output in the 1990s relative to the 1980s (Mathur *et al.* 2006; Chand *et al.* 2007; Bhalla & Singh 2009; Vakulabharanam & Motiram 2011), and of the slowing of yield growth (Chand & Pendey 2007; Bhalla & Singh 2009; Vakulabharanam & Motiram 2011). Some of this work has focused on individual state-level stories of crisis such as Punjab (Sidhu 2002) and Odisha (Pattnaik & Shah 2010), or success in Gujarat (Dixit 2009) or West Bengal (Harriss 1993). A rare exception is Gadgil and Gadgil (2006) who show that between 1950 and 2003 the impact of changes in rainfall has continued to have a significant impact on food-grain production and in turn on the growth of GDP, this despite the share of agriculture in GDP declining from 50 per cent in 1950 to 22 per cent in 2000. As more than 60 per cent of the population live and work in agriculture much consumer demand is linked to the fortunes of agriculture. Many industries, such as textiles and sugar processing are dependent on inputs from agriculture, and the rural economy is a significant consumer of industrial goods such as tractors, pump sets and electric generators.

Public investment. A key explanation for the *c.*1980 growth surge was the contemporaneous boost to public investment. The years 1979 and 1980 were, like the mid-1960s, characterized by drought, oil price shocks, rising food prices and a debt crisis. In contrast with the austerity of the mid-1960s India responded in the early 1980s with expansionary adjustment. A large IMF loan was taken out ($5.7 billion in 1981) that helped fund big increases in public investment in both 1981–2 and 1982–3. Private investment showed a strong response. Corporate investment, which had been stagnant in the 1970s, surged in the 1980s (McCartney 2009: Chp 7) led by private investment in machinery and equipment (the most productive element of investment) (Sen 2007: 41).

This was not just a story of liberating the private sector. The output share of the public sector peaked in 1991–2 at 26.1 per cent of GDP, which implies that the acceleration of GDP growth after 1980 was shared by the public sector. The public investment ratio peaked in 1986–7 at 12.5 per cent of GDP then gradually declined to 6.4 per cent by 2001–02. The public sector delivered a stable share of accelerating domestic output for 20 years even though its investment share halved, which demonstrates an impressive record of productivity growth (Nagaraj 2006). This was in stark contrast to the evidence for inefficiency in the public sector in the 1960s and 1970s. There is good evidence in the 1980s of this better efficiency of public investment. This included greater selectivity in new projects and the concentration of available resources in completing ongoing projects. There was an increase in the output growth of key state-produced industrial inputs such as coal, electricity, fertilizer, and cement. The growth in telecommunications measured by new telephone lines added and railway traffic after 1981 was evident (Nagaraj 1990).

There is also a lot of work on the narrower question of public investment in agriculture. Studies have found that public investment in agriculture was cut in the 1990s relative to the 1980s and that such cuts were an important contributory factor behind the slowdown in agricultural growth in the 1990s (Dhawan 1996; Gulati & Bathla 2001; Mathur *et al.* 2006).

Income distribution. After the 1960s stagnation debate, discussion of the impact of income distribution all but disappears and at most only some lingering influence can be teased out. Bhattacharya and Mitra (1990, 1991) offered an explanation based on income distribution and inequality between economic sectors. They noted that the rapid growth of the service sector in India from the 1980s was creating income and consequently consumption expenditure, which in turn was creating demand for consumer goods produced by the manufacturing sector (services accounted for less than 20 per cent of aggregate consumer expenditure in the 1980s). Incomes without corresponding manufacturing production, they suggested, would generate excess demand for imports or inflationary pressures and so render the service-led growth path unsustainable. There is little evidence, however, that the India economy was failing to produce consumption goods in the 1980s. Nagaraj (1990) shows that the growth rate of consumer durables output averaged 16 per cent per annum between 1980/81 and 1988/89 compared to only 7.4 per cent per annum for manufacturing as a whole. Rather than failing, the service-led growth path in India soared into an even more dramatic growth episode in c.2003.

State–business relations. Some scholars have studied the link between the acceleration in growth after 1980 and changing attitudes among government officials. Rodrik and Subramanian (2004) argue that before 1980 government rhetoric focused on socialism and pro-poor policies, and after 1980 they argue Prime Minister Indira Gandhi aligned herself politically with the private sector and dropped her previous rhetoric. This shift was made more explicit by the election of the pro-corporate and pro-private sector Rajiv Gandhi as prime minister in 1984. These changes were about attitudes rather than substantive policy reform, which had to wait until the 1990s. This view is related to a wider discussion about the Indian state becoming more pro-business after 1980 (Kohli 2006). The useful distinction here is that the government was not becoming more supportive towards the market per se but that they were specifically becoming more pro-business. A pro-market reform would focus on removing impediments to markets through trade and domestic liberalization which together would help new businesses start up and boost domestic and import competition on incumbents. A pro-business orientation is one that focuses on raising the profitability of established industrial and commercial establishments through easing capacity restrictions, removing price controls, and reducing corporate taxes. Rodrik and Subramanian (2004) argue that those firms with close links to the government through paying taxes or complying with regulations receive a significant boost when government attitudes become more favourable, even without actual policy change. They find that India in 1980 had very strong political and economic institutions for a country of its income level, including democracy, the rule of law, and adequate protection of property rights. This, they argue, meant that a small change in state attitudes towards the private sector could produce a large growth impact.

The problem with "attitudes" is that of collecting relevant evidence as changes in attitudes would have emerged during private meetings between the government and business. Relevant evidence is often more impressionistic and gathered by journalists through conversations and observation rather than rigorous evidence (Crabtree 2018). Rodrik and Subramanian (2004) do their best to test this hypothesis. They argue that if the causal mechanism is a shift in the attitude of central government then we should expect to see post-1980 growth being more pronounced in states where the ruling government was in the same party or in alliance with the central ruling party. They find indeed that states allied with the national government had growth rates in the 1960s and 1970s indistinguishable from others while in the 1980s and 1990s states allied with the central government had dramatically higher growth rates. This is a bit tenuous. More convincing is Sen (2009) who has concrete evidence that substantive policy changes did occur in the late 1970s and early 1980s that benefited the private sector and were a mix of pro-business and pro-market reforms. These related to a massive increase in public investment, liberalized access to cheaper imported capital goods and increased bank lending to the private sector. Other scholars have downplayed the importance of policy change in the 1980s leading to economic growth and argued that the surge in economic growth after 1980 and sustained growth into the 1990s and beyond was linked instead to earlier decades of successful state intervention in building capacity in sectors such as software, auto-components, and pharmaceuticals.

The policy framework constraint on growth. The earliest hint of liberalization, argues Nayar (2006), was in 1974 (a clearly different view to that discussed above) when government effort to nationalize the wholesale trade in wheat ended in failure and the government then started drawing back from its control of the economy. This was followed by a creeping devaluation of the rupee (by 20% between 1971 and 1975) and some minor deregulation of the domestic economy. Despite its limited scope Panagariya (2008) credits this "first phase of liberalisation" with average GDP growth rate of nearly 6 per cent between 1975–6 and 1978–9. Liberalization then continued into the next decade under Indira Gandhi. The freedom to import capital goods was increased, there was some easing of capacity constraints on domestic production and greater freedoms to engage in foreign collaborations. Reforms under Rajiv Gandhi after 1984 focused on domestic liberalization, easing licensed capacity constraints, reducing the bite of the MRTP, and raising the ceiling on small-scale enterprises. There was a particular push for exports, which included various tax and concessional credit incentives and the opening of more export processing zones (EPZs). The real exchange rate depreciated by about 30 per cent between 1985–6 and 1989–90. This liberalization was primarily aimed at the domestic economy as the effective rate of protection on imports remained very high into the late-1980s (Kotwal *et al.* 2011: 157).

The dramatic shift to liberalization occurred after 1991 when India accelerated domestic liberalization and opened up to international trade. The share of products subject to quantitative restrictions declined rapidly and average tariffs fell from more than 80 per cent in 1990 to 37 per cent in 1996. The Indian rupee was devalued against the dollar by 20 per cent in July 1991 (Topalova 2004). The controls on large enterprises under the MRTP Act were abolished and emphasis instead placed on unfair trade practices (with little practical effect). The new policy limited the extensive public-sector monopoly to only eight sectors based on security and strategic grounds. The RBI introduced the concept of automatic approval for FDI and the RBI was empowered to approve equity investment up to 51 per cent foreign ownership in 34 priority industries. Infrastructure was opened up to 100 per cent foreign-owned FDI for projects in construction and maintenance of roads, highways, bridges, toll roads, ports and harbours. Although the public sector continued to dominate the banking sector throughout the 1990s, private banks were permitted to operate and FDI up to 75 per cent foreign ownership was permitted. By the early 2000s 50 foreign banks were in operation (Panagariya 2004, 2008).

An evocative cover of *The Economist* magazine in the early 1990s showed a picture of a caged Bengal tiger. The clear implication being that economic liberalization (opening the cage) should unleash rapid economic growth. Panagariya (2008) does call the years 1988–2006 the "triumph of liberalization". But despite substantial economic liberalization after 1991 economic and productivity growth rates were no higher in the 1990s than they had been in the 1980s. By the end of the 1990s growth even showed signs of slowing down and returning to a much longer-term historical average of 3–4 per cent per annum. Those familiar with the wider literature on drivers of episodes of growth would not find the lack of link between liberalization and growth a surprise. Hausmann *et al.* (2004) for example, found that only 14.5 per cent of growth accelerations are associated with liberalization, while 85.5 per cent of growth accelerations are not preceded or accompanied by liberalization. This presents us with a double paradox that is hard to explain given the importance economists and policy-makers have attached to economic liberalization; growth without liberalization in the 1980s and liberalization without growth in the 1990s.

There have been various attempts to explain this apparent paradox. Bhagwati and Panagariya (2013) argued that liberalization over the 1990s had just not gone far enough to unleash the Bengal Tiger and should have been extended to the labour market, to agriculture, to energy and to FDI in retail. Dreze and Sen (2013) argued that liberalization was necessary but needed to be supported by vigorous public action in improving health, education, empowerment, and infrastructure to realize the positive impacts on economic growth. The paradox for some has been resolved by considering lags. In the short-term liberalization may lead to negative effects, especially among firms who are suffering from the effects of extra competition from imports and new entrants in the domestic market, resulting in the loss of markets and declining capacity utilization. This will lead to the bankruptcy of some inefficient firms. Other firms will be forced to upgrade technology, production processes and output mix to adjust to a more competitive global trading environment. It takes time for firms to utilize new capacity and new technology through learning-by-doing and by exploiting scale economies (Alfaro & Chari 2009; Virmani & Hashim 2011). There is good evidence of such a "J-curve" in India's GDP and productivity growth. Productivity growth in manufacturing was slow or stagnant in the 1990s and surged in the early 2000s (Virmani & Hashim 2011: 15). This occurred across a whole range of sectors including textile products, chemicals and chemical products, food products and beverages, motor vehicles, electrical machinery, and other transport equipment (Virmani & Hashim 2011: 22).

Looking at the effects of liberalization over time it makes sense to use more disaggregated data to study how liberalization transformed the economy at the micro-level. Such efforts also provide support for the J-curve effect. The study of company balance sheets for 15,500 firms between 1988 and 2005 shows that liberalization led to the bankruptcy of some older firms and to the substantial entry of new domestic and foreign firms (Alfaro & Chari 2009: 16). These new domestic and foreign firms entered a wide range of sectors including food, textiles, paper manufacturing, chemicals and plastic manufacturing, metals and industrial manufacturing construction and retail, tourism and media, financial services, real estate, and computing (Alfaro & Chari 2009). This was dynamism but dynamism at the margin. The economy in 2006 after 15 years of liberalization measures remained dominated by state-owned and traditional private-sector incumbents. The exceptions were the rising dominance of private firms in business and IT services, communications services, media, and health (Alfaro & Chari 2009). The growth of the telecommunications sector and with it, improved communications (the cell-phone revolution) and diffusion of the internet were clearly linked to liberalization, specifically the breakup of the government monopoly of telecommunications and the freedom to import telecommunication technology (Panagariya 2008: xxvii). The Air Corporations Act of 1953 merged all existing airlines other than Air India International to form Indian Airlines. The government maintained a monopoly over domestic flights and a sole carrier (Air India) was permitted to operate international flights. Reforms in 1997 freed entry into the airline industry and led to the entry of Spice Jet, Sahara, GoAir, IndiGo, and Kingfisher among others, which competed against the state-owned airline. Domestic private airlines were also allowed to fly abroad. There were also liberal bilateral agreements with major destination countries to allow greater reciprocal market access. The total number of passengers increased from 8.1 million in 1991 to 22.7 million in 2005 with the private share of the market rising from near nothing in 1991 to 80 per cent in 2006. By the mid-2000s India had 125 airports, including 11 international airports. Various of these were either constructed or run under public–private partnerships (Panagariya 2008: 97, 399). By 2017 India had been the world's fastest growing aviation market for three consecutive years and was poised to overtake the UK to become the world's third largest market behind the US and China. After growth of almost 17 per cent over the previous year by 2017 India's domestic air traffic nearly doubled to 117 million passengers with 100 flights taking off every hour compared with 67 in 2011.

There was some concern that FDI in the 1990s was actually reducing competition in industry. Between 1997 and 1999 for example nearly 40 per cent of FDI inflows into India were by global firms who wanted to buy up existing Indian enterprises rather than establish new firms and compete with incumbents. Such takeovers were concentrated in consumer goods such as food and beverages, household appliances, and pharmaceuticals. Multinational corporations (MNCs) were purchasing Indian firms to acquire marketing and distribution networks and sometimes the brand loyalty of established domestic firms. Coca-Cola, for example, re-entered India in the 1990s and acquired Parle, then the largest soft drinks firm with several established brands, nationwide bottling and distribution network. Gillette started in India by acquiring Indian Shaving Products and then took over Wilkinson and Harbanslal Malhotra and so acquired a near monopoly in shaving products (Kumar 2000). There was a more general worry that foreign firms with superior technology, marketing skills and financial strength would wipe out domestic firms. Over the 1990s liberalization of the automobile industry for foreign entrants led to the entry of almost all leading auto manufacturers to the country: Daewoo entered through a joint venture with DCM group, Ford with Mahindra, FIAT with Premier Automobiles, GM with Hindustan Motors, and Mercedes Benz with Telco. In all these cases the local joint-venture partners were later dropped by the MNC (Kumar 2000). Detailed firm-level evidence for the 1990s shows that these fears were not warranted. There is evidence that over the longer term liberalization reduced industrial concentration. It is true that the size of the average state-owned firm was increasing after 1991, but this was offset by the trend for the average manufacturing firm in India to become smaller in terms of assets, sales and profits (Alfaro & Chari 2009, 2012). These changes were clearly linked to the reform process. Average firm size declined more over the 1990s in those industries which were deregulated although the already large firms got even larger following such deregulation. Average firm size also declined significantly in industries that were opened up to FDI and trade liberalization (Alfaro & Chari 2012).

In the automobile sector while the pattern of joint ventures did not last long the entry of new producers stimulated the growth of a dynamic and competitive auto component sector. By 1999 the automobile industry produced a total of 4.5 million two- and three-wheel vehicles and recorded a turnover of $104 billion, which made India the fifth largest producer among developing countries. Many key global suppliers such as Delphi, Lucas-TVS, and Denso invested in India to follow global car manufacturers. Companies such as Ford, GMI, MB, and Toyota all encouraged their established suppliers to open manufacturing facilities in India. The growth of the middle class and optimistic predictions of its future consumption patterns was a draw for FDI in automobiles (D'Costa 2005). By the mid-1990s large business houses such as Tata (includes TELCO) and Birla (includes HML) as well as vehicle producers such as Mahindra & Mahindra set up joint ventures with global suppliers to produce key auto components. The component industry grew by an average of more than 20 per cent per annum throughout the 1990s. By the mid-1990s the Indian auto component sector comprised 400 formal and 5,000 informal sector firms. Much of this early growth was linked to liberalization of FDI combined with clear policy guidance for foreign investors. Until 1991 the government phased manufacturing program (PMP) forced foreign firms to achieve 95 per cent local purchase of inputs. Although the PMP was lifted in 1992 continuing high customs duties on imported automobiles and components continued to promote the sourcing of local inputs. Localization forced assemblers to use domestic small suppliers and upgrade their production capabilities, which raised technology and quality standards in the domestic component industry (Okada 2004).

Exports of software increased from $128 million in 1990/91 to $8.3 billion in 2001. Some attribute this success to specifically Indian advantages including the abundance of low-wage scientific and engineering manpower with English-language skills. By the late-1990s India's educational system churned out 75,000–80,000 software professionals annually (Patibandla & Petersen 2002). Liberalization was also important. Greater openness to FDI in technology sectors permitted the entry of a subsidiary of Texas Instruments (TI) in Bangalore in 1985. TI was the first private-sector firm to install its own satellite link. TI generated strong links with various local universities and research laboratories and stimulated the growth of local firms such as Tata Consultancy Services (TCS), Infosys and Wipro (all located in Bangalore). This successful entry was replicated by other firms. Hewlett Packard (HP) started operations in Bangalore in 1989 with ten people and by the late-1990s was employing 1,100 engineers. HP developed strong ties with Indian firms such as TCS as well as the Indian Institute of Science in Bangalore for its R & D activities (*ibid.* 2002). Firm-level data for 20 large Indian software firms over the 1990s shows that MNC presence in the sector and especially for firms with any sort of foreign collaboration had a positive link with productivity of domestic software firms (*ibid.* 2002). Migration has been crucial to this rise, both as an alleged constraint as software professionals left mainly for the US in the 1990s, but also later as they increasingly returned bringing with them new skills and international contacts (D'Costa 2016).

A TRIUMPH OF LIBERALIZATION OR
SOMETHING A BIT DARKER? 2003 ONWARDS

After 2003 the Indian economy appeared to suddenly shift gear. This was a surprise to contemporary observers. India was still recovering from a number of significant external shocks including the more marginal impact of the 1997 Asian financial crisis, and more importantly the international sanctions imposed after India and Pakistan conducted nuclear tests in 1998 and the bursting of the US dot.com boom in the early 2000s, which had so benefited Indian software firms. There is an exuberance to the reporting of economic growth statistics after 2003, although with much less rigour (as with *c*.1980), in order to demonstrate a statistical break.

Table 2.3 Economic growth in India, 2003–09 (ave. % per annum)

GDP	9
Manufacturing	10
Agriculture	5
Services	10
Capital goods	14.3

Source: Nagaraj 2008: 56.

Annual growth in beverages, textile products, basic metals, transport equipment, and electric and non-electric machinery (see Table 2.3) all exceeded 10 per cent (Nagaraj 2008: 56). There was a turnaround in the growth of agricultural output, from 1.0 per cent per annum between 1997 and 2003 to 4.9 per cent per annum between 2003 and 2008 and 3.6 per cent per annum between 2008 and 2012 (Mohan & Kapur 2015: 3).

India's investment rate increased from around 25 per cent of GDP in the second half of the 1990s to 33 per cent in 2006/07. This rise in investment was almost entirely financed from domestic savings, which increased from 23.7 to 34.8 per cent of GDP during the same period. The share of wages in GDP declined in the three decades prior to the early 2000s then declined more sharply between 2005–06 and 2011–12. This squeeze on wage growth boosted corporate profitability (Roy 2016: 36) which in turn boosted corporate savings. This has in turn been linked to the greater support from the state to private business (noted earlier in the chapter). Tax reforms improved government revenue collection and the better financial performance of public-sector enterprises turned around public savings (Nagaraj 2008; Walton 2011). Annual productivity growth (as measured by TFP) increased from 2.7 per cent between 1997 and 2001 to 3.3 per cent between 2002 and 2007 and further to 3.6 per cent between 2008 and 2011 (Mishra 2013: 57).

This growth was also supported by rising consumption, a striking demographic transition (5 million extra young people entering the labour force per year), a surge in exports (from $80 billion to $160 billion between 2002 and 2005) and a rise in foreign direct investment (FDI) (from $6 billion to $40 billion between 2002 and 2007). India became more integrated with the global economy. India's exports-to-GDP ratio increased from 14 per cent in 2002 to 25 per cent in 2009. Between 2003 and 2008 the current account deficit as a share of GDP averaged only -0.3 per cent and inflation only 5 per cent (Mohan & Kapur 2015: 3).

A less benign view of the economic boom starts with an observation on the changing composition of production and exports. The share of manufacturing products in total exports in India declined from 80.7 per cent in 1999–2000 to 61.4 per cent in 2013–14 (Roy 2016). The 2000s saw a rise in the share of resource-based production and exports which has important implications for the growth story. These are what Walton (2012) calls the "rent-thick" sectors. Such sectors include real estate, infrastructure, construction, mining, telecoms, cement, and media. The years after 1991 saw much of the licensing and regulatory framework being removed for manufacturing. Rent-thick sectors were different. Resources required permissions to undertake investment and business activity. Infrastructure projects, mining and spectrum licence allocation required government permissions or contracts. Large projects were likely to require environmental impact assessments, which are then verified by the state. Sectors such as IT/software, engineering firms, pharmaceuticals, finance and banking required more limited interaction with the state (Walton 2011; D'Costa 2018).

The shift to resource-based production and exports and the close relation of these sectors to the state and politics tightened the link between politics and business over the 2000s. This created more opportunities for corruption and so the ability of incumbent business to use the political process to their own benefit by preventing contracts, licences or permissions going to new entrants or other outsiders (Walton 2011). National scams came to a head in 2010 with a report from the Comptroller and Auditor General of India (CAG) on the 2007–08 3G spectrum allocations for mobile phones which caused a presumptive loss to the Treasury of $31 billion (Walton 2011). A feature of growth in the 2000s was the sharp rise in extreme wealth, most notably in the number and size of India's billionaires. Using the annual billionaire list published by Forbes, Gandhi and Walton (2012) find that there were only two billionaires in India in the mid-1990s with a combined wealth of $3.2 billion. By 2012 there were 46 with a combined wealth of $176.3 billion. Total billionaire wealth rose from 1 per cent of GDP in the mid-1990s to 22 per cent at its peak in 2008, and fell to 10 per cent in 2012 in part due to the Global Financial Crisis. In the US and UK by comparison it was between 4–6 per cent. Overall 43 per cent of billionaires (60 per cent of total billionaire wealth) originated from rent-thick sectors and this ratio increased over the 2000s (Gandhi & Walton 2012). Subramanian argues, "Some of the infrastructure investments were funded by reckless and imprudent lending by public-sector banks, which funneled resources to high-risk, politically connected borrowers." (2018: 34). Walton (2011) argues this wealth accumulation means that India in the 2000s was coming to resemble the Robber Barons of the US in the late nineteenth century, where individuals such as Carnegie, Vanderbilt, and Rockefeller then generated wealth through unethical practices and the abuse of monopoly power. For Bhagwati and Panagariya (2013: 52) the similarity is not so apparent. The nineteenth-

century US economy, they point out, was not subject to labour, regulatory, and social legislation at the federal level. India has a longstanding
commitment to eradicating poverty underpinned by universal adult suf-
frage. Railways remain a public sector monopoly and the government is
a dominant producer in coal, steel, petroleum, engineering, electricity,
and banking. In the US "gilded age", sectors such as steel, oil, sugar, and
meatpacking were dominated by large corporations whereas in contemporary India they are far more competitive sectors (Bhagwati & Panagariya
2013: 54).

Even if the comparison to nineteenth-century America is one too far,
many scholars have argued that the rapid growth in the 2000s was associated with rising inequality underpinned by closer business–state links that
was leading to an economy becoming less competitive and less dynamic.
The previous section showed that there was significant new entry of firms
in the 1990s, this was followed by virtual stagnation in the 2000s along
with rising industry concentration and so declining competition (Walton
2011: 47). Firms were able to boost profits and market share in sectors
such as pharmaceuticals and steel without attracting new entrants. There
is a consequent debate about whether this combination was evidence of
firms with large market shares being able to control the market (and perhaps the state) or of successful, efficient and profitable firms expanding
their market share. Using regression analysis, Mody *et al* (2011) find that
the profit rate is more closely linked to the sales growth of firms rather
than their market share. A proxy measure of efficiency (the sales-to-assets
ratio of a firm) shows that more efficient firms have more persistent profits. Together these results support the view that dynamic efficiency rather
than market power was the main reason behind rising corporate profits after 2003. This process can still of course be associated with rising
inequality but the cause is arguably more benign. There is also no evidence that firms linked to big business houses behaved differently from
stand-alone firms. The top 50 business houses were actually less able to
sustain high rates of profits than other firms (Mody *et al* 2011).

State capacity. It is not easy to measure state capacity. Some corners of the Indian state performed well in the 2000s such as the Telecom Regulatory Authority of India (TRAI), the Securities and Exchange Board of India (SEBI) and the Insurance Regulatory and Development Authority (IRDA). Greater transparency over the functioning of the state emerged through the Right to Information (RTI) Act passed in 2005 (Subramanian 2007). More generally, state capacity as measured by the ability to prevent theft and collect electricity bills, to solve criminal cases, or to collect customs revenue, was declining over the 2000s (Subramanian 2007: 209). The Indian state continued to be unable to mobilize the necessary tax revenue to fund its own expenditures. Cross-country analysis indicates that the general government revenue–GDP ratio in India is low (around 10% of GDP) even accounting for its per capita income. The Indian state is unable to tax the wealthy. The peak income tax rate in India applies to annual income of Rs 1 million and above which was almost 11 times per capita incomes in 2013. The corresponding OECD average was 4 times per capita income (Mohan & Kapur 2015). Only around 3 per cent of Indians pay income tax, including only about half of all doctors. A significant reform was the constitutional amendment to implement the Goods and Services Tax (GST) in 2016. This is a value added tax on goods and services that was labelled "the greatest fiscal policy reform in Indian economic history" (Subramanian 2018: xxxiv). The GST has widened the tax base and is likely to lead to greater revenue buoyancy in future years. The centralization and unification of the GST has helped create a single national market to replace the tax system that fragmented India along state lines.

The Global Competitiveness Reports compile indices, ranging from 1 to 7 (7 being the best) to measure various aspects of governance. Table 2.4 compares the reports from 2006/07 and 2014/15 which reveals a widespread deterioration in state capacity, across the quality of institutions, judicial independence, favouritism in government decision-making, waste in government spending and an improving if low measure of the reliability of the police. It is an apparent puzzle, why growth took off after 2003 despite the lack of improvement in state capacity.

Table 2.4 Declining state capacity, 2006/07–2014/15

Measure of governance	2006/07	2014/15
Quality of institutions	4.5	3.8
Judicial independence	5.9	4.2
Favouritism shown in decisions of government officials	3.6	3.4
Wastefulness of government spending	3.6	3.5
Reliability of police	1.9	3.6

Source: World Economic Forum, *The Global Competitiveness Report, 2006–07* (2006) and *The Global Competitiveness Report, 2014–15* (2014).

Public investment. The episode of growth after 2003 was linked to some specific increases in public investment. The centrally run schemes, the National Highways Development Project (NHDP) and Pradhan Mantri Gram Sadak Yojana (PMGSY) improved road connectivity after 2000 between major cities and within rural areas. The NHDP was centred around the so-called "Golden Quadrilateral", which aimed to connect Delhi, Mumbai, Chennai, and Kolkata with four-lane highways. The project was started in December 2000 and by January 2007 had converted 5,521 km into four lanes (Panagariya 2008). By 2012 the NHDP had invested $71 billion (Khanna 2016). Investment in roads increased from 0.4 per cent of GDP in the late-1990s to around 1.2 per cent by the late-2000s (Mohan & Kapur 2015).

Public investment was not the driver of rapid growth after 2003 as the 2000s saw a gradual privatization of infrastructure investment. The share of infrastructure spending to GDP increased from 5 per cent in 2006–07 to 6.3 per cent in 2008–09 then declined to 5.4 per cent in 2011–12. Unlike in earlier years this increase was driven by the private sector. The share of total infrastructure spending by the public sector declined steadily, from 73.9 per cent in 2006–07 to 59.1 per cent in 2011–12 (Mohan & Kapur 2015: 16). In agriculture as well total gross capital formation as a percentage of agricultural GDP increased from 12.9 per cent in the five-year period ending in 2003–04 to 17 per cent in 2012–13, but was mainly driven by the private sector (Deokar & Shetty 2014).

Income distribution. In relation to the 2003 episode of growth there has been an increase in studies exploring whether economic growth has been accompanied by rising inequality (Sarkar & Mehta 2010), and if so, how that inequality is structured according to discrimination (Banerjee *et al.* 2009), class (Vakulabharanam 2010), caste (Thorat & Newman 2007), and between states (Baddeley *et al.* 2006). Other studies have looked at the link between income distribution and economic growth, such as the political economy explanation for the slowdown after 2011 from Sen and Kar (2014).

While discussion of the causal impact of inequality has faded, with some exceptions, from discussion in India, it has gained much more widespread interest elsewhere. For example, Joseph Stiglitz has argued that inequality in the United States was an underlying cause of the 2008 Global Financial Crisis. Growing inequality, he argued, redistributed incomes from the poorest (who would be more likely to consume) to the richest (who were more likely to save) and to sustain consumption demand and so economic growth required an "artificial prop, which in the years before the crisis, came in the form of a housing bubble fuelled by Fed policies" (Stiglitz 2013: 106). It is not surprising, however, that this debate has had so little traction in contemporary India. In India, unlike the US, monetary measures of poverty are falling (Datt & Ravallion 2010) and the debate is almost entirely about the extent of that fall, not the fact of it (Deaton & Kozel 2005). In India, again unlike the US, real wages among the poorest have been rising not stagnating over recent decades (Kijima 2006; Sarkar & Mehta 2010) and consumption amongst the poorest in India is increasing over time (Deaton & Dreze 2009), although there are concerns that the rising prices of privatized education and health are crowding out consumption of nutrition, health and other important necessities (Pal 2013). It is easy to exaggerate the impact of consumer consumption on the Indian economy. Although the average annual growth of consumer expenditure in India on durable goods was 10 per cent over the 2000s, India remained a story of traditional consumption, not of shopping malls in Mumbai. The share of durable goods in total consumer expenditure rose from 2.8 per cent in 2000–01 to only 3.9 per cent in 2009–10. The share of more traditional non-durable goods and services still accounted for over 90 per cent of consumer expenditure by 2009–10 (Roy 2016: 37).

Agriculture–industry linkages. The macroeconomic link between agriculture and the 2003 episode of growth is often neglected. For example, Deokar and Shetty (2014) argue that 2004–05 was a turning point for agriculture. The average growth rate of output increased from 2.4 per cent between 1994–5 and 2004–05 to 4 per cent until 2013–14. They seek to explain the policy causes of this – which included the launching of the National Horticulture Mission, reforms to the agricultural extension system, launch of the Bharat Nirman Project in 2005–06 (to upgrade rural infrastructure), and efforts to boost credit to agriculture in three years after 2004–05 – rather than explore the macroeconomic significance of this shift. There are some exceptions, for example, Balakrishnan (2014) suggests but offers no rigorous empirical evidence that the poor harvests between 2008–09 and 2012–13 contributed to the slowdown of GDP and higher inflation in India in the late 2000s.

Institutions. The conventional view is that formal institutions such as written contracts, laws protecting private property rights, and functioning courts are necessary preconditions for investors to feel secure in making long-term productive investments. More important in explaining growth in contemporary India, however, are informal institutions in the form of personalized deals between political and economic elites (Sen & Kar 2014: 6). The early 1990s saw a strengthening of the predictability of the deal environment especially at the micro level. The dismantling of the industrial licensing system in 1991 removed an important source of uncertainty. The discretionary/case-by-case nature of private investment decisions, and access to imports having to seek government permissions was done away with. There is also evidence that some deals became more open and transparent in sectors such as pharmaceuticals and IT. This pattern fits well with the evidence on substantial entry of new firms in the 1990s (Mody *et al.* 2011).

We have seen that there was a shift in the pattern of growth in the 2000s towards sectors such as construction, real estate, communications, mining, banking and insurance and within manufacturing towards refined petroleum. A sharp increase in the global price of various minerals increased the value of licences allocated by the state to extract those minerals. These sectors required close collaboration between government and big business. This was most evident in corrupt deals political and economic elites struck in sectors such as bauxite, coal, iron ore, manganese and natural gas in Jharkhand, Karnataka, Goa and Odisha (Sen & Kar 2014). The slowdown in economic growth (to 3.4% per annum between 2011 and 2013) was, argue Sen and Kar (2014), a consequence of the popular discontent arising from the excessive corrupt incomes earned by political and economic elites after 2003. This discontent was variously reflected in mass mobilization against land acquisition (and dispossession) efforts in Odisha and West Bengal (D'Costa & Chakraborty 2017), and organizations such as the Supreme Court and CAG investigating corruption. In response to the controversy an activist Supreme Court banned iron-ore exports and the CAG investigated corruption in the allocation of 2G mobile phone licences and coal mining licences. This auditing frightened off business investors and increased the burdens on legal compliance. Increasingly, they argue, the ruling party at the centre lost the authority to credibly commit to new deals with investors in the face of popular and legal challenges. Investor perception of investment risk started increasing after 2006, and corporate investment and so economic growth declined as a consequence (Sen & Kar 2014: 22). A measure of economic uncertainty (combining a measure of press coverage of economic policy uncertainty and a measure of the disagreement among major economic forecasters regarding key macroeconomic variables such as inflation and the budget deficit) showed a sharp rise from the second-half of 2011. This rise was closely matched by declining business confidence and investment projects after 2010 (Anand & Tulin 2014).

Other evidence shows that political uncertainty as a characteristic feature of politics in the 2000s is exaggerated. There was a distinct change in politics from the 1990s onwards, which saw political fragmentation dating from the late-1960s being partially reversed. The decline of Congress during the 1990s saw the emergence of a relatively stable two-party (alliance) system. The number of seats won by Congress plummeted from 232 in 1991 to 114 in 1999 (from 415 in 1984) but the number of seats won by the Bharatiya Janata Party (BJP) showed a near equivalent increase, from 120 in 1991 to 182 in 1999. Congress revived in the 2000s to mirror the decline of the BJP, who fell to 116 seats in the same year. In 2014 the collapse of Congress (to 44 seats) was mirrored by the surge in support for the BJP (282 seats). The combined share of votes won by the two main parties (47.4–56.6%) remained very stable over the 1990s and 2000s. The choice for 2014 elections was frequently presented as being one between Narendra Modi (BJP) and Rahul Gandhi (Congress) and their regional allies; it saw a small (less than 3%) increase in their combined share of the votes and a negligible increase (0.73%) in their combined seat share.

This decline in political instability gave politicians and political parties a greater incentive to consider the longer term. The BJP went into the 2004 election reasonably convinced it would win, as did the Congress in 2009; both headed relatively stable coalitions largely constructed before the elections. This was in sharp contrast to the earlier 1990s when unstable coalitions put together largely after the elections were faced with the constant threat (and reality) of collapse. This gradual stabilization of Indian politics can be characterized as a shift from "roving" to "settled" bandits (Olson 1993). Politicians facing a high probability of losing office in the near future ("roving bandits"), whether democratic or authoritarian, face an incentive to maximize plunder in the short run. A leader with a monopoly of power and a reasonable expectation of surviving in office and winning subsequent elections ("stationary bandit") will have an incentive instead to promote economic growth. A stationary bandit will conduct "theft" through predictable taxes or bribes leaving producers with an incentive to generate incomes (Olson 1993).

3

Measuring economic and human development

This short chapter will present some of the sources of statistical data for key economic and human development fundamentals of the Indian economy discussed in this book, including industry information, poverty, population, height, literacy and health.

BUSINESS AND INDUSTRY

The Annual Survey of Industries (ASI) is conducted every year by the Indian Ministry of Statistics. The survey conducts a sample of all registered factories employing 10 or more workers using electric power, or 20 or more workers without using power. The surveyed factories are those registered as factories under the 1948 Factories Act and so comprise the organized (registered) part of Indian manufacturing. All firms employing 100 or more workers are surveyed annually and smaller factories are sampled. Plants report on the value of output, materials and fuels. There have been some changes in methodology and industrial classifications over time and there were noted problems with the collection of data in 1996–7. This makes it difficult to compare data over time.

Another source of data is the Prowess database collected by the Centre for Monitoring the Indian Economy (CMIE) from company balance sheets and income statements. This covers about 10,800 firms in the organized sector, those registered companies that submit financial statements. This includes firms in a wide range of industries including mining, basic man-ufacturing, financial and real estate services, and energy distribution. One problem is that apart from some financial data which goes back to 1989, the Prowess database only goes back to 1995 which makes it hard to study the before and after impact of liberalization in 1991. An advantage over the ASI data, which is based on annual samples, is that the Prowess data covers the same firms over time, which makes it easier to see how firms adjust in response to policy and other changes. However, unlisted foreign firm's data is only available if firms choose to disclose financial information; some, such as McDonalds and Coca Cola refuse to do so. Data is collected on firms classified across 62 industries by size of firm, by assets and sales, profitability and ownership (foreign, public or private). ASI is confined to manufacturing firms, whereas Prowess also includes service firms includ-ing defence, restaurants, hotels and IT services (Alfaro & Chari 2009).

CENSUS: POPULATION, EDUCATION AND LITERACY

Much of the data regarding human welfare in India, such as literacy, health and population growth comes from the census. India conducted its first national census in 1872 and has conducted one roughly every ten years since. Other Asian countries started much later and/or have endured long gaps between censuses. In Pakistan since independence a national cen-sus has only been carried out in 1961, 1972, 1981, 1998 and 2017, the last had been planned and postponed in both 2001 and 2008. The statistical agencies in India are staffed by highly competent statisticians and the cen-sus today relies on 2.2 million enumerators, most of whom are teachers, to visit every household in India. Data collection efforts are much less exposed to political interference than other parts of the Indian state and are very transparent in their methods.

The census data shows that India until well-into the late colonial period had appalling levels of mortality, very low levels of literacy and slow rates of economic modernization. The census in 1871 estimated India's population at 255 million. There was no sign of a demographic transition over the next 50 years. Between 1881 and 1921 fertility and mortality rates both remained very high. Life expectancy was 23.67 for men and 25.58 for women in 1871–81, and by 1911–12 this had fallen to 19.42 for men and 20.91 for women. In 1891 the literacy rate was 6.1 per cent (0.5% for women) and 30 years later, in 1921, still only 8.3 per cent (2% for women). The share of the population living in towns of over 5,000 people rose only slowly, from 9.2 per cent in 1881 to 10.1 per cent in 1921. This slow growth of urbanization was concentrated in the main capital seats of Calcutta, Bombay, and Madras and also in Hyderabad. There were widespread declines in other urban areas. It was only after 1911–12 that there was sustained growth in the overall urban population. Given these outcomes it was perhaps not surprising that between 1834 and 1920 more than 20 million people left India, mainly to serve as indentured or contract labour, to Fiji, Mauritius and elsewhere (Habib 2006).

Table 3.1 shows the very slow increase in school attendance in India over the 60 years to independence and the faster rate of improvement thereafter.

Table 3.1 Average years of schooling in the population aged 25+ years

	1890–01	1950–01	1999–2000
UK	4.23	7.32	9.35
India	0.20	1.20	4.77

Source: Broadberry & Gupta 2010: 272.

The slow progress of educational attainment can be partly explained by the minimal levels of government spending. Per capita expenditure on education and the share of education in total expenditure was low in British India compared to both the UK and other British colonies, and even compared to the princely states in India and to other underdeveloped countries. What little the colonial government did spend, however, was heavily weighted towards secondary education (14–18 yrs) and higher (18+ yrs) education. The percentage of the population in secondary/higher education was greater in India than in France and Japan and only marginally below England and Wales. Table 3.2 shows that the share of secondary and higher education in total government expenditure on education in India was significantly higher than in Indonesia and Japan from 1890 right up until the 1970s or 1990s. As Chapter 5 shows this legacy-pattern of education continued after 1947.

Table 3.2 Expenditure on secondary and higher education as a percentage share of total government expenditure on education, 1890–1990

	India	Indonesia	Japan
1890	61.2	18.8	14.8
1910	62.3	18.5	24.2
1930	59.5	21.4	30.8
1950	57.3	28.2	59.6
1970	75.5	36.2	62.9
1990	56.9	58.8	66.9

Source: Broadberry & Gupta 2010: 272.

According to the 1951 census, 9 per cent of the female population and 27 per cent of males were literate. The perceived neglect by the colonial government had led to a determination in 1947 to provide free and compulsory education for all children up to age of 14 by 1960. Indeed, this aspiration was written into the Indian Constitution. After 1947 the government returned to this pledge on numerous occasions but continued to fail to achieve it. It was not until the 2000s that India started to approach universal school enrolment, and even then only among the earliest years of primary schooling. The literacy rate rose to 52 per cent by 1991. The 1990s saw an increase to 65 per cent in 2001 which was the highest absolute increase in any decade going back to the 1880s (Kingdon *et al.* 2005). Even in traditionally, poorly performing states such as Bihar female literacy rose 12.3 percentage points, Uttar Pradesh 18.6 percentage points and Rajasthan 23.9 percentage points, although by 2001 literacy for women still remained low in these states at 35.2 per cent, 43.9 per cent and 44.3 per cent respectively. In Gujarat which did well economically over the 1990s overall literacy rates increased by only 3.4 percentage points (from 73.1 to 76.5%) (Kingdon *et al.* 2005: 133–4). There were reasons for optimism at the beginning of the twenty-first century. The future of literacy is driven by the literacy of young women, who will later become mothers. In India the literacy of mothers has a robust link to school attendance and literacy of children (especially girls). Between 1992/3 and 1998/9 literacy rates among rural girls aged 6–9 rose 16.5 percentage points (from 47.1 to 63.6%) and among urban girls aged 10–14 literacy rates reached 90.7 per cent (Kingdon *et al.* 2005: 134).

In theory the Indian census follows the UNESCO definition of literacy: the ability to read and write with understanding a short simple sentence relevant to everyday life. The census in India, however, does not have the resources to assess literacy to this degree. Instead the 2 million plus census enumerators ask every household head (or senior member) to report whether each individual in the household is literate. It is not clear what "literate" would mean to each head of household. One may only give information on literacy among male members if they are the ones who work outside the household and are therefore perceived to have a practical need for literacy. Estimates of literacy may be exaggerated for the purposes of portraying a household as more cultured and of higher status, or reduced if it is assumed low literacy might prompt the government to intervene with new schools, scholarships or other forms of welfare. The head of household, particularly if illiterate themselves, may have no reliable means of estimating the literacy of others. Kothari and Bandyopadhyay (2010) have asked the question "Can India's 'literates' read?" and define literacy to mean the ability to decode a grade 2 level text competently, if not perfectly. Their 2002 research was conducted across randomly selected villages in Rajasthan, Uttar Pradesh, Madhya Pradesh and Bihar and covered almost 18,000 individuals. In the first round of data collection they replicated the census method and found a literacy rate of 68.7 per cent, including female literacy of 55.7 per cent and male literacy of 80.4 per cent. In the second round of data collection they measured literacy by demonstrated reading ability. By this measure the literacy rate dropped by between 20 and 43 per cent (Kothari & Bandyopadhyay 2010: 715). Ninety per cent of children who had completed first grade (6–7 yrs) were reported as literate by the census method, although among those completing the first grade only 0.6 per cent were found to be good readers and only 27 per cent were able to read a little bit. Even after completing grade 5 (10–11 yrs), 25 per cent of students could not read at all, and only 12 per cent had become good and regular readers (Kothari & Bandyopadhyay 2010). Rigorous evidence on the quality of education is hard to come by. The Indian government was long reluctant to participate in large-scale testing exercises such as Trends in International Mathematics and Science Study (TIMSS) or the Programme for International Student Assessment (PISA). What evidence is available is discussed in Chapter 5.

POVERTY AND CONSUMPTION

Official poverty estimates in India are based on regular consumer expenditure surveys conducted by the National Sample Survey Organisation (NSSO). The method of random sampling of households was pioneered in India during the 1940s and 1950s. The NSSO conducts large consumer expenditure surveys of hundreds of thousands of households every five or six years and smaller surveys annually. The official poverty estimates are based on the larger surveys and count the number of people living in households with monthly per capita total expenditure below a poverty line specific to the state and whether the household is urban or rural (Deaton & Dreze 2005). According to these official estimates the headcount measure of poverty in India between independence and the 1970s fluctuated between 45 per cent and 65 per cent of the population. While following a similar trend in rural and urban areas poverty was consistently about 10 per cent higher in rural areas. There was a rise in the first half of the 1950s and in the second half of the 1960s, and a fall from the mid-1950s to the mid-1960s. Poverty was stable at around 65 per cent of the population throughout the 1970s and between c.1980 and 2017 poverty fell more or less continuously.

The design of Indian poverty surveys has evolved over time, under continual and transparent discussion. The length of the period over which consumption is reported by those being interviewed is significant for measuring poverty. The NSSO adopted a uniform 30-day recall period after conducting experiments in the 1950s. The NSSO ran a new series of experiments in the early-1990s by randomly assigning households to one of two questionnaires with different reporting periods. There was a questionnaire with a seven-day reporting period for items purchased regularly (food, paan, tobacco), 365 days for less frequent items (durable goods, clothing, footwear, institutional medical care) and 30 days for everything else. This method gave poverty counts that were only half those derived from the questionnaire with a uniform 30-day reporting period. People declared more consumption of those regular items (such as food and tobacco) when recalling consumption over seven rather than 30 days and slightly more purchases of infrequent items (such as durable goods and clothing) when recalling consumption over 365 rather than 30 days. This was an interesting result, but the experiment offered no guidance on which was the most accurate method (Deaton & Dreze 2005). The consumer expenditure survey for 1999 faced the dilemma of which survey design to use. Eventually a compromise was reached in which, for food, paan and tobacco each household was asked to report all items over both a 7-day and a 30-day period, and the traditional 30-day reporting period for durables, clothing, education and institutional medical expenses was replaced by a 365-day period. As well as not being comparable in method with earlier surveys, the outcome of these changes were not easy to anticipate.

The final results for the 1999 poverty estimates based on the new method showed a sharp fall in measured poverty from 37 per cent in 1993/4 to 27 per cent in 1999/2000 among rural households, from 33 to 24 per cent among urban households and from 36 to 26 per cent across all-India (Deaton & Dreze 2005). These estimates had been eagerly anticipated among researchers who were anxious to ask some big questions about the impact of liberalizing economic reforms since 1991 on poverty and inequality. The sharp falls in poverty and changes in the method of poverty estimation led many to question whether political manipulation of data rather than poverty-reducing economic growth was at work.

The open process of data collection in India and consequent relative ease with which researchers were able to access the data and published methodology for calculating these poverty numbers allowed external verification of these official estimates. Researchers found various ways of adjusting the 1999 estimates to make them compatible with earlier estimates of poverty. One method was to extrapolate results from parts of the survey where the data collection methodology had been left unchanged. The volume of careful and technically adept statistical probing of the official estimates was impressive. These re-estimations tended to agree the official estimates of poverty reduction were exaggerated, but Deaton (2003) has argued that most of this decline was real, and others that the decline in poverty was only one-half of the official decline (Sundaram & Tendulkar 2003), or that there was only minimal decline in poverty over the 1990s (Sen & Himanshu 2004). Other scholars traced the evolution of variables related to poverty (such as agricultural yields, development spending by the government and inflation) and used these to predict poverty rates in the 1990s. The results from this indirect method found slightly slower poverty decline in the 1990s compared to the 1980s (Datt *et al.* 2003).

Once consumption has been measured through these surveys the levels are compared against an official poverty line. The resulting measures of poverty is termed a head count ratio (HCR), which records the proportion of the population that falls below the poverty line. From the late-1970s to the mid-1990s the Planning Commission used only two poverty lines for per capita household expenditure: Rs49 for rural households and Rs57 for urban households at 1973/4 prices which was close to the 15 per cent urban price differentials estimated at the time. These poverty lines were examined in 1993 by a group of experts known as the Lakdawala Committee. The committee produced recommendations for new poverty lines that were adopted in a modified form by the Planning Commission and used in official estimations for data going back to 1983. However, the new poverty lines used estimates of urban–rural price differentials that were considered too large to be credible. In Andhra Pradesh, for example, the 1999/2000 official estimates give a poverty rate of 27.2 per cent for urban areas and only 10.8 per cent for rural areas. Another identified problem concerned how prices were calculated: until 1995 inflation for agricultural labourers was based on patterns of consumer expenditure from a survey dating way back to 1960–61 (Deaton & Dreze 2005).

Another group of experts, known as the Tendulkar Committee, was convened in 2005. The committee modernized the basket of consumption goods for which the poverty line was constructed, adding monthly spending on education, health, electricity and transport, and also oversaw a change in the method of updating the poverty line. These changes had the effect of boosting official measures of poverty significantly, from 27.5 to 37.2 per cent in 2004–05. By this new measure official poverty in India fell steadily, from 37.2 per cent in 2004–05, to 29.8 per cent in 2009–10 and 21.9 per cent in 2011–12. There was an outcry as the Tendulkar panel estimated a poverty line based on daily per capita expenditure of Rs27 in rural areas and Rs33 in urban areas. These numbers were regarded as unrealistically low and were referred to as a "destitution line" rather than a "poverty line". Another (the Rangarajan) committee was formed which raised these limits to Rs32 and Rs47 respectively, which increased official measured poverty from 21.9 per cent in 2011–12 to around 30 per cent. These adjustments show just how many millions of Indian people are crowded at or around the very low poverty lines.

Table 3.3 shows that between 2004/05 and 2011/12 official poverty measures fell in almost all states of India (there were a few exceptions among the north-east states – in Mizoram for example poverty increased). Poverty fell rapidly in those states that had started with high levels of poverty, such as Bihar, Uttar Pradesh, and Odisha. Even in states with lower initial levels of poverty, such as Kerala and Goa there was clear progress. A few states such as Chhattisgarh and Jharkhand showed more slowly declining poverty. The 2000s was a decade of success in the fight against poverty. In 2017 yet another task force, this time chaired by Arvind Panagariya submitted a report to the prime minister using a methodology similar to that used earlier by the Tendulkar Committee.

Table 3.3   Official measures of head count poverty in India, 2004/05–2011/12

State	2004/05	2011/12	Percentage fall
Mizoram (north-east)	15.3	20.4	+5.1
Bihar	54.4	33.7	20.7
Uttar Pradesh	40.9	29.4	11.5
Odisha	57.2	32.6	24.6
Kerala	19.7	7.1	12.6
Goa	25	5.1	19.9
Chhattisgarh	49.4	39.9	9.5
Jharkhand	45.3	37	8.3
West Bengal	34.2	20	14.2

Source: Planning Commission

HEALTH AND NUTRITION

There is a large literature that examines the relationship between mean adult heights and living standards. Adult height can be thought of as a summary measure of the impact of nutrition, disease, and environmental conditions from conception onwards, and those same factors impact through their effect on the life of the mother. Height is a single measure of human development that captures a lot of information. Inequality in height may also be easier to measure than monetary incomes and so can serve as a rough estimate of inequality of income. People are more likely to be happy to be measured rather than reveal income as height data is both quick and simple to collect and is unlikely to have future implications for taxation (Deaton 2008).

A good source of data is from the third round of the National Family Health Survey (NFHS) in 2005/06, which was the first to collect data on men as well as women's heights and were directly measured by the enumerators and not self-reported. The data allows us to look at the link between height and age. Contemporary India by this indicator resembles historical Europe in that people attain their adult height only in their twenties, several years later than in contemporary developed countries. The results show that the mean difference between men and women between ages 20 and 54 is 12.5cm, a little less than the 14.2cm difference in measured heights in the United States for men and women 20 years or older, which may be surprising given other evidence that shows greater gender discrimination in India compared to the US. The results also show that Indians, who are among the shortest people in the world, are getting taller but that Indian men are doing so at more than three times the rate of Indian women. This is worrying evidence and suggests, contrary to the previous result, that gender discrimination is not improving over time and that this result could be linked to differential access to whatever improvements there have been in health or nutrition or both (Deaton, 2007). These results support the idea that poverty and well-being is about more than just income as there is no correlation between the rate of growth of per capita expenditure and the rate of change of men and women's heights at state level (Deaton 2007).

There is even less agreement on how to measure health than education. The most accurate method is to evaluate the health status of individuals through a comprehensive clinical evaluation. This is done in the US through the US National Health and Nutrition Examination Surveys. These surveys are too expensive to be duplicated on anything other than a small scale in India. In India household surveys have tended to ask respondents to assess their own health based on a rating from "excellent to poor health". Individuals tend not to have a reference group against which to make their judgement and their self-perceptions are influenced by values, background, and beliefs which in turn are influenced by socio-economic characteristics, such as wages and income. For example, people rate their own health contingent on how often they use healthcare facilities. Those with little experience of the healthcare system (the poorest) are more likely to report themselves as being in good health (than the richest) (Strauss & Thomas 1998).

Another method is to estimate the consumption of inputs correlated with health outcomes such as average calorie consumption. Calorie availability is computed by converting food quantities (both purchases and consumption from own production) into nutrient intakes using food-composition tables. This can be easily calculated using data commonly collected in many household expenditure and farm production surveys. The method, however, has problems: food is likely to be wasted and surveys often fail to fully capture the meals that are served to guests or employees. A related method is to ask respondents to recall ingredients that went into meals consumed over some particular time period. Eating habits in India tend to vary by day of the week (many people in India fast on particular days during the week) so a short 24-hour recall period may not be representative. A longer recall period such as one week or 30 days will raise problems with recall bias (Strauss & Thomas 1998).

Disease-oriented definitions of health status are favoured by many researchers. Some studies have drawn such data from health facility records. In low-income countries a large fraction of the population, often the poorest who have the worst health outcomes, do not use such facilities. Other surveys ask questions about specific health symptoms such as fevers, diarrhoea, or respiratory problems during a reference period. Such methods will have the same problems as any self-evaluations of health status, as a symptom of ill-health will not mean the same thing for all respondents (Strauss & Thomas 1998).

The method that has proved very useful in India in recent decades has been to measure health outputs, including height, weight and body mass index (BMI). The BMI is the ratio of weight (in kilograms) to height (in meters) squared. On average a prime-age male in the United States has a BMI of about 25. BMIs are considerably lower in poor countries and average between 21 and 23 in Vietnam, Brazil, and Cote D'Ivoire. In 2006 around 57% of men and 52% of women in India had a normal BMI (between 18.5–25). Such data is easily collected by minimally trained enumerators and is not subject to the same biases of truthful revelation or interpretation (Strauss & Thomas 1998). There is a debate about the extent to which height is influenced by nutrition and genetics (see Chapter 5).

In India the National Family Health Surveys (NFHS) have aspired to collect high quality information on demographic and health outcomes. The NFHS-3 in 2004–5 created a huge debate as it indicated that despite then 8 per cent annual economic growth child malnutrition was stuck at high levels. The survey also showed declining levels of childhood vaccination rates. The NFHS-3 represented a huge extra data collection effort even compared to NFHS-2 in 1998–9. The number of questions administered in the NFHS-3 to women in the 15–49 age group was more than 450 and so almost double that of the NFHS-2 (Irudaya & James 2008). The data on immunisation decline was controversial and was contested by many state health departments. The results, for example, showed an 18 percentage point decline in immunisation rates among the richest population groups in Tamil Nadu. Such results, however, have been questioned and are likely to indicate problems with the data collection (Irudaya & James 2008). Various verification methods are possible such as comparing the answers to simple questions asked to couples about how many children they have. The data show that men and women only disagree marginally in the answers to such questions and in such a huge survey this is good evidence that overall the data being collected was accurate (Irudaya & James 2008).

4

The form of the Indian economy

In perhaps the most widely cited political economy work seeking to understand the economic importance of India's social structure Pranab Bardhan wrote in 1984 that there were three dominant proprietary classes (DPCs). These DPCs were the industrial bourgeoisie, rich farmers and professionals. The "professionals" class included civil servants and private-sector white collar workers. Bardhan estimated that the three DPCs belonged roughly to the top two deciles of the population. In 1975/6 this was 5 per cent of rural households and 17.6 per cent of urban households by income or 3.8 million rural and 3.7 million urban households. Bardhan argues that the three DPCs were *the* dominant classes in India and had a key role in influencing the process of government policy making. The key hypothesis of Bardhan was that "when diverse elements of the loose and uneasy coalition of the dominant proprietary classes pull in different directions and when none of them is individually strong enough to dominate the process of resource allocation, one predictable outcome is the proliferation of subsidies and grants to placate all of them" (1984: 61). The result of this is that even with extensive resource mobilization through savings and taxation, "the bulk of these resources have been frittered away in current expenditures" (*ibid.*). The influence of the DPCs on government, he argued, was evident. For example, farmers receive direct subsidies to maintain farm support prices and subsidies to reduce the cost of fertiliser, irrigation water, and diesel. Indirect subsidies for the professionals can be seen in the growth of public-sector employment and salaries. Bardhan notes that since the beginning of the 1960s real per capita income of central government employees increased two and a half times faster than that of per capita income in the country. Bardhan argues that the "Indian public economy has thus become an elaborate network of patronage and subsidies" (*ibid*.: 65). There is a clear link here with the various discussions of public investment as a driver of economic growth in India (see Chapter 2). The DPCs compel the government to extend to them more generous subsidies, this forces the government to cut back on public investment and economic growth declines. The argument from Bardhan gives us a political economy explanation for the decline (but not increases) in public investment, but it is also a Marxist-influenced work on the economics of class divisions in India, and so can be contrasted with the works discussed in Chapter 1 that look at the impact of ethnic and linguistic divisions in India.

This section reviews the three DPCs identified by Bardhan and explores how we might extend his categorization to accurately reflect contemporary India.

THE INDUSTRIAL BOURGEOISIE

After the mid-1960s richer and better connected industrialists appropriated the bulk of government licences, freely violated regulations, and installed unlicenced capacity, and over the 1970s there was not a single instance of prosecution for such violations (see Chapter 2 for specific case study examples of this sort of interaction between the state and corporate sector). Sales of the top 20 Indian business houses as a proportion of GDP grew significantly faster than those of the private sector as a whole over the 1970s. A remarkable feature of India, in contrast to Latin America and elsewhere, was the relative unimportance of foreign capital and foreign firms. Foreign capital had a high market share only in a small number of industries, exceeding 50 per cent only in industries producing cigarettes, soap, detergents, typewriters, batteries, light bulbs and a few others. After the 1950s and especially after the state nationalization of the banking system in 1969, Indian state-owned created banks became the main source of finance to private industry. Much of this lending was allocated to politically influential firms who then often found it easy to default on repayments.

There is a large literature analysing the influence of India's capitalist class on the state. From its foundation in 1885 the Indian National Congress in 1885 was clearly influenced by big business. The Associated Chambers of Commerce (ASSOCHAM) founded in 1921 was the first pressure group in India that claimed to represent the whole of Indian business, native and European. It was followed in 1927 by the formation of the Federation of Indian Chambers of Commerce (Tripathi & Jumani 2007). The INC routinely consulted with these business associations as an input into its negotiating strategy with the colonial government. Leading members of the business community formulated the Bombay Plan of 1944 as a more market-oriented alternative to the socialist-oriented central planning envisaged by Nehru. The plan was not implemented but it contributed to ensuring that the business community was an active participant in policy making. This positive engagement in the 1940s, argues Chibber, was supplemented by a very practical demonstration of the economic muscle of the business class. Indian state autonomy after independence, he argues, was undermined by a highly organized and concerted offensive launched by the business class (Chibber 2003). When the newly independent government tried to propose legislation to regulate the flow of investment and punish non-compliant firms, it triggered an offensive by the class against the new state. This, he argues, resulted in "the two key elements in the new apparatus – a Planning Commission and the Industries Bill – were both in their final design, fashioned to accommodate business demands as much as possible" (*ibid.*: 146). Herring (1999) argues that, over the following decades, state developmental aspirations could be worked around by selective capitalists who infiltrated the state to their own benefit through ties to government officials based on family, school, marriage and caste. India had a "state committed to planning yet too democratic, soft and embedded, to govern the market" (1999: 3). An example would be the large industrial houses who applied for industrial licences and then sat on them rather than expand production to sustain shortages and their own monopoly profits.

Although the state did intervene extensively after 1947 (as was discussed in Chapter 2) much of this was concerned with raising state investment to establish new industrial enterprises in heavy industry. The state was supportive to those big capitalist enterprises that already existed. In particular, the state regulated FDI to ensure it entered India in a subordinate relationship to the benefit of domestic capital. Policy sought to ensure that ownership and control should be held in domestic hands and that Indian experts should increasingly replace foreign experts. Of the 324 foreign investment projects proposed between April 1956 and December 1964 only 15 (1.2% of total FDI) envisaged full foreign ownership. At the same time previously foreign-owned firms such as the large firms Union Carbide, Goodyear, Hindustan Lever, Philips India, and Dunlop took on a share of Indian ownership (Kidron 1965: 246).

Big business has changed since Bardhan labelled it a DPC. At independence it tended to be based in New Delhi or Calcutta and controlled by foreign investors, or by Marwari, Gujarati and Parsi groups. After the 1980s, the growth of textiles, cement, sugar, chemicals, fertilisers, pharmaceuticals, electronics, steel, and engineering facilitated the rise of new business groups. These were often first generation groups headquartered in the states, particularly Punjab, Haryana, Maharashtra, Rajasthan, Gujarat, Karnataka, Andhra Pradesh and Tamil Nadu. Many of these business groups emerged from investing profits from agriculture. These new businesses were less inclined to support national political parties (until the success of the BJP in 2014) and were more often closely linked to regional political parties (Basu 2000).

While liberalization was looked upon favourably by much of the emerging middle class over the 1980s and 1990s it was seen as a threat by various sections of domestic business. Liberalization implied greater competition from imports and the loss of easy profits from long cultivated government links in accessing licences and subsidies. Liberalization in the 1980s and 1990s was pushed through not with the support of big business, but instead:

> relied upon an institutional structure that placed extraordinary decision-making power in a tight circle of key officials. Economic liberalization was unleashed from the apex of the political system – first, largely at the direction of a triumphant Indira Gandhi following her return to power in 1980, and then later by Rajiv Gandhi in the mid-1980s. Prime Minister P. V. Narasimha Rao, who drastically increased the scope and pace of reform in the early 1990s, as well as the prime ministers who headed the United Front government that followed, took decisions in consultation with a relatively small group of senior civil servants. (Jenkins 2019: 140)

Many scholars argue that the power and influence of Indian business has grown enormously since the early 1980s. This power is reflected in their dominant share of total investment, increasing control over the media, and in the financing of elections. Indian business remains well organized through various chambers of commerce, such as the Confederation of Indian Industry (CII). Kohli (2012) argues that the increasing influence of business is reflected in a "pro-business political economy" and economic policy that is less concerned with maintaining open markets, vigorous competition and the free entry of new firms, and more about promoting the profits of politically influential incumbents. Evidence includes official sanction of the flouting of labour laws and casualization of the labour force and the striking shift in distribution from wages to profits at the all-India level that started in the late 1980s and then increased after the 1990s (Walton 2011: 42). Firms have hired short-term contract labour (see Chapter 5) and used labour contractors to keep wages low (Barnes *et al.* 2015). The ability of privileged incumbents to remain in business despite enormous debt was labelled by Subramanian (2018: 5) as "capitalism without exit". A new attempt to overhaul the national bankruptcy system in 2017 was quickly overwhelmed by cases and made few decisive resolutions (*ibid.*: 57). A specific manifestation of this alliance are the nearly 600 special economic zones (SEZs) created by the government of India between 2005 and 2010, which involved the use of eminent domain authority by the state to seize the property of (mainly) small farmers and hand it over to private companies. This allowed corporate developers to capture windfall profits by accessing artificially cheap land acquired by the state. Jobs for local inhabitants in SEZs were confined to poorly paid and insecure positions such as gardeners, drivers, guards or cleaners (Levien 2011). However, over the long term there has been much churning and the composition of the top 20 business houses has changed significantly. While corporates like Tata, Birla and Mahindra have long remained influential, there have been new entrants, including Infosys and Reliance, while some older firms like Shriram and J. K. Singhania have declined. This churning would not have occurred if policy was skewed to benefit and protect powerful incumbent businesses.

RICH FARMERS

As already mentioned, Bardhan (1984) listed "rich farmers" as a DPC, while acknowledging that "the empirical identification of the class of rich farmers is of course, arbitrary" (1984: 46). He settles on a particular arbitrary definition based on two different measures of size. The first is by cultivated holdings, "large and very large farm households cultivating holdings above 4 hectares, constituting 19 per cent of the rural agricultural population, accounted for 60 per cent of cultivated area and 53 per cent of crop output in 1975" (*ibid.*: 46). The second is by assets, "in 1971 about 20 per cent of cultivator households owning more than Rs20,000 in assets, accounted for 63 per cent of all rural assets" (*ibid.*). There is little reason to doubt the status of rich farmers as a DPC in the post-independence era, particularly after the mid-1960s. There was a fundamental change to a Green Revolution agricultural strategy between 1964 and 1967 (Vanaik

1990; Varshney 1998: Chp 3) which focused on the application of new technology to those best able to make use of it and a greater reliance on price incentives, including subsidized inputs and high and stable prices for outputs. The new technology was steered to regions where the DPCs were already influential and had the skills, resources and connections to markets to permit the easy adoption of biochemical and mechanical innovations. Although biochemical innovations (high-yield variety seeds (HYVs), chemical fertilisers, pesticides and the regulated flow of irrigation water) were in theory scale neutral, in practice, the middle/large farmers that make up the DPC were better able to secure the subsidized credit that allowed them to purchase the new inputs and technologies. Similarly, the costliness and scale bias of mechanical innovations (tractors, threshers, drills, mechanical pumps for irrigation) were also more easily used by the middle/large farmers. Between 1954/5 and 1971/2 the largest landowners (many absentee) statistically lost out to these enterprising middle-sized farmers in terms of both households and area controlled (Rudolph & Rudolph 1987: 343–4). After the mid-1960s, "class for itself" action was pursued with "relentless skill" as the economic strength of this class was translated into promoting class interests (Byres 1981; Harriss 1992). This process was reflected in the creation of the Bharatiya Kranti Dal (BKD) party, which entered a coalition to form the state government of Uttar Pradesh in 1969. The BKD had campaigned, mobilized and governed on the basis of reducing taxation on agricultural revenues, subsidizing agricultural inputs and raising prices for state procurement of agricultural commodities. The rise of the Janata Party (JNP) to power in the centre in 1977 marked the first time the rural interest had been the senior partner in government (Rudolph & Rudolph 1987). Charan Singh (leader of the BKD) became the central finance minister in January 1979 and presided over the March budget, dubbed the "Kulak Budget", which extended vast subsidies on inputs, taxation and credit to large farmers (Byres 1981). Increasing procurement prices benefited only a small proportion of all Indian cultivators as the vast majority of them depended upon foodgrain purchases for most of the year. One estimate produced by a high-level committee formed by the incoming BJP government in 2014 estimated that only 6 per cent of farmers in 2012–13 sold any foodgrains to procurement agencies (*The Hindu*, 17 February 2015). Those farmers also tended to be concentrated in a very few locations, in particular Punjab, Haryana, western Uttar Pradesh and coastal Andhra Pradesh.

Vigorous mobilization led by middle and large farmers who produced surplus crops purchased by the governement continued into the 1980s and 1990s (Varshney 1998: 114) and drew in smaller farmers and the landless and was largely non-party based. The Tamil Nadu Agriculturalists Association under the leadership of Narainswamy Naidu had a reported membership of 3 million by 1980. Politicians in subsequent years rose and fell according to their willingness to propitiate the farmers' lobby. Devi Lal in Haryana promised to write-off cooperative loans in his successful 1987 state election campaign. His strengthened rural political base helped him become deputy prime minister and agricultural minister in the Janata government between 1989 and 1991. The Janata government waived all loans under central jurisdiction up to Rs10,000 from commercial and regional rural banks and cooperative banks. The World Bank estimated that these measures cost $1.5 billion. In the Punjab, farmer campaigns centred around the prices paid for electricity, irrigation water and diesel and purchase prices paid by government procurement agencies (Varshney 1998).

In the early 1980s, when Bardhan labelled large farmers as a DPC, agriculture contributed around 40 per cent of GDP. By 2012–13 agriculture's contribution had dropped to around 15 per cent, although it still employed around half of the country's labour force. There has also been a sharp decline in the presence of large farmers. According to the agricultural census of 2010–11, holdings of 4 hectares and above accounted then for less than 5 per cent of the total and around 30 per cent of the operated area. Sub-division, usually through inheritance, left small and marginal farmers holding the rest. Despite this evidence of decline, farmers retain economic power in rural India. Even if incomes are lower, incomes of landless labourers and marginal farmers are even lower, and the ability to employ (or not employ) the 50 per cent of the labour force engaged in agriculture gives the larger farmers enormous influence in the rural economy and in local politics. Rich farmers have also invested in off-farm economic activities so landholdings are a less useful measure of their economic influence. This diversification has included money-lending, trading, transport, and other businesses and services. Examples include the Patels of Gujarat, Reddys of coastal Andhra, and Gounders of western Tamil Nadu (Lerche 2014: 26). The rise of regional business groups, noted earlier, was linked to investments out of agriculture and this diversification has narrowed the social and economic distinction between the industrial and agricultural DPCs. Investment in education (usually for sons) has spread the formerly agricultural DPC also into the professions and civil service. The political mobilization of farmers, so prominent in the 1980s and 1990s, faded away in the 2000s. Indeed, one of the most prominent farmer leaders, Mahendra Singh Tikait, who had organized a massive occupation of Delhi in 1988, died in 2011 almost forgotten (Jenkins 2019). The declining profitability of agriculture turned the attention of potential farmer leaders to industry and to the professions in search of investment and profit and their interests increasingly converged with those of the other DPCs.

PROFESSIONALS AND WHITE-COLLAR WORKERS

Bardhan argues that if physical capital can be the basis of class stratification, then so can human capital. India, Bardhan argues, has a long tradition of powerful bureaucratic functionaries, from the bureaucrats of Moghul India (fouzdars, subadars) to the continuing British traditions of a strong civil service. The class's proprietary nature rested on their scarce "property" – their "human capital in the form of education, skills and technical expertise" – from which they were able to extract rents in both the public and private sectors, reinforced by exclusive upper-caste networks and cultural traits (Bardhan 1984: 51–3). This was evidenced both by the "bureaucracy's diversion of investment away from mass education in order to 'protect their scarcity rent', and their bitter resistance to reservations for lower caste applicants in medical and engineering schools" (Chatterjee 2019: 187). Those rents for the bureaucracy were closely linked to the interventionist-development role of the state, state-owned enterprises, regulations, licences and the fact that the state employed two-thirds of all formal sector employs. Business and agriculture had to "approach these dispensers of permits and licences essentially as supplicants" (Bardhan 1984: 58). It may be tempting to conclude that economic liberalization after 1991 and the supposed withdrawal of the state has undermined the economic and rent-seeking role of state bureaucrats. There is also a striking degree of continuity. In terms of employment there has been little change in the bureaucracy, from 20 million employees in 1997 to 17.61 million in 2012, both of which are significantly higher than the 16.87 million bureaucrats that Bardhan labelled a DPC in 1984 (Chatterjee 2019: 189). The size of the elite Indian Administrative Service (IAS) has remained at 5,000 throughout. Civil servants have continued to enjoy lucrative salaries. With the civil service wage bill becoming the largest item of government spending by the 1990s, with real wage annual growth of almost 8 per cent over the second half of the 2000s (Nagaraj 2017: 165). Liberalization has opened up new avenues for bribery, corruption and obliging particular segments among powerful interest groups. Politicians have found a continued role as "fixers" for water and electricity services, gaining commissions on public works, providing political protection for local criminal leaders, in the transfer and appointment of public officials, and in facilitating investment through the provision of land and licences. The bureaucracy who implement the decisions of politicians shared in these corrupt incomes (Jenkins 1999). The shift in economic growth in the 2000s into "rent-thick" sectors (see Chapter 2) gave renewed importance for state bureaucrats in allocating licences, permissions, environmental clearances, land allocation in sectors such as mining, telecommunication, real estate and infrastructure (Walton 2011).

The professionals have seen their monopoly access to higher education progressively weakened. There has been a huge expansion in school enrollment (see Chapter 5) and in the number of institutions of higher education. Both schooling and universities have boosted access to non-traditional groups through centrally mandated reservations for other backward castes (OBCs). As was discussed earlier, recruitment into the professions now encompasses a broader range of elites, the sons of farmers are increasingly gaining access to elite education and joining the professions. Traditional groups still have an enormous advantage. In fieldwork in rural Bijnor district, western Uttar Pradesh in 2000–2002 Jeffrey *et al.* (2005) found that growing primary and secondary education was allowing some Dalits to challenge established structures of power but was more generally reinforcing inequalities based upon caste and class.

THE MIDDLE CLASSES: THE BARDHAN THESIS AND BEYOND

The years since 1991 have seen much discussion of India's middle class, which does not have an obvious parallel to the three DPCs of Bardhan. Instead of thinking through the lens of DPCs, Varma argued that the middle classes have been influential in India since independence and that 1947 marked the departure of the British in person, not a discontinuity of British-style governance. Varma argues that in 1947 the upper and middle class controlled state power, they ran the bureaucracy, legislatures, business and industry, media, and land in rural areas: "the interests of the middle class hijacked the agenda of the nation" (Varma 1998: 50). Middle-class leadership of the independence movement ensured that British institutions remained intact, such as the ICS (the pinnacle of middle-class aspiration) where the mode of selection remained the same as for the judiciary, the higher education system, and the armed forces. Between 1947 and 1956, 94 per cent of IAS officers were recruited from the professional and service classes. Public-sector employment grew from 4.1 million in 1953 to 16.2 million in 1983 (Fernandes 2006). At independence, 55 per cent of provisional parliament members were professionals (Fernandes & Heller 2006: 514). The Constitution of 1950 included a provision for universal, free and compulsory education until age 14. This was ignored by the middle class who had already acquired basic education. Instead the middle class pushed and achieved further growth in higher education. For the first two decades the growth in enrolment rate in higher education outpaced primary education. The number of universities increased from 27 in 1950 to 119 in 1975 (Fernandes 2006: 22). In *c.*1980 China had 80 per cent literacy compared to 50 per cent in India, while India sent six times as many to higher education than China. The marker of middle-class status, the English language, became "one of the most invidious systems of social exclusion" (Varma 1988: 58).

Liberalization set into motion a broader shift in national political culture which can be seen in highly visible images of changing trends in consumption practices, lifestyles and aspirations. These images have centred around the proliferation of commodities such as cell phones and washing machines. The cultural and economic standard for the old middle class would have been represented by a job in a state bank or in the Indian civil service, while members of the new middle class aspire to jobs in MNCs or foreign banks (Fernandes 2006). The new middle class represents a dominating image of India's transition to a committed liberalizing nation, or what D'Costa (2005) referred to as "ebourgeoisment". These representations have identified the rise of this new middle class with the success of economic reform. Emerging consumption practice represent an important set of everyday signs and symbols through which people make sense of the more abstract term "economic reform". The appeal of the new middle class rests on the assumption that other segments of the middle class and upwardly mobile working class, can potentially join it. The new middle class provides a normative standard to which other social groups can aspire (Fernandes 2006).

At the time of independence, the middle class was almost exclusively constituted by English-educated upper castes. One survey defined the "middle class" as those respondents who possessed two of the four characteristics: ten or more years of schooling, ownership of at least three assets out of four – television, motor vehicle, electric pumping set, non-agricultural land – residence in a pucca house built of brick and cement, and a white-collar job. The survey found that 20 per cent of the sample population was identified as belonging to the middle class. The upper castes account for about 25 per cent of the sample population, but constitute nearly half of the new middle class. About half of the middle class came from various lower-caste groups among the scheduled castes (SCs) and scheduled tribes (STs), and other backward castes (OBCs) and the religious minorities. Using the definition of middle class as those households belonging to higher-income groups, Sridharan (2004) estimated their number to have reached between 6 and 26 per cent of the population by the end of the 1990s, or between 55 and 248 million people depending on how wide the income bands are drawn.

By the 1990s economic liberalization, Varma argues, had been supported by and contributed to "the acceptance of a certain kind of lifestyle: insular, aggressive, selfish, obsessed with material gain, and socially callous" (1998: 132). This, Singh (2005) argues, is evident in the middle class living in gated communities with private water, security and schooling and paying little taxation. Media in India is owned by and tends to reflect the interests of the middle classes. Media professionals tend to come disproportionately from privileged backgrounds in terms of caste and class (Dreze & Sen 2013). Rural issues, for example, get around 2 per cent of the total news coverage in national dailies, whereas the interests of the minority middle classes, such as fashion and gastronomy, are well covered (Dreze & Sen 2013). The growth of civic organizations such as the Citizens Forum for Protection of Public Space represents an emerging trend in which the new middle class engages in a politics of "spatial purification" and claims public spaces by cleansing them of poor and working classes. Increasing pressures on urban space have produced significant conflicts between street-sellers and middle-class civic organizations demanding greater access to public street space (Fernandes 2006). The middle class voted in large numbers for the BJP and provided much of the support for Hindu nationalism while being opposed to the political assertion of the backward castes (e.g. the Mandal Commission Report, which led to the expansion of caste based reservations). Corbridge and Harriss (2000) argue that it is possible to describe both economic liberalization and

Hindu nationalism with sometimes contradictory but often surprisingly complementary agendas for the reinvention of India as "elite revolts". Both reflect the aspirations and vehicles for the middle- and high-caste Indians (Fernandes 2006).

It is often assumed that the middle classes necessarily benefited from liberalization, this assumption ignores the marked internal differentiation within the middle classes. The restructuring and privatization of the state sector, for example, has imposed costs on large fractions of the middle classes. Indeed, the shift from a state-managed to a liberalized economy threatened much of the traditional middle class. The All India Bank Employees Association (AIBEA) with a membership of around 550,000 in the mid-2000s represented a section of the middle class that has consistently opposed liberalization (*ibid.*:107). Subcontracting recruitment and payroll calculation to specialized companies represented the casualization of chunks of white-collar work. Middle-class employment remained dominated by the state. Formal-sector employment was only 7–8 per cent of total employment throughout the period from 1973 to 2000 and reached only 28 million people by 2000. The failure of the Indian economy to generate private-sector jobs (see Chapter 5) means that the state in 2018 still employs around two-thirds of formal-sector workers. There has been a marginal decline in employment in the state sector, from 19.5 million in 1995 to 17.5 million in 2011 (Ministry of Finance 2013). There were 166 million members of the middle class either dependent on state employment, or on public subsidies to agriculture (Sridharan 2004). Although it is growing in number and diverse in terms of its constituents, entry to the middle class remains difficult. A study of 71 villages in Rajasthan revealed the difficulty of escaping from the lowest income and occupational strata. Globalization and the growth of new opportunities seem to have largely bypassed the educated youth in these villages. About 1,000 individuals in these 71 villages graduated from high schools over a 12 year period and only one was able to become a software engineer, one a civil engineer, one a medical doctor, and one a practising lawyer in the district courts (Krishna & Brihmadesam 2006). Human resource managers at three Bangalore-based IT companies (MindTree, Philips and Sasken) compiled a list of software professionals who had been recruited at the entry level over the 5–10 years to the early 2000s and from these lists 50 employees were selected in each company through random sampling. More than three-quarters of the sample had fathers who were college graduates, only 18 per cent of respondents had fathers who only graduated high school and zero per cent less than high school. If having two educated parents is a requirement for entry to better-paying jobs, then only between 4–7 per cent of all rural Indians will qualify to gain entry (Krishna & Brihmadesam 2006).

UNIONIZED LABOUR

Indian unions are similar to those in the US and UK where unions tend to engage with employers at the firm level and the state role is restricted to the regulation of union bargaining and conflict. European unions by contrast aspire to engage in nationwide corporatist negotiation with the state and employer federations. Rudolph and Rudolph (1987) argued that Indian unions have weakened over time because of a process they call "involuted pluralism" where the number of unions increases while their average membership declines. Together this means that unions become less effective in standing up for member's interests. More unions make it easier for the government and management to divide and rule. Unions become distracted by inter-union rivalry in the workplace rather than representing workers to the management. As evidence of this Rudolph and Rudolph (1987) showed that the average membership of unions in India showed a long-term decline from 3,594 in 1927–8 to 710 in 1976. Teitelbaum (2006) argues that by contrast the Indian working class was highly mobilized in collective bargaining long after independence and continued successfully to negotiate bipartite agreements into the 2000s. He shows that the number of registered unions did increase from 11,312 in 1960 to 57,925 in 1995, but argues that this does not reflect the number of functioning unions in India (2006: 396). The Trade Unions Act of

1926 which governs the registration of unions in India allows any seven individuals to register as a union; the Act has no mechanism to verify the continued functioning or existence of unions that register; the penalty for non-submission of returns is only a maximum of Rs50 and there is no law for deleting registered unions that have become defunct. So at any given time thousands of unions may be registered but do not necessarily exist. A better indication is the number of unions submitting returns, which increased from 6,813 in 1960, to 10,324 in 1975, and declined to 8,162 in 1995 (*ibid*.: 396). Membership of functioning unions increased, with fluctuations, from around 4 million in 1960 to over 6.5 million in 1995 and members per functioning union increased from 589 in 1960, to 841 in 1980, and to 801 in 1995. This is very different from the involuted pluralism of Rudolph and Rudolph (1987). The fragmentation at the firm level is also less than suggested by their analysis: the vast majority of companies surveyed have only one or two unions operating in their factories and 64 per cent of them were currently bound by a collective bargaining agreement. Nevertheless, regardless of the states or periods chosen, the volume of strike activity in India is high by international standards and comparable to that of European countries with notably difficult industrial relations, such as France and Italy (Teitelbaum 2006: 408). Even in the modern, export-oriented automobile supply-chain firms, there has been a high level of industrial conflict since the 2000s, which included violent conflict at the Maruti Suzuki plant in Manesar in 2011 and 2012 (Barnes *et al.* 2015: 357).

THE MILITARY

Pakistan has experienced four successful military coups and has been ruled for around half its independent existence by military governments. Despite its poverty, low levels of literacy, bouts of political turmoil and a military with the same British colonial traditions as Pakistan, India has never been threatened by a military coup. The military clearly has less influence on popular conscience than in Pakistan. Although enormously popular there is little tradition of military strongmen entering civilian politics. There is also no political pressure or expectation on Indian prime ministers (as with US presidents) to have served in the military. Some of this is due to the much greater strength of the post-independence political leadership and ability of the Indian National Congress (INC) to lead political debate and demonstrated ability to take the big nation-forming and protecting decisions quickly after independence. The Constitution, the first general election and the first five-year plan were all launched in the first few years after independence, whereas it took 20 years for all three to be accomplished in Pakistan. The Indian nationalist movement held a wide and deep sense of legitimacy against which the army could never have competed. The army was instead seen as having been a long-term collaborator with the British colonial government. During the colonial period senior military leaders had regular and direct contact with the top echelons of the political leadership. After independence they had to report only to a civilian defence minister. In 1955 the post of commander-in-chief was dropped and instead each of the three services was given an independent chief with formal equality established between them. The Indian army is further divided into six separate regional commands. These changes have weakened the ability of the army to coordinate any effort at a military takeover. After the 1962 war with China and the 1965 war with Pakistan the military budget was increased from 2 to 4.5 per cent of GDP, but over the long run it has trended downwards, increasing again in recent years as India has started to aspire to some form of international Great Power status. The budget has never reached the levels of 6–7 per cent of GDP seen in Pakistan.

The army has a long history of providing assistance to civilian authority and is expected to perform various tasks such as relief supplies during floods, or restoring public order after riots. One estimate suggests that the army was called out on 476 occasions between 1951 and 1970 which increased to 369 times between 1981 and 1984 (Ganguly 1991: 22). In Pakistan the use of the army to quell civil disturbance and terrorism in 1977 escalated into a full-scale military coup. While the Indian army has been used on an ongoing basis in areas like Punjab in the 1980s, and Assam and Kashmir in more recent decades its use has always been more localized. During the national 1977 emergency for example the army remained in barracks and the police and various paramilitary organizations were utilized to implement the repressive interventions of Indira Gandhi's government (Ganguly 1991; Pardesi & Ganguly 2010). The Indian army have remained out of corporate business, unlike their equivalent in Pakistan. In the latter some generals have emerged as some of Pakistan's biggest businessmen and many served on the boards of private and public-sector businesses. Siddiqa (2007) argues that the Pakistan military now controls so much land and business that it has become increasingly independent of the state and even in itself has emerged as a "class" (Siddiqa 2007; Shah 2014).

Much of the rest of this book engages with other ways in which the Bardhan thesis has to be reconsidered in contemporary India. The Bardhan thesis focuses on classes and their resulting interests and this book supplements that approach by considering gender and caste. Caste remains important in the Indian economy, associations of higher castes often regulate the local economy but lower castes are now better organized, better represented in politics and are experiencing faster falls in poverty than the rest of the population (see Chapter 6). The rise of new business groups after the 1990s have also been concentrated among particular castes (Damodaran 2008). Gender remains crucial and the economy is often structured around the absence of women, absence from formal-sector labour, absence (although less so over time) from schooling and a more fundamental absence in terms of being "missing" (see Chapter 5).

A SINGLE INDIAN ECONOMY?

The Indian economy according to IMF estimates is the seventh biggest in the world as of 2017. Its total GDP is estimated at $2.3 trillion, compared to $2.7 trillion for the UK, $11.3 trillion for China and $18.6 trillion for the US. Even if we lack an objective measure of "diversity" it is probably safe to say that India's economy is more diverse than any of these. Gandhi and Walton (2013) found that over the last 20 years India has created enormous wealth among billionaires as a percentage of GDP and reached levels equivalent to Brazil, Russia or Saudi Arabia. This at the same time as 45 per cent of children were born underweight (see Chapter 5) and the percentage has barely shifted during these years of rapid growth. In 2012 the population of various states in India would have made them some of the most populous countries in the world, such as Uttar Pradesh (204 million), Bihar (99 million), Maharashtra (114 million) and West Bengal (90 million). It is at state level where solutions to political, economic and social welfare problems are increasingly sought. Voting turnout in the last three national general elections has remained between 57 and 59 per cent, while for state elections turnout is around 10 percentage points higher and has been rising. Recall that states have constitutional responsibility for crucial aspects of economic management such as law and order, agriculture, education and health.

Lost within the aggregate discussion of a single Indian economy are fascinating and very diverse stories of growth and development at state level. Punjab was the pioneer of the Green Revolution in agriculture in the mid-1960s and had all but eradicated absolute poverty by the 1990s. The state economy, although the richest in India by the early 1990s, experienced relative stagnation during the era of liberalization after 1991 and booming national economic growth after 2003. Bihar has long been regarded as a basket-case in terms of human and economic development. Since the mid-2000s it has been among the fastest growing states in India. Many have attributed this to the inspirational developmentally-inclined leadership of chief minister Nitish Kumar. In the 1960s Bangalore in the state of Karnataka was a quiet city noted for a pleasant climate and being a favoured place of retirement for army officers. By the 1990s it was the fastest growing city in Asia and is now home to one of the world's leading clusters of software development. Software exports, a high-tech service industry in a poor developing country, touched $82 billion in 2015 (see Chapter 6). The state of Gujarat (population 62 million) has been one of the fastest growing corners of the global economy over the last 15 or so years, experiencing rapid growth in agriculture and, unlike other parts of India, also in industry. Much of this has been led by foreign investment. Its charismatic chief minister Narendra Modi was propelled to national leadership as prime minister in 2014 promising to take this growth story to the whole country. Others have been more critical suggesting that rapid economic growth in Gujarat was established long before Modi and that such growth has not been translated into equivalent improvements in human development. The state of Kerala in the south-west of India has long been poor even by Indian standards with an average income level in the 1990s equivalent to poor countries in Sub-Saharan Africa. Kerala has only a minimal industrial base and spends no more on public services that other states in India. Yet Kerala has levels of human development far higher (life expectancy ten years longer) than the rest of India. Is Kerala a case study of how to achieve human development at low levels of development, or is it a case study of sacrificing long-term development and growth prospects for the sake of short-term populist welfare?

One way to make sense of state-level differences in India is to think in terms of a general North–South divide. Northern states have more "missing" women (see Chapter 5), higher fertility rates, a lower first age of marriage, and higher infant and child mortality. These differences have been ascribed to different patterns of kinship. In the North, spouses must be unrelated and are often located at distance from each other (marriage rules are exogamic); men tend to cooperate with and receive help from other men only when they are related by blood, frequently adult brothers; and women generally do not inherit property. In the North this means that marriage is often dominated by the search for alliances between males, often through business, and the dowry becomes the main marriage transaction. The south Indian system differs in respect to most of these principles and their consequences. In the South the preferred form of marriage is often between cross-cousins (marriage rules are endogamous); men are as likely to enter into social, economic and political relations with other men with whom they are related by marriage as with men to whom they are related by blood; and women sometimes inherit/ transfer property rights. Women are likely to be married to known persons in familiar households near to their natal home. Equality is more likely to exist between husband and wife when they are already related kin and women are less isolated after marriage and continue to interact with their natal kin more regularly than counterparts in the North (Dyson & Moore 1983). The southern marriage system by giving women more freedom of movement, greater ability to acquire and dispose of property, and support from kin networks is likely to give women more autonomy. This can be seen in the later age of marriage and lower fertility levels (shown by greater prevalence of contraceptive use) in the South. The greater ability of women to influence household food allocation and take children to doctors contributes to lower child mortality in the South (Dyson & Moore 1983).

A second way to think of state-level differences is in terms of historically constituted property rights. The pattern of property rights created by the British differed across colonial India (Banerjee & Iyer 2005). In much of northern India property rights to land and taxes were assigned to a few landlords (known as *zamindars*). In much of the South, across Madras, Bombay and also in Assam in the north-east, property rights to land and taxes were assigned directly to cultivators. Landlord-based systems required much less administrative machinery to be set up, so areas conquered in the early periods of British rule were likely to have landlord-based systems. As time elapsed British administrators were more likely to grant rights directly to cultivators. British administrators were influenced by political thinkers that emphasized the importance of property rights for strengthening the incentives of small family-farmers to boost investment and so production. Again, after the 1857 Mutiny the British returned to giving landlords revenue-collecting rights to gain their political support. This distinction, argue some, had an impact after independence as those areas in which land ownership was concentrated in the hands of a few elites had incentives to structure political institutions for their own benefit, i.e. to promote more extractive institutions.

In landlord-dominated areas peasant property was relatively insecure, which discouraged productive investments because of the risk of expropriation. By contrast in the other areas, the proprietary rights of peasants were stronger and based on explicit written contracts with the colonial state. Evidence does show a long-term difference between areas with the two varieties of property rights. Non-landlord areas after independence had higher agricultural investment, used more modern inputs such as fertiliser and yields, and had better health and educational outcomes. Where landlords had a freer role in setting terms for tenants they remained able to appropriate any gains in productivity which undermined incentives for peasants to invest. Landlord areas had local governments that were less concerned with mass welfare, which is not surprising if the state is dominated by a powerful minority. Control over peasants created a political ethos of class-based resentment in these areas, which persisted into the post-independence era. The Maoist/Naxalite uprisings in West Bengal, Bihar, and the Srikakulam district of Andhra Pradesh were all in landlord areas. Landlord-dominated villages had fewer primary, middle and high schools, lower literacy rates and higher infant mortality (Banerjee & Iyer 2005).

5

Human factors in the Indian economy

Economic theory and empirical evidence suggests there is a close link between economic growth and wider measures of human development, or as Pritchett and Summers (1996) wrote, "wealthier is healthier". Economic growth will generate incomes that can be spent by households on education, health or nutrition, or be taxed by the government to fund public spending on social services. Economic growth will also lead to the creation of more high-paid jobs and so increase the incentive for households to educate children, so they have a better chance of acquiring such jobs in later life. A debate has arisen in recent years about whether India is experiencing "growth without development", or as Dreze and Sen (2013: ix) put it, "that the growth process is so biased, making the country look more and more like islands of California in a sea of Sub-Saharan Africa". Bhagwati and Panagariya (2013) have argued otherwise, that economic growth has been generally inclusive and has led to reductions in poverty. This chapter will outline the human development story of the contemporary Indian economy using case studies of poverty and inequality, education, health, labour and employment, and gender, here focusing on the unusually low and declining level of female labour force participation and "missing" women.

POVERTY

Between 1950 and 1955 the poverty head count ratio (HCR) averaged over 50 per cent and fluctuated between 45 and 60 per cent until the early 1970s. The HCR then began a systematic decline lasting until the mid-1980s, after which there were further fluctuations around a modestly declining trend (see Chapter 3 for more details). However, despite this fall in the percentage, owing to steady population growth, the absolute numbers of people in poverty has risen, from 200 million in the early 1950s to 300 million today. The decline in poverty (HCR) had been general across all states between the early 1970s and into the 2000s, but by the late-2000s it was falling faster in those states, such as Bihar, Uttar Pradesh and Odisha, that had the highest initial levels of poverty.

Scholars have found various factors that explain this steady decline of poverty, including agricultural output, which through its impact on foodgrain prices impacted on poverty, as most of the poor are net buyers of foodgrains (Ahluwalia 1978); farm yields, state spending on development and inflation (Datt & Ravallion 2002); and expenditure on rural infrastructure, agricultural research and extension, education and irrigation (Fan *et al.* 1999). The relationship between agricultural output and poverty reduction varies sharply across Indian states, being for example much higher in Kerala than Bihar. In general, agricultural growth during the 1990s had the biggest impact on poverty in states where poverty was already below the national average (Cassen & McNay 2005) but this relationship changed in the 2000s. The availability of land is closely linked to employment and production opportunities in the rural economy and has a negative relation with poverty (Sundaram *et al.* 1988). As fertility is higher in poor households, inheritance may lead to greater fragmentation of land ownership across generations, so poverty may actually be causing access to land to decline over time (Van de Walle 1985). Population growth can lead to poverty in other ways. High population growth (hence a growing labour force) may increase competition in the labour market and so put downward pressure on wages. A household with a large number of members may be compelled to dilute spending on consumption, education and healthcare among its members. Being female, and belonging to other groups subject to discrimination, especially the STs and SCs very commonly translates into acute poverty: 50 per cent of the 206 million population of SCs and STs are poor. It is these structural reasons that make poverty so resistant to change and mean that economic growth alone is not the answer (Cassen & McNay 2005).

Poverty is measured by income in contemporary India, but it is not only manifest as a monetary phenomenon. Poverty is linked to inequality of access to public services and severe inequalities of outcomes in health and nutrition. According to the 2015–16 NFHS, 63 per cent of mothers with secondary or more education had at least four antenatal care visits over the past five years, compared to only 28 per cent of mothers with no education. Seventy per cent of the top 20 per cent of households by wealth had full immunisation of children between 12–23 months old, compared to only 52 per cent of households among the bottom 20 per cent.

EDUCATION

Economic theory, labelling education as "human capital", has long emphasized the importance of education in explaining economic growth. For India there is good evidence that technical change associated with the Green Revolution in agriculture in the mid-1960s based around new seed types, fertilisers, and pesticides was more pronounced in rural areas with good education. Farmers needed to read the instructions on the packet of fertiliser to use it efficiently (Munshi 2004). Literacy is a basic requirement for working even in exploitative textile factories: 99.7 per cent of the young women working in Tiruppur knitwear factories for example are literate (Neetha 2002). The benefits of education are more general. Education, especially among mothers, is closely linked to better nutrition, health and education among children (Aslam & Kingdon 2012). The long-established link between a mother's education and childhood outcomes does seem to have changed in India. Bhat (2002) has shown that almost two-thirds of the fertility decline in India is attributable to illiterate women. This, she argues, is still linked to education, but more indirectly, as the wider use of contraception is intended to reduce family size and so enable household resources to be focused on allocating that smaller number of children to attend school.

Figure 5.1 National adult literacy rates, 2000–04, (as % of population over 15 years)

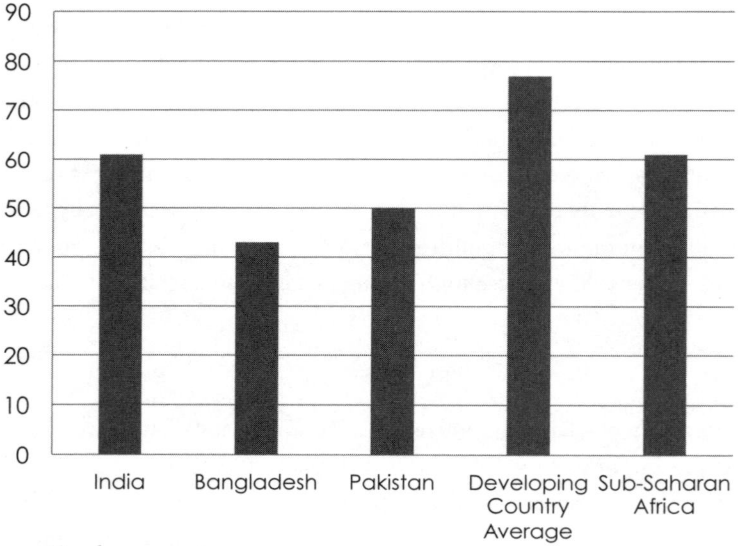

Source: Kingdon 2007: 169.

Some colonial nostalgists have argued that the legacy of the facility with the English language was an important benefit of British colonization. In fact, according to the 1951 census only 9 per cent of women and 27 per cent of men were literate and among these only a tiny fraction were literate in English. It was only after independence that Indian people acquired literacy in English or any other language. As mentioned elsewhere, the 1951 Constitution promised free and compulsory education to all children up to age 14 by 1960, but even today India has still not lived up to these promises. Figure 5.1 shows that India's adult literacy rate in the early 2000s was better than other South Asian countries, is equivalent to Sub-Saharan Africa and worse than developing countries in general. In India, progress had accelerated in the 1990s, which saw the most rapid gain in literacy of any decade in India going back to the first census in 1872, from 52 per cent in 1991 to 65 per cent in 2001. And in some states there was a very rapid increase: in Madhya Pradesh and Rajasthan literacy rates rose 20 and 22 per cent respectively. At least there was some general improvement across rich and poor states, urban and rural areas, and both men and women (Kingdon 2007: 178).

Chapter 3 noted that there are problems with literacy data in India. In recent decades India has acquired good survey-based attendance data from the NFHS-1 in 1993 and subsequent rounds in 1999, 2004 and 2014. Data on school attendance shows a widespread improvement in attendance rates across India in various age groups, in rural and urban areas, and for both males and females. Andhra Pradesh, Madhya Pradesh, Rajasthan and Uttar Pradesh saw increases in school attendance rates by over 25 percentage points between 1993 and 1999. In a few states, such as Orissa, West Bengal, Bihar and Gujarat there were actual declines in attendance rates for slightly older children, aged between 11 and 14, in urban areas (Kingdon et al. 2005: 136–7; Kingdon 2007). The ASER 2006 survey and Pratham 2007 found that progress had continued into the 2000s and that 93.4 per cent of all school-age children (aged 6–14 years) were enrolled in school. There is a striking problem among children aged 15–16 years, among whom the out-of-school figures rise to just over 20 per cent for both boys and girls. Enrolment in secondary education of 47 per cent remained well below the level predicted for a country of India's per capita income level (Kingdon 2007). This rapid growth in school-age attendance has not been matched by the growth in teacher numbers (until the para-teachers scheme; see later discussion) which has resulted in ever more overcrowded classrooms, reaching more than 60 pupils per teacher in some states (Goyal & Pandey 2012). Despite rising literacy and enrolment there are (like health) striking inequalities across, caste, gender and religion. A survey of 33,000 rural households across 16 states showed that the enrolment rate for Hindu boys and girls was 84 per cent and 68 per cent; for Muslim boys and girls, 68 per cent and 57 per cent; for Dalit boys and girls, 70 per cent and 55 per cent (Borooah *et al.* 2005).

Supply of education

A pressing problem is the chronic underfunding of primary education. The share of central and state spending on education in GDP averaged 3.4 per cent between 1989/90 and 1990/91, declined thereafter to 2.69 per cent in 2005/06, increasing to 3.8 per cent in 2013 (Tilak 2008; Goyal & Pandey 2012). Although there are pockets of STs and SCs still deprived of primary schools this low spending is not most obviously manifest in a physical shortage of primary schools. A typical survey finds that only 2 per cent of households sampled live more than 2km from their nearest primary school (Goyal & Pandey 2012). A more striking problem at primary level is with the physical quality of educational facilities. A survey in the mid-1990s found that not a single school visited had full use of the building; there were signs of prolonged decay, pending repairs, incomplete construction, and lack of maintenance, and school furniture being appropriated for private use by the school teachers or other influential local residents (Dreze & Gazdar 1996). Absent schools tends to be a problem later in the education system. There is an enduring shortage, which in 2002–03 amounted to one-fifth as many secondary schools (those with grade 10 classes, 15–16 year olds) as the number of primary schools (Kingdon 2007). The scarcity of secondary schools means that places are rationed through higher fees and entrance (ability) exams which often means that government secondary schools tend to be accessed by wealthier students (Kingdon 1996b).

The low level of education spending is exacerbated by patterns of education spending. Between 1950–90 around 25–30 per cent of combined central and state education expenditure was allocated to higher education. This was higher than even developed countries and, as Chapter 3 shows, this pattern of spending goes back deep into the colonial era. This spending built an education system that was aiming to produce engineers, scientists, and managers for the publicly-owned industrial plants and the elite civil service, not to achieve mass literacy. In other countries the historical story has tended to be the opposite pattern, with mass literacy preceding the rapid expansion of higher education. In 1900, for example, most North American and European countries had full primary enrolment and were only then expanding secondary education (Goyal & Pandey 2012).

The Sarva Shiksha Abhiyan (SSA) or campaign for universal education was launched in 2001 as a central government programme to create universal primary education (6–14 years) by 2010. The scheme provided funding for the salaries of additional teachers to reduce the pupil to teacher ratio to 40:1, teacher training and grants for teaching materials. There were also targeted interventions to close caste and gender gaps in school attendance, such as free textbooks to girls and low-caste children (Kingdon 2007; Goyal & Pandey 2012). The government's eleventh five-year plan in 2007 launched a programme called SUCCESS, which aimed to achieve universal access to secondary education to all students by 2015 and universal retention (no drop-outs) by 2020. The programme again aimed to provide the necessary infrastructure and resources to increase the capacity of the system (Tilak 2008). However, the structural bias in education spending has remained entrenched. Primary education's share of total education spending has remained stagnant. SUCCESS was not implemented by state governments and nearly half the allocation made in 2007/08 was returned to the central government unused (Tilak 2008). The government's emphasis remained on elite education: in 2004–05 the central government planned a huge increase in education spending directed to setting up 16 new, centrally-funded universities and three new Indian Institutes of Technology (IITS), in Andhra Pradesh, Bihar and Rajasthan. The Eleventh FYP planned to establish 30 new central universities, eight new Indian Institutes of Technology (IITs), seven new Indian Institutes of Management (IIMs), ten new National Institutes of Technology, three Indian Institutes of Science Education and Research (IISER), 20 Indian Institutes of Information Technology, and two Schools of Planning and Architecture (*ibid.*). These plans have been largely successful and the expansion has continued after the Eleventh FYP.

There have been efforts to boost primary education at state level, some more successful. The 1996 Education Guarantee Scheme (EGS) launched by the Government of Madhya Pradesh aimed to expand the number of primary schools in rural and tribal areas of the state. The EGS offered villages a school and funding for a teacher within 90 days of a village council (*panchayat*) requesting a school, providing land for it and identifying children willing to attend. Within three years 30,000 new schools had been established in the state. Data from the NFHS in 1992/3 and in 1998/9 suggest that primary school attendance in rural areas of Madhya Pradesh increased from 61 per cent to 85 per cent of households (Johnson & Bowles 2010).

One of the traditionally poorly performing states, Bihar, made significant efforts to improve education after the mid-2000s when more than 20 per cent of girls over the age of 10 years were not in school. Nitish Kumar as chief minister of Bihar gave unprecedented attention to primary education from 2005 to 2010. The allocation of funds for activities linked to the Sarva Shiksha Abhiyan (SSA) increased ten-fold, which led to the recruitment of 300,000 teachers, the building of 100,000 classrooms, the expansion of the mid-day meals scheme and increased spending on textbooks. Summer camps were established to give daily classes in numeracy and literacy to encourage girls not enrolled in school to attend. The proportion of children out of school in Bihar dropped from 20 per cent to 6 per cent in four years (Banerji 2011). Significant problems remained, however. One survey in 2009 showed that in sampled districts only 65 per cent of enrolled children were found present in school during the survey; less than 50 per cent of teachers were found able to meaningfully summarize a standard Grade 5 text; and only 57 per cent of children in Grade 5 could read a Grade 2 text fluently (this after five years of schooling) (Banerji 2011).

Demand for education

As noted in the last section low enrolment was not solely a consequence of the lack of physical school infrastructure. Why parents choose or demand education is important.

One survey found that more than half of the parent-respondents did not feel school was useful. These attitudes stemmed from a lack of history of education in the community and the absence of any jobs for educated workers (Chandrasekhar & Mukhopadhyay 2006). Studies do confirm that the financial returns from education can be very low for the poorest families who may only have options to work as casual labourers. There is no incentive to acquire education higher than primary schooling for a casual worker as the cost of this education will not be recouped in the form of higher wages later in life (Dutta 2006). For women there are lower or even negative returns, as less than 20 per cent of women work for wages. There are low returns from education in traditional agriculture and self-employment, and women still work mainly in the household so there are only limited gains to household production from education (Fulford 2014).

Non-attendance is clearly related to economic factors. Household poverty, the direct costs of education and whether the school serves a mid-day meal, all influence school attendance. Family financial constraints necessitating that children work outside the household was given as a reason for non-attendance by a third of sampled parents in another survey (Borooah *et al.* 2005: 1378). Household composition is important too. The presence of children below the age of five reduces the probability of a sibling going to school, suggesting that older children may be dropping out of school to help with childcare. Equally, the presence of household members over the age of 60 reduces this impact by providing alternative sources of child care (Chandrasekhar & Mukhopadhyay 2006). When both parents are literate, children tend to attend school regardless of their religion or caste (Barooah *et al.* 2005) and the impact of the mother's education is more pronounced for girls' school attendance (*ibid.*). These results imply that illiteracy can cascade down from one generation as the children of illiterate parents don't attend school.

Quality of education

The Public Report on Basic Education (Probe Team 1999) was the first serious evidence-based study of the quality of primary schooling in India.

Based on a 1996 survey of schooling facilities in 242 villages in five northern states, Bihar, Madhya Pradesh, Rajastan, Uttar Pradesh and Himachal Pradesh, Probe found poor school infrastructure (see Figure 5.2).

Figure 5.2 PROBE 1996 report on schooling (% of schools with resources)

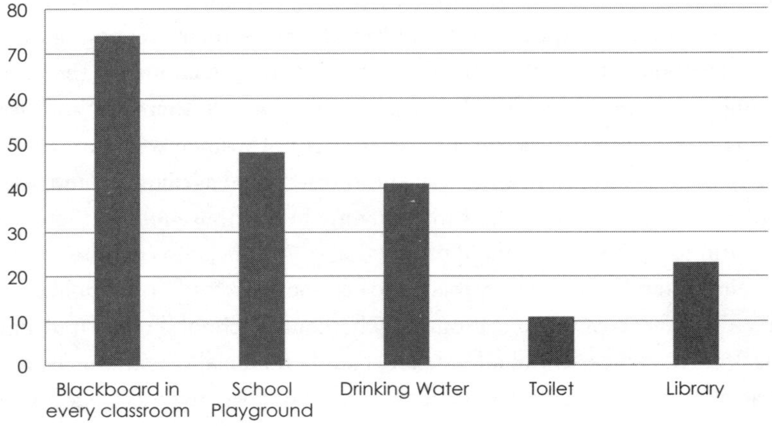

Source: Public Report on Basic Education (Probe Team 1999).

A later report, the Annual Status of Education Report (ASER) 2005 found some improvements. By 2005, 66 per cent of primary schools had water (up from 41 per cent in 1996), and 42 per cent had functioning toilets (up from 11 per cent in 1996). This improved infrastructure was in part due to the District Primary Education Project (DPEP) which began in the mid-1990s and was continued by the Sarva Shiksha Abhiyan after 2001 (Kingdon 2007).

There was no national-level data on learning available until 2006 when the educational NGO, Pratham carried out a survey of learning achievement using a sample of 330,000 households. Pratham visited 20 homes in each of 30 randomly selected villages across 549 Indian districts and interacted with all children between the ages of 6 and 16 in the sample houses. The survey found that 47 per cent of children who were in school and studying in grade 5 (10–11 yrs) could not read the story text at a grade 2 (7–8 yrs) level of difficulty. In arithmetic, 55 per cent of grade 5 and nearly 25 per cent of grade 8 (13–14 yrs) children could not solve a simple division problem (three digits divided by one digit). There was also significant inter-state variation. From the sample of grade 5 children in the north Indian states of West Bengal, Haryana, Bihar, Uttaranchal, Chhattisgarh less than 50 per cent of children were able to do a simple division problem (Kingdon 2007). Das and Zajonc (2010) give the first (since 1970) internationally comparable measure of cognitive skills for Indian children enrolled in Grade 9 (14–15) from Rajasthan and Orissa. The results show that the median enrolled child in these two states is failing to meet a basic international low benchmark of mathematical knowledge: 42 per cent in Rajasthan and 50 per cent in Orissa. Given that gross enrolment in India in lower-secondary schools was then 53 per cent, this study left out half the children of the relevant age group. Adjusting these figures for the testing of out-of-school children done by Pratham shows an even lower rate of educational achievement. The results show that India came forty-ninth out of a 51-country sample, with only Ghana and South Africa scoring worse. The results also showed that the top 5 per cent of performers in India did far better than other low-income countries and did fairly well even when compared to high-income countries. This combination makes the test score distribution the second most unequal in the world after South Africa. Hence, as the title of the study put it, while "India is shining", "Bharat is drowning" (Das & Zajonc 2010). This suggests that the elitist bias in education is much more pervasive that just a disproportionate amount of spending on higher versus primary education.

There is clear evidence of teacher failings in schools which is likely to be a contributory factor to poor educational outcomes. In 1994 Dreze and Gazdar (1996) made unannounced visits to primary schools across four districts of rural Uttar Pradesh, where they found two-thirds of teachers absent and the school day lasted on average only three hours (together amounting to a school year averaging only 75 days per year). With no effective teaching taking place in any of the schools during visits, they were in practice little more than child-minding centres. It is hardly surprising then that across all those schools surveyed attendance was below 50 per cent of those officially enrolled, or as noted above, parents were not finding education "useful" (*ibid.*). There has been little sign of improvement since then, or that Uttar Pradesh might have been a special case. In 2003 Kremer *et al* (2005) made three unannounced visits to each of 3,700 schools in 20 major states and found that on average 25 per cent of teachers in government primary schools were absent from school on a given day and of those teachers present only half were found to be teaching.

Public and private schools

A significant development in Indian education in the recent past has been the growth of fee-charging private schooling (Kingdon 1996b). The data concerning the enrolment numbers in these schools, however, must be treated with some caution as there are clear financial and job security incentives for government schools to claim larger than actual enrolment numbers and so a greater proportion of school-age children. State-school teachers are meant to be allocated to schools on the basis of a pupil-teacher ratio of 40:1 so if student numbers are truthfully reported to have dropped (implying a shift to private schools) then spending on the school could be reduced and teachers could be transferred to other schools or lose their jobs (Kingdon 1996b). In addition, some children may attend private schools in the morning, for a better education, and then attend government schools for the mid-day meal. Such joint enrolment would also enable children to be eligible to take examinations as a government pupil and so later gain access to government secondary schools (Tooley & Dixon 2007).

Given these data caveats there is widespread and consistent evidence for the rise of private schools. More reliable evidence on school enrolment can be found in household surveys as households have no incentive to mislead enumerators about the type of school children are attending. The discrepancies are massive. In the city of Patna in Bihar in the early 2010s the official enrolment in the 350 government schools was 100,000 children and there were officially nearly 16,000 out-of-school children.

The actual number of school-age children was 1.8 million. This implied there were likely to be hundreds of unaccounted for private schools (Rangaraju *et al.* 2012). Similarly, an earlier household survey carried out by the National Council of Applied Economic Research (NCAER 1994) confirms the divergence between official and household survey findings of school enrolment across all Indian states. The difference was between 10–30 per cent in Haryana, Punjab, Kerala and Uttar Pradesh (Kingdon 1996b: 3309).

The growth of private schooling has dramatically accelerated over time, particularly in primary education and in urban areas. In urban India, up to 60 per cent of the increase in primary school enrolment between 1978 and 1993 was absorbed by private schools and this increased to almost 96 per cent between 1993 and 2002. Even this dramatic increase is an underestimate, as it takes no account of enrolment growth in the numerous unrecognized private schools that are excluded from official statistics. In rural India, the rate of expansion of private schooling has been much slower, although even here it reached almost 25 per cent of the total in the late 1990s (Kingdon 2007: 186). Another area of private enterprise not captured in official figures is the private tuition and coaching industry, which accounts for a significant share of household educational spending in India. Survey evidence shows that in urban Uttar Pradesh on average 23 per cent of household educational expenditure (including fees, books, uniform, travel) of secondary and higher education students was spent on private tuition or coaching. A survey in 1991 from a sample of 928 students of Grade 8 (13–14) in government and private schools showed that 34 per cent reported taking private tuition (Kingdon 1996b) and since then, the private tutoring business has only grown further.

The view that private schools cater only to children of the elite in high-cost residential areas has been challenged: a survey of the slum areas of North Shahdara, Delhi found 256 schools of which only 71 schools were government and almost half of children were at private schools (Tooley & Dixon 2007). Similarly, private schools cannot be explained solely by the absence of government schools. Rangaraju *et al* (2012), using the Google map of Patna in Bihar, show that more than 1,000 private schools existed within a 1 kilometre radius of 111 government schools, and so could hardly be said to serve only those areas that lack a government school.

There has been an impressive effort to compare the academic attainment of students in private and government schools. One typical example is a study of schools in Hyderabad. Tooley *et al.* (2007) surveyed private schools in India between 2003 and 2005. Researchers selected three from 35 of the poorest zones in the city with a population of about 800,000 across an area of about 19 square miles. A team of eight specially trained researchers recruited from a local NGO were asked to physically visit every street and alleyway in the area during the mornings of a school day looking for all primary and secondary schools. When a school was located the researcher called unannounced and had a brief interview with the head teacher, checked physical school facilities and visited one Grade 4 (9–10 yrs) to observe teaching activity when a normal lesson was timetabled. Finally, a stratified random sample of around 150 schools was selected from those found in the census and several hundred students (Grades 4/5) randomly selected from within these. Questionnaires were prepared for students, families of the students, teachers, and school managers/head teachers and data was collected on background variables, such as household income and wealth indicators, years of parental education, caste/tribe, religion and parental motivation. Mathematics and English were tested for these students. There were limitations to the research: more than one unannounced visit would have been better to gauge the extent to which teachers were teaching over a prolonged period; and researchers were also prevented by head teachers from physically counting the students present in the school at the time of the visit. There are other similar and impressive studies, of the slum areas of North Shahdara, in East Delhi (Tooley & Dixon 2007), of urban Lucknow in Uttar Pradesh (Kingdon 1996a), and of Patna, Bihar (Rangaraju *et al.* 2012).

The findings of these school surveys indicate that private-school students already have advantages over those children that remain in government schools. They are less likely to be from SCs and ST households, are more likely to be male and have parents educated above primary school, are more likely to have fathers in occupations other than agricultural labour, and come from households that own more land than the sample average. These factors are also likely to influence children's school attainment. Wealthy families, for example, are more likely to provide private tuition for their children (Goyal & Pandey 2012). Consistently, the various studies found that the "raw" mean scores of primary-level children were highest in private schools. These differences were large. In Hyderabad mean scores in mathematics were about 22 percentage points higher in private schools over government schools. This advantage was more pronounced for English language, which is not unexpected as private schools are far more likely to teach in English (Tooley & Dixon 2006). In Patna less than 43 per cent of children in Grade 4 (9–10 yrs) of government schools could perform the subtraction sums that more than 93 per cent of private school students could accomplish (Rangaraju *et al.* 2012: 34). However, these differences fall sharply when the background of students is taken into account: adjusting for student background implies that 44–80 per cent of the difference in attainment is explained by student intake (Kingdon 1996a; Goyal & Pandey 2012: 70).

These surveys defined teaching as when the teacher was present in the classroom supervising the class in some activity (Tooley *et al.* 2007). In every study, private primary school teachers were more often present in schools and teaching than in government schools (Tooley & Dixon 2006). In the Hyderabad study, for example, over 90 per cent of teachers in private schools were teaching at the time of the researcher visits compared to less than 75 per cent in government schools (*ibid.*: 453). There is some evidence that other (physical) teaching inputs are better in private schools. The majority of government schools had a blackboard and drinking water available. While government schools tended to do much better on the availability of separate toilets for boys and girls, private schools had more availability of fans, seats and desks in classrooms. Private schools were also more likely to be in a proper brick or stone building with a tiled roof, or similar construction, rather than a tent, open space or temporary building (Tooley & Dixon 2007; Goyal & Pandey 2012; Rangaraju *et al.* 2012). While student characteristics are important, teacher characteristics seem to have less influence on pupil attainments. Over 90 per cent of government school teachers are trained while the majority of private school teachers in both rural and urban areas in all states are untrained (Goyal & Pandey 2012). Age, gender, education, number of years of service, number of days of in-service training in last school year, whether a teacher's appointment is on a contract basis and whether the teacher is a resident of the village, all explain very little of the variation in standards of teaching between schools (Goyal & Pandey 2012).

A common criticism is that private schools are exclusionary. Nambissan (2012) for example argues that private schools "are inherently unjust and discriminate against the rights of children" (2012: 51). Survey evidence shows that at the upper-primary level, the average cost of sending a child to a private school in 2006 was more than three times that of a government school (Hill *et al.* 2011: 99). But these studies also consistently show that private schools are typically cheap. The typical cost of private schools in Hyderabad was about Rs70–90 per month (approx. £1), which was about 4 per cent of the monthly wage for someone earning the minimum wage (Tooley & Dixon 2006) and in Shahdara, East Delhi monthly fees ranged between 5–9 per cent of the monthly wage for a worker earning the minimum wage (Tooley & Dixon 2007). Not all students pay fees. Around three-quarters of private schools told researchers that they offered free or concessionary places, which amounted to nearly one fifth of all places (Tooley & Dixon 2006, 2007; Tooley *et al.* 2007). Surveys found little difference in the balance of boys and girls in private schools (Tooley & Dixon 2006, 2007).

Survey data tends to show smaller class sizes in the private sector (Tooley *et al.* 2007; Johnson & Bowles 2010). For example, among private schools the pupil–teacher ratio was 22:1 compared to 42:1 for government schools, and for 13 per cent of government primary schools the ratio is above 100:1 (Rangaraju *et al.* 2012). Private schools in slum areas manage to charge low fees despite smaller class sizes than government schools. The reason is that private schools pay much lower average salary levels and make more intensive use of teachers. Using data on five different states shows that in the early to mid-1990s private school teachers' monthly pay was about 40–50 per cent of government teachers' pay, and by 2002 this ratio was down to about 20 per cent. The private sector pays market wages and government schools pay government mandated wages (Kingdon 2007). The combination of the more intensive use of teachers (lower absence) and lower salaries means that private schools can produce the same level of numeracy skills as government at less than half the cost of government schools (Kingdon 1996a: 75).

We lack data from the studies of schools in slum areas on teacher turnover and whether this was undermining educational performance of children (Sarangapani & Winch 2010). At the very low salaries found by the various studies by Tooley of slum school teachers it may be the case that teachers have high levels of frustration and job turnover (Sarangapani 2009). There is little evidence that the slum schools themselves are unstable and survey evidence shows that the mean year of establishment for recognized private schools was over a decade before the surveys (Tooley & Dixon 2007; Rangaraju *et al.* 2012).

The learning outcomes between private and government schools can be overdrawn. A study of learning outcomes in government and private schools in Uttar Pradesh and Madhya Pradesh found that in both systems the majority of students performed poorly and a few do very well (Nambissan 2012). In both school systems there was little difference in test scores between grades 4 and 5 indicating that very little learning took place over the teaching year (Goyal & Pandey 2012). Tooley has been criticized by some scholars as having conceptualized education as a commodity where through the means of a commercial transaction money is exchanged for educational opportunities. Education may be more properly seen as preparation for life in a particular society and so less about individual benefit and of more interest to other members of that society. Education should be both a public and a private good. Tooley has nothing to say about how people relate to each other, in terms of mutual respect, moral regard, and fraternity and how such values could be undermined by the profit-seeking motivations of private education (Sarangapani & Winch 2010).

A crucial driver of differences in effort and attendance among teachers in private schools stems from differences in employment status. Privately funded schools were far more dependent on teachers employed on short-term contracts (Johnson & Bowles 2010). Teachers in private schools argued that temporary contracts created anxiety stemming from a fear of dismissal and so teachers made more effort to please parents and the head teacher (*ibid.*). In a private school teachers are accountable to the head teacher who can fire them and also to parents who can choose from a wide selection of alternative private schools. In a government school the chain of accountability is much weaker. Teachers have a permanent job with salaries and promotions are not related to performance. This contrast is clearly seen by parents (PROBE 1999).

Teachers (especially in government schools) are also politically well represented. The Indian Constitution reserves one-twelfth of the seats in state legislatures for teachers. In Uttar Pradesh the share of teacher MPs has reached nearly one quarter of the state parliament and several chief ministers, including Mulayam Singh Yadav, Kalyan Singh, and Mayawati as well as many education ministers were also former teachers (Kingdon & Muzammil 2009). A survey of teachers in Uttar Pradesh shows that almost one-third of them personally knew a teacher-politician. Teacher politicians maintain close links with the teacher community and actively help them in matters relating to appointments, transfers and disputes. Survey evidence showed that almost two-thirds of district education officers report suffering from such political interference. There is a clear statistical link between "political connections", measured in terms of whether a teacher knows or has met a teacher politician, and "reduced effort" in terms of lower levels of self-reported teaching time. Students taught by either a unionized or a politically connected teacher have lower achievement scores (Kingdon & Muzammil 2013). The unionization of teachers is a government-sector phenomenon. Interview evidence shows that around

85 per cent of government-school teachers, but only 5.1 per cent of private primary school teachers are unionized (Kingdon & Muzammil 2013: 257). The political strength of teacher unions can be seen in the changing patterns of teacher salaries and other education spending. Between 1973/4 and 1995/6 the basic salary of a qualified primary school teacher grew by 5 per cent per annum in real terms. Teacher salaries are higher relative to per capita income than in other countries and has squeezed out other forms of educational spending. The share of wage costs as a proportion of total public expenditure on education increased from 74.7 per cent in 1960–01 to 97.3 per cent in 1987–8 and has been locked in as a constraint ever since (Kingdon & Muzammil 2009: 140).

Policy interventions

This section reviews potential policy solutions to the problem of education: para teachers, increased community and parent power, pupil subsidies, teacher attendance bonuses, and the 2009 Right to Education Act.

The para-teacher scheme allows schools to appoint low-cost and untrained teachers on a temporary contract using central government grants. By 2004, 500,000 had been appointed, in varying degrees across states, with large numbers in Andhra Pradesh, Bihar, Chhattisgarh, Jharkhand, Madhya Pradesh, Rajasthan, and Uttar Pradesh and few in Kerala, Tamil Nadu and Karnataka (Kingdon 2007; Kingdon & Sipahimalani-Rao 2010). Para teachers are paid much lower wages (only 14 per cent of regular teaching salaries in West Bengal) so have helped reduce teacher–pupil ratios (Kingdon & Sipahimalani-Rao 2010: 61). Para teachers have much lower levels of absenteeism and tend to be hired locally so have shorter distances to travel to school. Through the need to regularly renew their contracts they face greater pressures of accountability than regular teachers (*ibid.*). Regular teachers performed better than para teachers in language and mathematics in Bihar and Uttar Pradesh, but when controlling for teacher education, training and experience para teachers did better than regular teachers in Bihar, but not in Uttar Pradesh. These positive effects are likely to be underestimates as para teachers are more likely to be posted to more remote schools and to more deprived communities (*ibid.*). Para teachers may boost educational performance as compared to an absent regular teacher, but it is difficult to see how an untrained and very low-paid teacher can sustain improvements over the longer term.

There are few means available for parents to punish absent or under-performing teachers in India. Even were parents to remove children from a school, the salaries of government teachers are not linked to the number of pupils they teach. There are various ways to change this, such as by making teachers accountable to a school committee or body of parents. Parents may be better informed than distant education bureaucrats about teacher absenteeism or poor classroom performance, and also be more willing to expend time and energy to remedy such problems (Pandey *et al.* 2008). This process is not easy as teachers will certainly be better educated than parents and are extremely likely (as discussed above) to have good political connections which could make parents reluctant to make any effort to enforce accountability (Banerjee & Duflo 2006). Increased community participation was given a central place in the Sarva Shiksha Abhiyan (SSA). The SSA mandated the formation of village-level committees that would receive public funds for spending by schools and would provide a mechanism to increase monitoring of teachers (Banerjee *et al.* 2007).

Evidence shows that such committees do not function as planned. In Madhya Pradesh for example committee members are often appointed rather than elected and have become a means of channelling public money intended for uniforms and textbooks into politically influential parts of the village (Johnson & Bowles 2010). Such committees rarely meet and the wider community has little awareness of their roles nor tends to participate in their oversight roles (Goyal & Pandey 2012: 272). In Uttar Pradesh only 2 per cent of parents could name members of the school committee, more than 85 per cent of respondents could not name a household member who had ever attended a village meeting and of those who have attended only 5.8 per cent mentioned education when recalling which issues were discussed at the last meeting (Banerjee *et al.* 2007: 1369).

Researchers conducted a large randomized control trial of schools in 610 *gram panchayats* (village councils) across three states (Madhya Pradesh, Uttar Pradesh and Karnataka). A sample of school committees were given an intensive information campaign about the roles and responsibilities of education committees. Researchers returned a year later to gauge the impact of the intervention. There were minimal impacts on pupil achievements and attendance of teachers in school (Pandey *et al.* 2008). The poor results could be explained by the fact that parents had such low expectations from government schools that they only allocated little time and thought into trying to improve matters. Poor parents in rural areas are not very likely to understand what the private (and social) return to education would be after ten years of schooling. It may also have been the case that teachers are seen as too powerful to be subject to greater effective oversight by parents. Education did not seem to be as important among parents as the provision of mid-day meals in schools, which were valued by parents and resulted in greater attendance by children. But parents then showed no comparable energy in pushing teachers to attend and teach the pupils now present in class (Banerjee & Duflo 2006).

The costs to households of children attending school can be substantial even for "free" government education. In 1999/2000 the total costs of "free" government primary education (fees, books, stationary, uniform, footwear and transportation) ranged from $14 to $51 (typically being higher in urban areas). These costs do not include the opportunity costs of any lost earnings opportunities in the case of child labour which may amount to around 10–15 per cent of the monthly per capita consumption expenditure of a rural household and 15–30 per cent for older school-age children (Goyal & Pandey 2012). Although there are a wide range of incentives for children to attend school, such as free uniforms and textbooks and attendance scholarships for girls, between 50–90 per cent of children do not receive them and of those parents that do, 70–90 per cent are not satisfied with their quality (*ibid.*). In areas of Uttar Pradesh and Madhya with low levels of literacy all girls in grades 1–5 are entitled to free school uniform each year. In practice these benefits are rarely received

(Pandey *et al.* 2008). The case of Bihar offered a successful example of efforts, including scholarships, to increase pupil enrolment, but it had little impact on teacher attendance or learning achievements.

A randomized experiment was implemented by the NGO Seva Mandir in rural Udaipur where most government schools had only a single teacher. The average absence rate in 2003 of 44 per cent meant the entire school would often be closed. Seva Mandir selected 60 random schools and gave teachers a camera with instructions to take a picture of themselves with their students every day at opening and closing time. The cameras had a tamper proof date and time function. Teachers received a bonus as a function of the number of valid days actually attended. The teacher received a salary of Rs1,000 monthly if they were present at least 21 days a month and a bonus of Rs50 a day up to a maximum of Rs1,300 per month. In the remaining 60 control schools teachers were paid Rs1,000 per month. One unannounced visit was made every month to measure teacher absence. The absence rate of teachers in treatment schools declined from 36 to 18 per cent and increased teaching activity among those teachers actually present. The cost was $6 per child per year and showed that the combination of a clearly defined task, simple incentives and a commitment to implementation could be quite powerful (Banerjee & Duflo 2006).

Another large-scale randomized evaluation of a teacher performance pay programme was conducted in Andhra Pradesh in 2005. This intervention gave a bonus (equal to 3% of a teacher's annual salary) dependent on improvement in test scores. The study was conducted in 300 randomly selected government schools in rural areas (100 of which were given no bonuses and served as the comparison group). Tests were conducted in schools in 2005 and follow up tests in 2006. The bonus payment was a function of the average improvement of all students to prevent teachers focusing only on stronger students. To prevent exclusion of weaker students from taking the test a zero improvement score was recorded for any student who took the baseline test but not the end-of-year test. To reduce cheating, tests were conducted by external teams of evaluators, the identities of students taking the test were verified and the grading was done at a supervised central location. The bonuses had a significant impact on test scores in mathematics and language and that impact was still evident two years on. The results show that better educated and better trained teachers responded to incentives and that incentives can boost the effectiveness of other school inputs including teacher human capital (Muralidharan & Sundararaman 2011).

The Right of Children to Free and Compulsory Education Act was passed in 2009. Provisions of the Act include that 25 per cent of seats in private schools be reserved for government-sponsored poorer students and that all schools that remain unregistered close within three years of the Act coming into force. The latter provision was non-credible, ignored the large numbers of children in low-cost unregistered schools and has not been achieved in practice. Closing down unrecognized schools would mean forcing 60 per cent of children out of their existing schools in some areas. There were also unrealistic administrative burdens for unregistered schools to become registered. Section 23 of the Act makes it compulsory for teachers to be trained, which if enforced would make unregistered schools unsustainable. To replace its existing teachers with trained teachers and pay them a salary on a par with the salary earned by trained teachers in government schools would force low-cost schools to increase average fees by 560 per cent (Rangaraju *et al.* 2012). In Bihar for example state funding for all those children currently in unregistered schools would have enormous financial implications: 83 per cent of children in private schools are in unregistered schools; multiplying this number by the average per child, per annum expenditure that Bihar spends on education would require the state government to increase its education budget by around 200 per cent (*ibid.*).

The studies show that parents left to themselves, or even supported by efforts to strengthen local governance and oversight of governments, is not enough. The studies show that there exist interventions impacting the incentives faced by teachers that have real impacts on learning outcomes at low costs. Resources and political will directed towards government schools are necessary to improve learning outcomes.

HEALTH

There are huge variations in the availability of healthcare in contemporary India (Baru *et al.* 2010). For example, life expectancy in Kerala in 2001–05 was 74 years and in Uttar Pradesh, 62 years; infant mortality 13 and 69 per 1,000 live births; population per government hospital bed 1,299 and 20,041; and proportion of children aged 12–23 months fully immunized 75 per cent and 23 per cent (*ibid.*: 51). The all-India immunisation coverage of 43.5 per cent in 2005–06 hid considerable variation across socio-economic groups. Immunisation among the top 20 per cent of households by income was 71 per cent, or almost three times that among the lowest 20 per cent of households. Among STs the immunisation rate had increased from 26 per cent in 1998–9 to only 31 per cent in 2005–06 which showed no decline in inter-caste gaps (*ibid.*).

There are various factors responsible for these high levels of health inequalities. The government has traditionally invested very little in public health, leaving much of it up to the free market. Between 2004 and 2006 for example per capita health expenditure was around $35, of which only $6.50 was accounted for by the government (*ibid.*). The private sector has gained a dominant presence in medical education and training, medical technology and diagnostics, the manufacture and sale of pharmaceuticals, hospital construction and the provision of medical services (Selvaraj & Karan 2009). Even though public health facilities are supposed to be free (as with education) many people choose to pay private providers. There are widespread perceptions of poor quality, high absentee rates, long waiting times, and lack of courtesy among public-sector providers (Das & Hammer 2007). The public-sector share of total outpatient care declined from 26 per cent in 1987–8 to 20 per cent in 2004 and in hospitalization the decline was from 60 per cent to 40 per cent over the same years.

A consequence of the growing dominance of the private sector has been that the share of household out-of-pocket expenditures (OOPs) is very high and rising. OOP include direct payments for consultations, diagnostic testing, medicines, and transportation. It is estimated that 80 per cent of total health expenditure and 97 per cent of private expenditure (indicating the lack of insurance) are borne through OOPs. This imposes huge financial burdens on households. In 2004–06 the average direct health expenditure on outpatient care per treated person in rural areas was nearly 20 per cent of total annual household consumption expenditure and around 30 per cent for the poorest groups (Baru *et al.* 2010). These results indicate that a large majority of the economically vulnerable population, and even a sizeable section of the middle class, are susceptible to catastrophic health spending especially if an earning member of the household is afflicted with serious hospitalization. There are widespread reports of corruption in public health services in terms of bribes demanded for admission and treatment in public institutions, in the recruitment, promotion and transfer of personnel, admission to medical/paramedical education, procurement of drugs and technology. In rural areas close to 40 per cent of health expenses for hospitalization is financed through borrowing. A survey of nearly 500 households in Udaipur, Rajasthan showed that nearly 29 per cent of households identified health expenditure as their major source of financial stress (Banerjee & Duflo 2007). Poverty data for 2004 showed that as a result of healthcare expenditures an additional 35 million people fell below the poverty line (Selvaraj & Karan 2009). In rural and urban India rising OOP health expenditure is resulting in lower spending on clothing, footwear and education especially among lower income groups (Pal 2013). The largest component (70–80%) of OOPs are for the purchase of medicines. Some states have been able to lessen the cost of medicines, for example, in Tamil Nadu the Medical Supplies Corporation (TNMSC) has been successful in improving drug procurement, distribution and controlling costs of medicines in the public services, having adopted a list of the essential drugs to be provided to the public sector health system (Baru *et al.* 2010).

There is no clear evidence for the superiority of private-sector healthcare. An intensive survey of healthcare providers and patients in rich, middle-income and poor areas of Delhi, which lasted over two years and conducted interviews with 300 households weekly for 35 weeks and monthly for another eight months, made a census of all medical practitioners within a 15-minute walk of the surveyed households. The availability of healthcare was not found to be a problem as the average household could choose from 80 providers within a 15-minute walking radius. The average household visited a doctor once every two weeks, and the poor visited more than the rich. However, there are concerns with quality as only 52 per cent of visits to private-sector doctors are to "doctors" holding a Bachelor of Medicine and Bachelor of Surgery (MBBS) degree while providers in the public sector all hold an MBBS degree (Das & Hammer 2007). Private-sector providers are very responsive to patient expectations but the quality of advice, suggested treatments and prescriptions is limited by the low (often unqualified) competence of the provider. Meeting patient expectations implies that private doctors often give excessive prescriptions and that private care is characterized by unnecessary diagnostic tests, repeated consultation and superfluous surgery (Selvaraj & Karan 2009). Doctors in Delhi spend on average 3.8 minutes per patient. While non-MBBS providers knew fewer of the important questions to ask and the examinations they needed to perform than qualified doctors, they did perform approximately all those they knew. Private practitioners completed only 60 per cent of the questions and examinations that they knew to be important (Das & Hammer 2007). The poor receive low-quality care from the private sector because doctors do not know much, and receive low-quality care from the public sector because doctors do not do much. However, in poor areas despite the lower competence of providers in the private sector, the quality of advice patients receive compares favourably to the public sector. The results suggest that improved medical services for the poor is more to do with encouraging doctors to fully utilize existing medical resources than a need for better medical training. For the private sector improved medical services is more likely to come from improving information to consumers and reducing demand for extensive and inappropriate treatment (Das & Hammer 2007).

Interventions and policy

A public health intervention to address a communicable disease is a good example of a "public good". Interventions such as immunisations confer external benefits as the more children immunised the less likely other children are to get the diseases. This is an example of an externality and such effects will not be taken into consideration by private providers of healthcare seeking profits. Communicable disease control is also important on equity grounds as the prevalence of diseases such as malaria and tuberculosis (TB) tend to be higher among poorer income groups (Hammer *et al.* 2007). Individual and household attitudes to hygienic practices, such as making sure children are immunised, boiling of water, and breastfeeding are important inputs into health status. Public health campaigns to change behaviours related to these practices are also public goods and are best served through public health interventions.

One very successful public health campaign was discussed in Chapter 1. In 1947 India suffered 75 million cases of malaria and 800,000 deaths. In 1953 the Indian state, backed by the WHO, launched a public health campaign based on spraying DDT during peak transmission periods in May and September. By 1961 the number of malaria cases had dropped by more than 90 per cent across northern India (Cutler *et al.* 2010). A more enduring failure of public health is that related to the drivers of diarrhoea. Diarrhoea is the second leading cause of child mortality in the world after pneumonia. India has the highest global number of child cases, which included an estimated 237,482 deaths from diarrhoea in 2008. Diarrhoea is related to poor hygiene and sanitation. In 1990 it was estimated that only 7 per cent of India's rural population had access to an improved sanitation facility and 66 per cent access to an improved water source. Fifteen years later these figures were 18 per cent for sanitation and 81 per cent for improved water. However, piped water is not enough to prevent diarrhoea if households prefer to engage in open defecation, or if water is stored in contaminated vessels. The presence of piped water to a household significantly reduces but does not eliminate diarrhoea. Handwashing has been shown to have a large, negative and highly significant effect on the incidence of diarrhoea (Fan & Mahal 2011: 353) and is a classic illustration of the importance of public good campaigns to alter attitudes and behaviours.

There is a longstanding problem in allocating resources to preventive public health activities in India. As with the successful treatment of mosquitoes, for example, it is not clear that people will recognize the absence of illness as a result of government policy, making it hard for politicians to take credit for the successes of the programme. Curative care, by contrast, is specific to an individual so can more easily be attributed by the patient to a specific government service. Curative hospitals are physically prominent and enable politicians to take credit for opening them. India has been able to construct a physical supply of healthcare facilities, but in a competitive political system like India this means that less, and too little, is likely to be spent on public goods such as communicable disease control by public health measures. Indeed, a rough estimate is that only 5 per cent of government health spending goes to public health measures (Hammer *et al.* 2007).

Expenditure on the health sector comprised 1.15 per cent of GDP in India in 2018, one of the lowest in the world. There are significant vacancies in public primary health centre (PHC) posts leading to severe staff shortages. Even among those in post absentee rates were 18 per cent among doctors, 15 per cent among nurses, and 30 per cent among paramedics (Chaudhury *et al.* 2006). Banerjee *et al* (2008) report on a randomized evaluation of an incentives programme to improve assistant nurse midwife (ANM) attendance at rural clinics. The study was implemented between the NGO Seva Mandir and the state and local health administration in Udaipur district, Rajasthan across 100 villages, 1,000 households and the private and public healthcare centres. Despite high poverty and low population density the average household was only 1.53 kilometre from the closest public facility; there was no reported problem with affordability; and on average a visit to a sub-centre cost the patient only Rs33 and a PHC/CHC visit only Rs100 for visits involving operations and tests (Banerjee *et al.* 2008: 489). Nevertheless, the public healthcare system in the region had failed to provide health services: more than 75 per cent of people needing medical care went to more expensive traditional healers and private providers (Banerjee *et al.* 2004). Absenteeism by medical staff was identified as one reason for this low attendance by patients – a 2003 survey showed that sub-centres were closed on average 56 per cent of the time (Banerjee *et al.* 2008). The incentives intervention programme sought to improve monitoring. A member of the community was paid to check once a week (monitored by the survey team) on unannounced days, whether the medical personnel were present in the health centre or in the village doing health visits. The weekly monitoring system was put in place in 143 randomly selected clinics for eight months and the results were publicized among the local community. The monitoring and publicity had no impact on staff attendance rates, which showed that community monitoring and the dissemination of evidence on poor public service provision was by itself not enough to affect change (Banerjee *et al.* 2004: 125).

In November 2005 the NGO Seva Mandir and the government of Rajasthan agreed to a programme in which Seva Mandir would monitor the attendance of nurses across 135 villages. This time monitoring was combined with incentive payments. Any nurse absent for more than 50 per cent of the time on monitored days would have their pay reduced and nurses absent for more than 50 per cent of the time on monitored days for a second month would be suspended from government service (Banerjee *et al.* 2008). In the first six months of the monitoring programme attendance increased dramatically. The greater presence of nursing staff, however, had no impact on the number of patients treated, or the number of patients attending the government clinics (*ibid.*: 495). Over time the positive impact declined because the local government allowed nursing staff more "exempt days" when they were not required to be present, such as vaguely defined "health surveys" or "immunisation work". The state government was providing official excuses for absence and undermining the incentive system that had been set up (*ibid.*: 498). The optimism, in the previous section, about incentives for teachers needs to be tempered by the recognition that teachers and nurses may seek to undermine any intervention to their own advantage. Nurses had been able to direct political pressure on politicians and civil servants to undermine the monitoring system. Villagers who had long ago given up on public healthcare (they were not attending the clinics in greater numbers even when nurses were present) were not generating countervailing local political pressure to enforce attendance at health clinics.

Any reform effort in the future needs to address this underlying lack of demand for publicly provided healthcare (and government schooling) (*ibid.*). This story is not just one of apathy among medical professionals. In some cases, the job assignments of nurses were poorly defined in a way that made increased absence almost unavoidable. Nurses often did not live in the village where they were employed in a clinic and found it difficult to attend daily via poor public transport. It is often also expected for nurses to visit all the hamlets near their assigned village once a week, again by poor public transport and in debilitating hot weather. In these cases, there may also be a need to rationalize job descriptions (Banerjee & Duflo 2006).

The Congress-led United Progressive Alliance that won election in 2004 recognized many of these problems, which led to the formulation of the National Rural Health Mission (NRHM) in April 2005. The NRHM aimed to address issues such as underinvestment in human resources and infrastructure and also the quality of public health provision. The practical aims included more female health professionals, increasing community participation through the involvement of local community monitoring institutions and strengthening capacities for data collection to facilitate evidence-based planning, monitoring and supervision. It has also initiated several measures to improve accountability, such as greater local political control and auditing. By 2010 the NRHM had been extensively evaluated (Husain 2011), which revealed enormous gaps and inter-state variations in the success of the programme (Baru *et al.* 2010). Surveys found a substantial shortfall in the supply of essential drugs to the healthcare centres which were not regularly available in three quarters of the PHCs surveyed in Uttar Pradesh. Data from the health ministry revealed that 11 per cent of the PHCs did not have a doctor, rising to 17 per cent in more backward states. At the CHC level, only 25 of the required specialist posts had been filled. Community monitoring had failed to elicit any appreciable change in attendance or effort among medical professionals (Husain 2011).

A more difficult challenge than building more physical health facilities is how to improve the quality of care. Training has little impact. A doctor with an MBBS degree is only 1.5 percentage points more likely to perform the nine specific tasks involved in diagnosing and treating diarrhoea and coughs than a less qualified colleague. For these nine tasks, the probability that the tasks are completed by the provider is 15 percentage points lower in the public than private sector (Das & Hammer 2007). Hospital provision has its problems too. Large and often urban-based hospitals can be difficult to access for remote villagers and tend to focus too much on curative rather than preventative healthcare. In contemporary India hospitals do offer some advantages. In a hospital peer observation and monitoring often leads to better attendance among professionals (Chaudhury et al. 2006). Research in Andhra Pradesh shows that doctors tend to work more effectively and with greater commitment in settings where they have colleagues to work with and equipment and opportunities to use their skills and education. Hospitals are hard to justify on equity grounds as about 75 per cent of the healthcare infrastructure in India is located in urban India, whereas 65 per cent of the population and the bulk of those living in poverty are in rural areas (Husain 2011). Without a fundamental shift in the way that nurses and doctors are paid, monitored and rewarded in the public sector, perhaps the best policy option is to help patients become better consumers of health care. Private providers will do what the patient asks even when they know better. A key change is to stop patients asking for unnecessary treatments. How to do this among often poorly educated patients is not clear. Patients will be better served in public-sector hospitals provided they can get advice from doctors serving in hospitals, although again, access to hospitals is often very difficult for the poorest (Das & Hammer 2007).

NUTRITION

It is often forgotten but *mal*nutrition or "bad" nutrition can equally refer to a diet of excess driven by prosperity, leading to problems such as obesity. Obesity, compounded by sedentary lifestyles among certain groups in India, is a rising problem. In 2005–06, an estimated 12.6 per cent of women and 9.3 per cent of men were measured as being "obese" (Jose 2011: 96). The more commonly discussed problem in contemporary India, however, is that of malnutrition measured by the slow gain of height, weight and circumferences of head and upper-arm. The World Health Organisation (WHO) have developed common standards of height and weight by age and gender to measure malnutrition. The three most widely reported indicators of child malnutrition are the proportion of children stunted (low height for age), underweight (low weight for age) and wasted (low weight for a given height, regardless of age).

Malnutrition can lead to health problems ranging from liver problems, anxiety, to attention deficit among school children. Micro-nutrient deficiency resulting from inadequate levels of iron, folate, iodine, and other vitamins may lead to conditions such as anaemia, bone deformities, and night blindness. Malnutrition makes a child susceptible to infections often responsible for child deaths such as diarrhoea, pneumonia and measles (Panagariya 2013). Maternal malnutrition leading to maternal short stature and iron deficiency anaemia increases the risk of death of the mother in childbirth and accounts for at least 20 per cent of maternal mortality. Maternal malnutrition is associated with the increased risk of intrauterine growth retardation leading to the birth of low birth weight (below 2.5kg) babies. In 2000 almost 8 million children born in India had low birth weights, which accounted for more than 40 per cent of all low birth-weight births in developing countries (Jose & Navanaatham 2010). Maternal malnutrition is also related to the rising burden of chronic diseases for children in their later life such as cardiovascular diseases, type-2 diabetes, high blood pressure, and some forms of mental illness during adulthood (Jose & Navanaatham 2010).

There are two striking problems in contemporary India: first, that malnutrition is at very high levels, and secondly, that little progress has been made in reducing malnutrition. The incidence of malnutrition among women in India is one of the highest in the world. In 2005/06, over 35 per cent of women between 15 and 49 years had a BMI below 18.5 (classed as underweight). Of 23 countries in Sub-Saharan Africa with comparable data, only Eritrea has a worse outcome (Jose 2011: 96). Improved BMI has been shown to be marginal for women, people of lower caste and the poorest 20 per cent of the population (Jose & Kavaneetham 2008: 65). Between 1998–9 and 2005–06 (as measured by various rounds of the NFHS) the percentage of children classified as underweight declined only marginally at the all-India level, from the globally high level of 46.7 to 45.9 per cent (Deaton & Dreze 2009). The 2015–16 NFHS showed an improvement in this trend, to 35.7 per cent.

The most obvious driver of household nutrition status is household income, which can influence food security, dietary intake, and access to healthcare (Harriss & Kohli 2009). There is some evidence for this relationship. Between 1992–3 and 2005–06, the proportion of children underweight in the bottom 20 per cent of households by wealth declined from 61 per cent to 53 per cent; among the top 20 per cent of households the drop was from 35 per cent to 26 per cent (Desai & Thorat 2013: 20). This fall continued into the 2015–16 NFHS to 49 and 20 per cent respectively. Income (or wealth) matters, but it is not everything. There is, however, no consistent link between nutrition outcomes and economic performance among Indian states. Kerala, Tamil Nadu and Andhra Pradesh have performed better than higher-income states like Gujarat, Maharashtra and West Bengal. While poor states such as Madhya Pradesh, Bihar and Orissa have performed poorly, the poor north-east states like Assam have better nutritional outcomes and some even outperformed Kerala (Radhakrishna 2005). Malnutrition declines slowly with improvements in the standard of living and even persists among the top income groups (*ibid.*).

This lack of a strong relationship between income and nutritional outcomes comes out more strongly when making international comparisons, revealing a particular India puzzle. A scatter plot of the prevalence of malnutrition against a measure of income shows a negative relationship among a large cross-section of countries. This test shows that India (and Pakistan) are both outliers in the sense that they have much greater levels of child malnutrition than we would expect given their income levels. The proportion of children in India with low weight-for-age was higher in 2005–06 than in Ethiopia, a poorer and drought prone country. This relationship also shows up as a puzzle over time, as economic growth reduces malnutrition in India must less than expected when compared to other countries (Walton 2009: 17). The differences are explained by the fact that income and poverty are not the only determinants of nutritional outcomes and other factors, which themselves are not perfectly linked to income are important.

Some of this problem is related to caste. According to NFHS-3 data almost 48 per cent of ST children are malnourished compared to around 34 per cent among other caste groups (Thorat & Sadana 2009). Several studies have identified discrimination in the access by SC patients to public health services and schemes related to food security for school children. Health service personnel may not visit SC families, or choose to hold health camps for mass vaccinations and other health interventions away from SC dwelling areas in villages (*ibid.*).

Some of the malnutrition story is related to failures in specific states. Since the 1970s striking differences have emerged between states in India. Between 1974 and 2001 Kerala reduced the level of undernutrition in children (1–5 years) by 57 per cent, Andhra Pradesh by 47 per cent, Tamil Nadu by 43 per cent, Orissa by 25 per cent, and Madhya Pradesh by only 9 per cent (Harriss & Kohli 2009: 10). Despite these reductions, by the early 2000s, even in Kerala, the best performing state, almost 30 per cent of children remained malnourished, and in Madhya Pradesh almost 64 per cent (Radakrishna 2005, 2009). There is a broad consistency between the trends in child malnutrition across states and various related factors such as female literacy, availability of public goods such as water supply and sanitation, and the prevalence of immunisation and institutional birth deliveries (Harriss & Kohli 2009: 12). Together these results imply that malnutrition is driven by deeper determinants of the status of women (see Chapter 4) and the ability of the state government to provide broad-based public services.

Panagariya (2013) highlights another India puzzle by comparing various health indices for mothers and children in India with Chad and the Central African Republic (CAR). Figure 5.3 shows that Chad and the Central African Republic do considerably worse on almost all measures of mother and child welfare, yet India has a much higher official rate of child malnutrition.

Figure 5.3 Child welfare indicators: Chad, Central African Republic and India, 2009

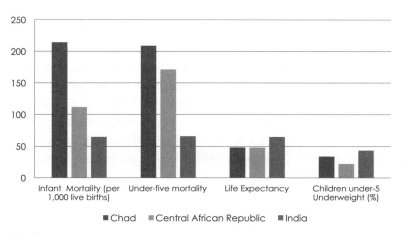

Source: Panagariya 2013: 100.

To explain these apparent anomalies Panagariya turns to the data on malnutrition. The currently accepted approach starts by defining a height norm for children of a given age and gender then classifying as stunted all children of the same age and gender in a given population who are below this norm. These norms are based on the assumption that children from different races, ethnicities, cultures, time periods and geographical locations would be identical in terms of height distribution if they had the same nutrition. The World Health Organisation (WHO) developed height and weight standards using a reference population based on data from 8,440 healthy breastfed infants and young children from Brazil, Ghana, India, Norway, Oman and the United States. These standards were adopted in 2006 and are now widely used (Panagariya 2013). Panagariya argues that any particular population of children may be shorter than the children in the reference population because of genetics. For example, good diets have led Japanese people to become taller over time but they have remained 12–13cm shorter than adults in the Netherlands. African men and women, by international standards, are exceptionally tall despite low incomes, high infant and child mortality rates, low per capita calorie availability and low female literacy rates (Deaton 2007). How significant a factor is genetics?

In the 1970s the official poverty line (more like a line measuring absolute deprivation) was 50+ per cent of the Indian population. By any global or health-related standard, poverty in India was then deep and pervasive. It is only over the past three decades that India has been experiencing sustained rapid economic growth and within the last decade that India crossed the threshold (just) into becoming a lower-middle-income country. It is still the case that around 70 per cent of the population live on $2 a day or less. The generational effect whereby low-income mothers are smaller so are physically constrained to have smaller daughters who in turn are constrained to having smaller children later in life is still likely to be influential. The portion of stunting in India that is due to a process of gradual catch-up may still have some way to go even among now wealthy families (who may have been much poorer in the recent past) (Gillespie 2013: 104).

In his discussion Panagariya looks at overall averages of malnutrition among children. In doing so he misses important dynamics that happen within the household over time. Jayachandran and Pande (2013) have noted that there are significant variations in patterns of stunting within families. Using data from comparable household-level surveys for 25

Sub-Saharan African countries and for India between 2004 and 2010, they show that height-for-age differences only appear with the second-born child and become even more pronounced with subsequent births. This gap they identify can account for the entire India/Africa height gap. This gap is not a consequence of family, parental characteristics, or whether the child is male or female. Genetic differences should be uniform across all births and not vary with the order. Analysis of food consumption patterns for Indian and African mothers shows a relatively greater decline in food consumption among Indian mothers during second and subsequent births. This decline is concentrated only among pregnant Indian women and the decline in consumption is not experienced by their husbands. Women's food consumption and BMI decline with successive pregnancies. This would likely affect fetal health and the well-being of breastfed children. It is also the case that prenatal check-ups, maternal iron supplements, childbirth at a health facility, child vaccinations, and postnatal check-ups decline with birth order in India but not in Africa. Later in childhood there is also evidence that parents spend less on the education of second and subsequent children in India. A preference for earlier born children is observed in many societies and in India may be reinforced by a cultural norm of eldest son preference. Once the family in India has a son parental inputs decline with subsequent pregnancies (Jayachandran & Pande 2013: 79).

Using data from 240 households across six representative villages in southern India, Behrman and Deolalikar (1987) find that calorie consumption and nutrient intake improved with real income growth in the mid-1970s. Afterwards things changed. Between 1972/3 and 1993/4 per capita consumption of cereals showed a decline of 12 per cent in rural areas and 5 per cent in urban areas. This was crucial because cereals are important in the Indian diet and provide approximately 60 per cent of calorie and protein intake. There were significant regional variations in these trends, in rural Gujarat, Haryana, Madhya Pradesh, Punjab, Rajasthan and Tamil Nadu the fall was more dramatic, between 18 and 30 per cent (Rao 2000: 202). Minimum necessary calorie intake is roughly 2,400 calories for a rural and 2,100 for an urban prime age male. By the 2000s the daily calorie consumption of the bottom 30 per cent of income earners (1600–1700 kcal) was well below these norms (Radhakrishna 2005). Figure 5.4 shows that there were striking regional variations without an obvious pattern. By the 2000s, calorie availability was lower in the high human development states (Kerala, Tamil Nadu and Karnataka) than the rich states (Gujarat, Maharashtra, Haryana and the Punjab). Low-income and low human development states such as Bihar and Madhya Pradesh did not do particularly badly in terms of average calorie consumption (Cassen & McNay 2005).

Figure 5.4 Calorie availability in Indian states, 2000

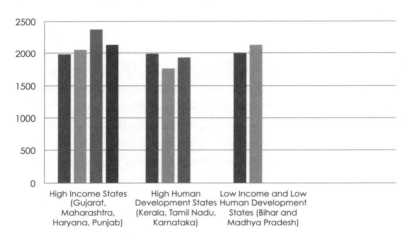

Source: Cassen & McNay 2005: 198.

For Patnaik (2007) these findings are evidence that actual poverty is much higher than the official or related estimates of poverty discussed in Chapter 3. She emphasizes how rising costs of healthcare and education (discussed earlier in this chapter) were squeezing food consumption among the poorest. There is supporting evidence for this proposition. Per capita rural and urban food expenditure increased during the 1970s and 1980s then fell steadily in the 1990s and 2000s. This was despite a steady rise in per capita total expenditure between 1970 and 2000 across all social classes. Expenditure was rising but less of it was going on calories

(Radhakrishna 2005: 1818). The focus of Patnaik on cereals as the driver of malnutrition is too narrow. The poorest 30 per cent of population experienced some increase in per capita consumption of cereals (from very low levels) over this period, while it was the middle 40 per cent and top 30 per cent of the population who experienced the decline in their per capita consumption. The decline was sharper for the top 30 per cent in both rural and urban areas (Rao 2000: 202). Another explanation for declining cereal consumption is that people were diversifying their food spending and consumption patterns. There were large increases in per capita consumption of vegetables, fruits, milk and meat (Hanchate & Dyson 2005: 234). Food diversification may be beneficial from a nutrition perspective if it enhances nutritional status by increasing intake of micro-nutrients, even if not adding much calories to the diet. For all-India the data suggest only modest improvement, or even some stagnation in the nutritional content of the average diet during recent decades (Hanchate & Dyson 2005). Despite the general diversification of diets micro-nutrient deficiency remains common in India. Up to 80 per cent of the rural population receive less than half of vitamin-A requirements, the lack of which can cause blindness. Iron deficiency anaemia is common amongst men and women. The widespread cereal-based, vegetarian diet has a low iron content and large shares of men and women do not eat iron-rich meat on a regular basis. The absorption of iron is inhibited by various typical aspects of Indian cooking such as the "overcooking" of vegetables, consumption of milk immediately after the main meal and drinking tea on a regular basis. Phytates found in cereals, nuts and legumes also significantly reduce iron absorption (Jose 2011: 100). While income and poverty undoubtedly impact diet diversification it is not everything. Only 45 per cent of men and 58 per cent of women in the top 40 per cent of income groups regularly consume fruit. Gender is also important. More men than women are regular consumers of milk, fruit, and meat (*ibid.*: 100). These dietary habits are also prevalent in young children. In three sample states (Karnataka, Bihar and Tamil Nadu) infant feeding contains few iron-rich foods and tends to be characterized by a monotonous diet (Menon *et al.* 2009: 63).

Nutrition and sanitation

The link between sanitation and nutrition is only recently becoming more widely appreciated. The conversion of food intake into nutritional outcomes depends on access to safe drinking water, healthcare and hygiene. This focus can also help explain the problem highlighted by Panagariya as he does not consider it a major factor that could contribute to explaining differences in child nutrition status between children in India and Sub-Saharan Africa (SSA). This explanation for this difference might be that 53 per cent of the Indian population defecates in the open, which is both much higher than in SSA and occurs in a country which has much higher population density than in SSA (Gillespie 2013).

There are two key causal mechanisms linking open defecation to malnutrition: diarrhoea and chronic enteropathy. Living in an area of poor sanitation will increase the likelihood of an individual ingesting faecal pathogens, which is a well-known cause of diarrhoea. As well as increased mortality (in India diarrhoea caused the deaths of 212,000 children below the age of five in 2010) diarrhoea can also cause stunted growth due to loss of consumed nutrients. The second and less well understood mechanism is environmental or tropical enteropathy. This is a clinical condition resulting from the ingestion of faecal bacteria, which damages the wall of the small intestine weakening its ability to absorb nutrients. The condition also prompts energy- and protein-consuming immune responses to fight the resulting infections, so is continuously debilitating. The condition is difficult to identify and measure. The impact can be malnutrition of various forms without the experience of diarrhoea (Spears 2012; Chambers & Von Medazza 2013). This problem has, historically, not been unique to the developing world. In c.1910, the prevalence of hookworm among schoolchildren in the southern US states was around 40 per cent. Children walking barefoot were routinely exposed to worms while walking in fields fertilized with human faeces. Hookworm infections caused anaemia and stunting in children (Geruso & Spears 2014).

The provision of sanitation in India is poor. Between 60–75 per cent of Indian households do not have access to indoor piped water, water supply for at least three hours per day, and access to a flush toilet. There has been some improvement in sanitation over time, especially in access to flush toilets. The 2011 census lists about 36 per cent of households with indoor toilets, compared to 18 per cent in 2001 (Desai & Thorat 2013). The growth in the population and the large fraction of the population who choose not to use indoor toilets means that (using the 2001 and 2011 national census) the percentage of households defecating in the open in India has only declined slowly over this decade, from 63 to 53 per cent. A UNICEF-WHO estimate shows that the number of people defecating in the open peaked at 664 million in 1996, then declined to 605 million in 2001. At this rate India will eradicate open defecation in 150 years (Spears 2012: 2). The distribution of open defecation by wealth quintile is also skewed. The wealthiest 40 per cent of Indians are ten times more likely than the poorest 40 per cent to use improved sanitation (Chambers & Von Medazza 2013). The most important variable for our discussion of malnutrition is the density of open defecation in a child's local area, measured as the number of people defecating in the open per square kilometre (Spears 2012). The key point is that sanitation matters more in areas of high population density. While the percentage of households defecating in the open declined between 2001 and 2011, most Indians (52.9%) live in districts where the density of open defecation increased (*ibid.*: 6).

The statistical results demonstrating the link between sanitation and child nutrition are robust. Spears (2013) finds that sanitation predicts child height even after accounting for other important determinants of child health, including levels of income, mother's literacy, immunisation, knowledge about oral rehydration therapy, access to healthcare facilities, measures of governance, prevalence of breastfeeding and accessibility of water. This result holds across different sub-regions of the world, showing that the result is not driven by geography or genetic differences. The results do help solve Panagariya's highlighted problem. India's open defecation rate (55%) is more than double that in Nigeria (26%) and higher than many of the poorest countries in the world such as Congo, Malawi, Burundi and Rwanda (Spears 2012; Coffey *et al.* 2014). Panagariya notes that the incidence of stunting among children (based on WHO standards) is higher in India than in Chad, in spite of infant mortality being much lower in India. Sanitation, others argue, accounts for the average height difference between children in South Asian and SSA countries (Spears 2013). While a statistically average child in Chad is exposed to about seven neighbours who defecate in the open per square kilometre, in India this figure is over 200 per square kilometre. Spill-over effects mean that having a toilet may be of little use if neighbours are not using toilets (Desai & Thorat 2013). If one identifies the "top" 2.5 per cent of the Indian population as those who live in urban homes with flush toilets that are not shared with other households, whose mothers are literate and have been to secondary school, and whose families have electricity, a radio, a refrigerator, and a motorcycle or car, even these relatively rich children are shorter than healthy norms. This is not surprising and is not a reflection of genetics, but of the fact that many households living near these rich children defecate in the open (Spears 2013: 11). In West Bengal, Hindu households are wealthier than Muslim households but Muslims are 40 per cent more likely to defecate in pit latrines or toilets than Hindus. Muslims are more likely to use indoor toilets themselves and are more likely to have neighbours who do. The entire gap between Hindu and Muslim child mortality can be accounted for by this sanitation externality. Again, these patterns are not driven by household ownership of assets, parental education, or urban residence (Geruso & Spears 2014).

If sanitation access is improving why is open defecation still so prevalent? The 2014 SQUAT survey (a rural survey about Sanitation Quality, Use, Access and Trends) conducted interviews in villages in Bihar, Madhya Pradesh, Rajasthan and Uttar Pradesh across 3,235 households and 22,787 household members to ask about the defecation behaviour of each member of the household. These five states are home to 40 per cent of India's population and to about 30 per cent of the world population who defecate in the open (Coffey *et al.* 2014). The survey showed that open defecation is common even in households that have access to an indoor toilet. Of all interviewed households 80 per cent had at least one member who defecates in the open, and even 48 per cent of households with a work-ing toilet had at least one member who defecates in the open (*ibid.* 2014). Government efforts to construct toilets have had only a limited impact: only 9 per cent of households reported receiving money or materials from the government for building a toilet and 60 per cent of households who did had at least one household member who still defecated in the open (*ibid.*). Of people who defecate in the open 47 per cent explain that they do so because it is pleasurable, comfortable and convenient, as do 74 per cent of those who have a toilet in their household and defecate in the open. There is a general failure to recognize the health benefits of latrine use: 51 per cent of those who defecate in the open report that widespread open defecation would be at least as good for child health as toilet-use by everyone in the village, and only 26 per cent of respondents had any clear understanding of the possible causes of diarrhoea (*ibid.*). Furthermore, access to water is not the constraint on construction of toilets that many assume. The survey shows that less than 1 per cent of men and 5 per cent of women who defecate in the open cite lack of access to water as the rea-son not to use a latrine. The results indicate that most households in India could afford to build the kinds of inexpensive toilets commonly used in poor countries (*ibid.*).

The call for policy-makers is to recognize open defecation and lack of sanitation and hygiene as powerful and persistent causes of under-nutrition. In 2013, before becoming prime minister, Modi argued that India should build "toilets before temples". The policy he launched once in office, via the Nirmal Bharat Abhiyan (NBA) sanitation programme, aims to ensure an open defecation-free rural India by 2020 and if that were achieved "much of the undernutrition of Indian children would disap-pear" (Chambers & Von Medazza 2013: 17).

Policy interventions

The Public Distribution System (PDS) is a large-scale rationing pro-gramme intended to increase food security at national and household levels. The Indian government procures foodgrains, mainly wheat and rice from farmers, rice millers and others, which are then stored as a buffer stock or distributed to consumers at "fair prices" through specially licensed shops (Mooij 1998). The PDS has its origins during wartime rationing after 1939 to ensure food availability to urban areas. The scheme was expanded in the mid-1960s as the government intervened more in agriculture, purchasing output at guaranteed prices to motivate farmers to invest in new Green Revolution technology (*ibid.* 1998). The scheme then expanded rapidly and by the end of the 1980s the PDS was selling 18 million tonnes of foodgrains (about 10 per cent of national production) through more than 350,000 fair-price shops, three-quarters of which were by then in rural areas (*ibid.*).

The PDS has helped ensure there has been no large-scale famine in India since independence but it has not eliminated widespread hunger and malnutrition. By the early 1990s across states there was very little connection between the allocation of foodgrains through the PDS and the percentage of people below the poverty line. People in high poverty states like Orissa, Uttar Pradesh and Madhya Pradesh received a per capita allocation of foodgrains from the PDS of less than 10 kilos per year, while in lower poverty states like Kerala, Andhra Pradesh and Tamil Nadu per capita distribution ranged from 20 to 63 kilos per person (Mooij 1999: 627). By the 1990s a large proportion of the PDS foodgrains failed to reach poor consumers at rationed prices and leakages were prevalent across India. This occurred when subsidized foodgrains were not sold to consumers at rationed prices but instead diverted onto the free market. In states such as Bihar, Haryana, Orissa and the Punjab, up to 88 per cent of wheat and rice leaked out of the subsidized system into the market. Even in the better performing southern states such as Kerala, Karnataka and Tamil Nadu, the figures were still up to 40 per cent (*ibid.*: 628). The proportion of the bottom 40 per cent of households getting any PDS benefit declined from 50 per cent in 1993–4 to 33 per cent in 2000–05, while leakages from the PDS doubled (Himanshu & Sen 2013).

In response to these perceived failings the central government in the early 1990s tried to reduce expenditure on the PDS by raising the price (by

40 per cent) of rationed foodgrains and shifting to making the PDS more targeted towards poorer consumers. Together these changes reduced the percentage of the population accessing the PDS from 72.6 to 23.5 per cent in urban areas and 68.3 to 29 per cent in rural areas (*ibid.* 2013). After 2004 there was a revival in the PDS. Many states implemented reforms to improve the delivery infrastructure. In Chhattisgarh message alerts sent to mobile phones reported grain movements to citizens, electronic weighing machines were used to weigh rations and lists of ration-card holders were put on public display. These reforms increased the coverage of the PDS by nearly two million individuals and led to a big and widespread increase in consumption of rationed rice (Krishnamurthy *et al.* 2014). Reforms in other states have included making higher payments to those running fair price shops to increase their viability, handing over management to local governments or self-help groups, computerizing records, setting up functioning grievance redressal procedures and mobile phone text information about stocks of foodgrains held by any outlet (Khera 2011a). After 2004 the proportion of the poor accessing the PDS increased. In Bihar the proportion of households accessing the PDS increased from 2 per cent in 2004–05 to 43 per cent in 2011–12, and grain leakages declined from 97 per cent in 2004–05 to 20 per cent in 2011–12. Overall the national percentage of households accessing PDS cereals increased from 24 per cent in 2004–05 to 45 per cent in 2011–12 and over the same years grain leakages declined from 55 to 35 per cent (Himanshu & Sen 2013: 49). Those states seeing big improvements included Chhattisgarh, Madhya Pradesh, Orissa and Uttar Pradesh which were all dysfunctional at the beginning of this period (Khera 2011b). By the second half of the 2000s the PDS lifted an extra 55 million people out of poverty annually (Himanshu & Sen 2013).

The Mid-Day Meal Scheme (MDM) was launched in 1995. Under this central government scheme cooked mid-day meals were to be introduced in all government and government-aided primary schools to provide pupils with a minimum of 300 calories and 8–12 grams of protein each day of school for a minimum of 200 days. The aim was to reduce classroom hunger, improve the nutritional status of primary school children and boost school attendance. A Supreme Court order in November 2001 directed lagging states to implement the scheme to all primary schools within six months. By 2006 MDM was near universal across India and was providing a lunch to about 120 million children every school day. Some states went beyond the mandated minimum: Kerala and Tamil Nadu, for example, allow the destitute and aged to participate in the MDM (Kingdon 2007).

Some early critics of the MDM scheme argued that lack of food was not a major constraint on children's school attendance and that the poverty of the parents was responsible for poor attendance. Such children would also be required for work during the agricultural season and the school meal was unlikely to be comparable to potential earnings for a child outside school (Singh 2004). These criticisms were untenable in light of the significant increases in school attendance following the introduction of MDM. One survey conducted between January and April 2003 across Chhattisgarh, Rajasthan and Karnataka found that in 76 of 81 schools MDMs were being served regularly and that school enrolment increased by nearly 15 per cent after MDMs were introduced. In the first year of class in Rajasthan, girls' attendance increased by almost 30 per cent and 78 per cent of teachers revealed that afternoon attendance was the same as morning attendance (Dreze & Goyal 2003). In another survey in Rajasthan after the launch of the MDM almost all children from the lowest castes were attending school (Garg & Mandal 2013). Some studies have reported the prevalence of caste discrimination in MDM, such as students from SC and ST groups being made to sit away from upper castes, or being served left-over food. There has been little evidence of this in surveys, although many higher-caste children have left government for private schools and the MDM may have helped prompt this shift (*ibid.* 2013).

Some have criticized the MDM for the minimal nutritional value of the meals served (Singh 2004). There certainly is evidence of corruption and poor-quality food being served. One survey of the MDM in Delhi, for example, which was extended to all students enrolled in government primary schools through centralized kitchens operated by NGOs, and by

2013 it was feeding 1.29 million primary school students, used laboratory reports of MDM samples, field surveys, kitchen experiments and reports from a third-party monitoring institute (Shukla 2014). The survey showed that only 1 per cent of 466 MDM samples tested in 2010/11 satisfied the prescribed nutritional norms in terms of calories, proteins and vegetables. This increased to 5 per cent of MDM samples in 2011/12 and 17 per cent in 2012/13 (*ibid.*). The Delhi government was not monitoring food quality and had failed to act on negative assessments from auditors and activists. NGOs have never been punished for these poor efforts and the same NGOs were later granted a three-year contract extension. The Delhi NGOs make significant profits from compromising on the quality and quantity (weight) of food served in the MDMs and government grain deliveries that should have gone to kitchens was often sold directly to flour and rice mills and substituted for inferior alternatives. School teachers are clearly complicit in this corruption (*ibid.*). Despite these evident problems, the extreme poverty and malnutrition among disadvantaged children means even compromised MDMs can have beneficial effects. Survey evidence shows that on a school day ST children had more food intake than on a non-school day (Garg & Mandal 2013).

Some have argued that MDMs may disrupt classroom activities and media reports have suggested that teachers have been asked to spend time cooking instead of teaching (Singh 2004). Rather than MDMs disrupting precious learning in return for minimal nutrition benefits, the survey evidence has shown that cooks have generally been appointed in all sample schools and that there were no cases found of teachers doubling as chefs, although teachers did spend time organizing and supervising the MDMs (Dreze & Goyal 2003). Facilities are often poor. When the scheme was launched many schools experienced a shortage of utensils, relied on donations, or asked children to bring plates from home. In Rajasthan many children were found to be eating on pieces of paper torn from their notebooks, or textbooks (*ibid.*). The quality of school meals was significantly better in Karnataka where most cooks had the assistance of a helper, and by 2001 almost one-third of schools had a specially built kitchen. To replicate the Karnataka model nationwide and cover the recurring costs of a national mid-day meal programme covering all children enrolled in government schools would add up to approximately 0.1 per cent of India's GDP (*ibid*.). MDMs have in practice contributed to improving the learning environment, helped reduce classroom hunger, promoted regular attendance and fostered egalitarian values (Dreze 2004).

State aid, cash transfers and benefits

Over the past twenty years cash transfers to the poor have been implemented in countries like Brazil and Mexico and have been seen by many to be a great success. This has prompted much debate in India. A cash transfer is the direct transfer of a regular sum of money to specific individuals or families. This is usually done electronically directly from the government to an individual's bank account. Some cash transfer programmes are conditional, such as that households will only receive a given sum if children attend school on a regular basis, or receive regular medical check-ups. Cash transfers can be given to groups with particular characteristics, such as the low paid, elderly or unemployed. The main argument for cash transfers is that it costs less to deliver a rupee to a beneficiary than an elaborate, leaky, system of physical procurement and distribution like the public distribution system (PDS). Others argue that the preferences of male household members may predominate regarding decisions on how such cash is spent, on alcohol rather than food for example. Studies do show that the PDS does lead to higher calorie consumption by households (Himanshu & Sen 2013).

The technology of cash transfers has improved significantly and a secure payments infrastructure can now deliver cash transfers. In India the Aaddhar card offers people a biometrically unique identity and by the end of 2015 900 million such cards had been issued. This is supplemented by the recent drive, known as the Jan Dhan, to persuade people to open bank accounts. By December 2015 there were 195 million such accounts. There are also close to 1 billion mobile phones in India that are increasingly being used to make payments and operate bank accounts. India also has a long and relatively successful series of experiments with paying wages under the NREGA (National Rural Employment Guarantee Act) programme directly into bank accounts which reduces leakages and has led to significant cost savings.

Joshi (2016) argues that cash transfers financed by eliminating government subsidies (on food, fertiliser, and employment) would be good for growth by aligning prices more closely with costs in these sectors. He argues that cash transfers will not necessarily be wasted on alcohol and other non-essential consumption. Trying to make cash transfers conditional on poverty would face the difficulty of identifying the poor by income or by assets and by excluding a large fraction of the population would generate controversy about the cut-off point and also lock-in long-term opposition among those paying taxes but not benefiting. Better, argues Joshi, would be a universal basic income paid via cash transfers. In 2014–15 he suggested this could entail a cash transfer of Rs17,500 to each household per year at a cost of 3.5 per cent of GDP. This compares to the annual cost of selling goods produced or procured by the public sector (food, fuel, fertiliser, iron ore, water, electricity and rail journeys) at below market prices of more than 4 per cent of GDP (Joshi 2016: 210). A cash transfer of this magnitude would, argues Joshi, reduce poverty and significantly enhance the income security of the very poorest in India.

EMPLOYMENT: AN INDIAN CRISIS?

This section outlines three distinctive features of employment and the productive sector in India – slow employment growth, the informalization of labour and the small size of production enterprises – that together have been labelled by some as a specific "Indian problem". The formal sector in India refers to that part of production and employment that is licensed, that, in 2018, is likely to pay the new Goods and Services Tax (GST), and where labour is employed and more likely to work in decent working conditions, with a contract, regular hours, holiday entitlement and other benefits.

India has experienced slow employment growth since independence. Formal employment in the primary sector grew annually by 1.6 per cent in the decade before economic liberalization (1983–94) and by -0.34 per cent in the post-liberalization decade (1994–2004). The manufacturing sector saw slow growth throughout, and the tertiary or service sector, slower growth after 1994. The cumulative impact was that by the 1990s the formal sector was tiny in relation to the rest of the economy. Formal-sector employment in 1991 was 26.73 million and had barely increased to 27 million by 2003. Despite this ten plus years of liberalization two-thirds of the total was in the public sector, and the share had remained unchanged since 1991 (Joshi 2004: 4176).

It was easy to attribute slow employment growth to India's purposefully capital-intensive industrialization strategy in the 1950s and 1960s. The emphasis on sectors like oil-refining and steel-making generated industrial output but much less employment (Chakravarty 1987). The industrial stagnation from the mid-1960s and in the 1970s could not have been expected to generate much employment (Ahluwalia 1985). When GDP growth accelerated in the 1980s continued employment stagnation became a more intriguing puzzle. With faster growth the Indian economy seemed to become even less able to generate good jobs and the employment elasticity (the increase in employment for every 1% rise in GDP) actually declined after 1980 and showed no increase in the 1990s (Mazumdar & Sarkar 2004: 3019; Kannan & Raveendran 2009: 83–4). The Indian economic boom between 2003/04 and 2008/09 saw rapid (7.5%) annual growth in employment in the organized manufacturing sector, but this proved short-lived and employment growth subsided after 2008–09 (Goldar 2011). This was "jobless growth" (Bhalotra 1998). In agriculture, the employment elasticity was low but positive until the 1990s, after which further output growth was associated with shedding labour from the sector. Between 2004/05 and 2009/10, 14 million workers left agriculture and a further 14 million departed between 2009/10 and 2011/12.

Typically for a developing country, output growth in India has long remained higher in manufacturing and services than in agriculture. The share of agriculture in GDP consequently declined from 44 per cent in 1978 to 28 per cent in 2004. As implied by the figures above, employment change was slow. The share of employment in agriculture declined from 71 to 57 per cent over the same period (Bosworth & Collins 2008: 57) and further to 53 per cent in 2010. There was little more than a lethargic tug of labour from manufacturing. While the share of manufacturing output to GDP increased from around 10 per cent in 1951 to 33 per cent in 1991, the share of employment increased from 11 to only 16 per cent (Bhalotra 1998). In the first half of the 2000s the economy did manage to create 12 million jobs in manufacturing, of which 7.5 million were accounted for by textiles, wearing apparel and leather products (Thomas 2012). Over the longer term India had missed the labour intensive manufacturing growth trajectory characteristic of many other Asian economies. In South Korea and Taiwan between the early-1960s and late-1970s manufacturing employment rose by 11 per cent and 8.5 per cent per annum respectively, resulting in the share of manufacturing in total employment rising from 8 to 22 per cent and from 16 to 32 per cent respectively. Employment growth was around double that of India in much of East Asia and China over the 1980s and 1990s (Mohan 2002).

An optimistic reason for the slow growth of India's employment during the second half of the 2000s was the rapid growth of education. There has been a steady increase in the ratio of students to the relevant age range in India, from 20.5 per cent in 1993/4 to 26.6 per cent in 2009/10. This took potential workers directly out of the labour force. The expansion of primary and secondary schooling that occurred mainly in the first half of 2000s drew nearly 3 million teachers, often young women into employment (Thomas 2012; Mehtrotra *et al.* 2013). The success story in terms of output growth was services and this created some bright areas in terms of employment. During the 1990s more than 13 million jobs were created in trade, hotels, transport and communications. In the latter half of the 2000s 4 million new jobs were created in services, mostly in retail trade, which employed almost 36 million people by the end of the decade. Over the same years the boom in urban retail and residential building and infrastructure created more than 18 million jobs in construction. The employment guarantee programme (NREGA) created more than 2.5 million jobs during these years (Thomas 2012).

Another standout feature of what job creation did take place in India is that it was almost wholly in the informal sector. The share of industrial workers in the informal sector increased from 71.25 per cent in 1978/9 to 78.42 per cent in 2000/01. This was driven not just by the expansion of employment in the existing informal sector, but also by sectors replacing formal with informal workers, which was widespread in key industry groups such as textiles, food, beverages and tobacco, wood products, leather, and machinery and equipment (Marjit & Kar 2009: 66).

Figure 5.5 The size of firms (number of employees) in India and other large developing countries, 2009

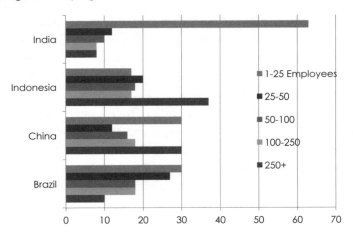

Source: Fernandes & Pakes 2009: 149.

The third distinctive feature of Indian employment has been the relatively small scale of enterprises. Figure 5.5 shows that the vast majority of industrial establishments and employment are in enterprises employing less than 25 people and this group is dominated by firms employing less than 10 workers (Nagaraj 2000b). By contrast, in Taiwan and South

Korea during their eras of rapid industrial growth from the 1950s to the 1970s small-scale enterprises lost ground to large firms employing more than 500 workers (Little *et al* 1987). This pattern was replicated in the later industrial growth stories of the Philippines, Indonesia, Thailand and Malaysia (Hasan & Jandoc 2010: 7). Similarly, by the late-1990s almost half of Chinese manufacturing employment (then some 60 million people) was in factories with an average size of about 100 workers (Mohan 2002: 229).

The story of one of India's most rapidly growing states, Gujarat, demonstrates these features in striking detail. Between 2000 and 2008 Gujarat's GDP grew by around 11 per cent per annum, with double digit growth in both manufacturing and services. While the share of manufacturing reached almost 40 per cent of Gujarat GDP the state failed to turn this into jobs. Across the 1990s and 2000s growth of formal-sector employment was only 0.5 per cent per annum and the employment share of manufacturing only reached 22 per cent of the total. More than half the state labour force remained in agriculture. The share of the informal sector in employment at almost 90 per cent was little different from the all-India average (Hirway & Shah 2011).

The ultimate implications of "The India Problem", of slow employment growth, a growing informal sector and the small scale of production, are profound. This difference is brought out strikingly by Bramall (2007) in a comparison to China:

[The] growth of rural industry in China is one of the most dramatic changes that has occurred in the developing world over the last 25 years. Rural industrialisation has transformed the Chinese countryside and engineered a remarkable reduction in the level of absolute poverty. By the end of the century, close to 200 million rural citizens were employed within the rural non-farm sector, and many of these new industrial workers had been lifted out of (income) poverty in the process [...] it is this ascent from poverty that demarcates the China of the new millennium from the economies of sub-Saharan Africa and South Asia. (Bramall 2007: 322)

The orthodox view and critique

The orthodox view of economists, such as Besley, Burgess, Lucas, Fallon, Goldar and Zagha, seeks to explain the "India Problem" and the big differences with China principally in terms of labour market regulations. Labour legislation in India, argues the orthodox view, has raised the cost of employing labour and so slowed the growth of labour demand. In India by the late 1990s there were 45 different national and state-level pieces of labour legislation. These covered minimum wages, conditions of work, payment of benefits, procedures to resolve industrial disputes, conditions for hiring and firing workers, and the conditions to close establishments (Zagha 1999). The Industrial Disputes Act (IDA) 1947 and amendments of 1976 and 1982 make it illegal, except with prior government permission, for firms employing more than 300 (later 100) workers to dismiss employees. Permission to retrench was rarely granted and failure to comply with the law threatened a substantial fine and a prison sentence for an employer (Zagha 1999; Ahsan & Pages 2005). These laws are costly and confusing. A "wage", for example, is defined in 11 different ways in 11 different laws. Legalistic labour disputes usually take more than a year and often up to 20 years to settle. Restrictions on dismissal make employers more reluctant to hire, and generates a preference for the use of (flexible) capital rather than (fixed) labour. The labour laws also hinder the free (re)allocation of labour within an enterprise in response to changing market and production conditions. The IDA requires employers to provide "notice of change" such that no employer can re-assign an employee within the workplace without giving 21 days notice.

Labour legislation has also been blamed for the small-scale nature of production and the prevalence of the informal sector. Labour laws and the costs they impose on employers tend not to apply to small-scale or informal firms so give employers an incentive to keep firms small or move them into the informal sector out of the purview of regulation. The requirement to establish a pension fund is waived for firms with less than 20 employees. Prior approval from the government to retrench in any firm is not required for those with less than 100 regular workers. Any firm of 25+ workers must inform the local employment exchange of any vacancies. The 1948 Committee on Fair Wages fixes minimum wages, guides wages in particular sectors, and applies indexation and bonus payment rules only in the organized sector. The Industrial Employment (Standing Order) Act requires firms of more than 100 workers (in some states 50) to specify to workers the terms and conditions of their employment. The Contract Labour Regulation and Abolition Act regulates the service conditions of contract labour in firms of 20 or more employees providing for some basic welfare amenities and provisions against the delay in wage payment.

There is widespread empirical support for the orthodox view. Fallon and Lucas (1993) found that the 1976 amendment reduced formal sector employment by 17.5 per cent for a given level of output. Besley and Burgess (2002) found that Indian states amending regulations in a more pro-worker manner experienced lower output and employment growth and lower investment and productivity in manufacturing. Ahsan and Pages (2005) estimate that states who strengthened central regulations through pro-worker amendments experienced an 11 per cent decline in manufacturing employment relative to other states. They estimate that if the retrenchment permission legislation were lifted, about 880,000 registered manufacturing jobs would be created in India.

The corollary of these arguments is that employment growth should respond positively to any efforts to liberalize labour markets. There have been gradual changes to the legal framework in this direction, particularly since general liberalization was launched in 1991. One example was the The Micro, Small and Medium Enterprises Development Act 2006 which exempted micro- to medium-sized enterprises from inspection under various pieces of labour legislation, including the Maternity Benefit Act, the Factories Act, the Payment of Bonus Act, and the Payment of Wages Act. Goldar (2011) shows that taking the top five states in terms of their ranking in a labour reforms index, the growth rate of employment in the organized manufacturing sector was more than double (7.5% per annum) that of those five states with the least labour market reforms. The result is a weak one and employment growth appears more closely associated with the growth of output and investment than labour market liberalization (Nagaraj 2011).

However, there are severe empirical problems with the orthodox view. Studies looking at the impact of the 1976 amendment, such as Fallon and Lucas (1993), have overlooked the fact that the sections of the Amendment requiring official permission for lay-offs were contested in state and supreme courts for the next 25 years. One section, for example, was found unconstitutional by the Supreme Court in 1978, an amended version only being declared valid in 2002. Various other sections were upheld in amended versions by the Supreme Court only by the early-1990s (Bhattacharjea 2006, 2009). Even the likely impacts of the operational parts of the act have been overestimated. The much heralded 1976 and 1982 amendments that made it mandatory to seek government and other approvals for retrenchment only imposed minimal financial burdens on firms, usually around 15 days of compensation at 50 per cent of basic wages for every year of employment. Sacking workers is easily affordable. Large parts of the labour force were never covered by the IDA so have always been "flexible". Workers on fixed-term contracts, or those only casually employed (for less than 240 days in a given year), were never considered as workers under the IDA and have always been exempt from the requirement for severance pay, mandatory notice, or retrenchment authorization (Ahsan & Pages 2005). The IDA Act was also not applied to managerial and supervisory staff (Kannan & Raveendran 2009).

The 1980s onwards saw significant "reform by stealth" that led to labour markets becoming flexible in practice, if not in formal law (Nagaraj 2004). The key event empowering employers was the large-scale defeat of the Bombay textile workers in 1982–3. The strike was followed by the loss of 75,000 jobs in Bombay and 100,000 in Ahmedabad. And in Gujarat 66 textile mills were illegally closed, in violation of the IDA, and many

workers never received any redundancy payments. After the Bombay textile strike, lock-outs have caused more workdays to be lost than strikes,
something often used by management as a means to effectively close
down production units (Sundar 2004). The setting up of the National
Renewal Fund in the 1990s to finance mainly retrenchment of workers in
public-sector enterprises was seen by employers as a signal of the government's tacit support for similar initiatives in the private sector (Nagaraj
2004). In a survey of about 1,300 manufacturing firms across nine industry groups Sharma (2006) found that 27 per cent of firms had downsized
their workforce indicating significant employment flexibility. There was
also a distinct shift in the judiciary that contributed to the weakening of
trade union power. Indian courts historically gave pro-labour verdicts,
but from the 1990s onwards judgments tended to favour employers. Agi-
tations, demonstrations, bandhs, and processions were more frequently
curbed by legal judgments. In 2001 the Supreme Court over-ruled an earlier judgment which made it mandatory to eventually transform contract
labour into permanent employees (Sood *et al.* 2014).

Contract workers and casual/temporary workers are defined as those
working for less than 240 days in any 365-day period, they are not considered as employed under the IDA, so are exempted from any severance pay,
mandatory notice or retrenchment authorization (Ahsan & Pages 2008).
There has been an ongoing substitution of permanent workers by contract
workers despite existing job security legislation. The share of contract
workers in total organized employment increased from 10.5 per cent in
1995/6 to 25.6 per cent in 2009/10. The share of contract labour has risen
to above 40 per cent in states such as Gujarat, Orissa and Andhra Pradesh.
The textile industry shifted from being a male, unionized and formal sector in the 1970s to informal, small scale and female after the 1980s. In the
Tiruppur knitwear cluster, for example, by the late-1990s 96 per cent of
workers were employed as "casual" in predominantly small-scale enterprises (Neetha 2002). Contract workers are not just a phenomenon of the
small or informal sectors. In firms with more than 500 workers close to
50 per cent of workers were contract workers by 2009/10 (Ahsan & Pages

2008). Reflecting this de facto liberalization of labour markets, firm surveys (using for example World Bank Investment Climate data) found that firms do not list labour market regulations as a constraint on their operation (Ahsan & Pages 2005; Panagariya 2008).

The impact on working conditions of this shift is more muted than we might guess as the shrinking formal sector is not a haven of good employment conditions. The NSSO employment/unemployment surveys demonstrate the poor quality of even formal sector employment. In 2011–12 for example 77.5 per cent of the workforce employed in the organized manufacturing sector had no written contract and this rose to 91 per cent for female workers. Only 42.7 per cent of regular workers are entitled to any paid leave, 60 per cent of regular workers and 93 per cent of casual workers are not eligible for any social security benefits (Sood *et al* 2014: 61).

The expectation was that economic reforms after 1991, which reduced distortions in factor and capital markets and the de facto more flexible labour markets, would lead to Indian industry becoming more labour-intensive so employment growth would become more tightly linked to industrial output growth. This did not happen. As discussed above, employment growth remained slow after 1991. Within the formal manufacturing sector there was an ongoing decline in the labour intensity of production after 1991. Overall labour intensity fell from an average of 1.45 workers per machine in the 1980s to 0.33, or one worker per three machines, in the 2000s. Even among traditionally labour-intensive industries such as tobacco products, footwear, knitted fabrics, manufacture of furniture and food products labour intensity fell, from an average of 3.34 in the 1980s to 0.78 in the 2000s (Sen & Das 2015). This decline in labour intensity was reflected in the share of labour income in value added which fell from around 53 per cent in 1980–1 to about 31 per cent in 2009–10 (*ibid.*). As well as traditionally labour-intensive sectors becoming more capital-intensive, traditionally capital-intensive sectors such as automobiles, auto-parts, and petroleum refining, as well as skilled, labour-intensive services such as software, pharmaceuticals and banking have recently grown rapidly (Dehejia & Panagariya 2013).

A second explanation for the "India Problem" highlights supply-side constraints. These include infrastructure bottlenecks, poor skill levels and low literacy rates among workers as possible reasons why firms are substituting labour for capital (Panagariya 2008). To explain declining labour intensity over time we would need supply-side constraints to have become worse over time. As already discussed, infrastructure and education have improved in India noticeably over the last decade, so cannot be an explanation for the sustained recent decline in labour intensity that has been observed across all sectors of Indian manufacturing (Sen & Das 2015).

A third explanation is that the increase in real wages relative to the cost of capital has induced firms to substitute workers in favour of machines. There is good evidence for both sides of this argument. While the Indian economy has not been good at creating new jobs, there has been rapid growth in real wages, especially in rural areas since the mid-2000s. This wage growth has contributed to falling poverty (see Chapter 3). The real wages of female casual workers (employed in activities other than public works) in rural areas grew at an average of 5.5 per cent between 2004/05 and 2009/10 (Thomas 2012: 42). A key factor behind rising wage inequality was that the demand for skilled workers grew faster than the supply. The share of university graduates employed in new sectors such as finance and IT increased as did their employment in traditional sectors such as textiles and machinery equipment. While the labour force did become more educated and skilled over time this progress lagged behind rising labour demand for skills. This led to shortages, rising wages and an incentive to use machines rather than labour (Kijima 2006: 111). The second side of the proposition is that the cost of capital has declined. Trade liberalization since the 1980s did indeed reduce the cost of imported capital equipment and put pressure on domestic producers to become more cost-competitive. Import licensing was abolished for most machinery and equipment and manufactured intermediate goods. The import-weighted customs duty rates fell from an average of 97 per cent in 1990–01 to 29 per cent in 1995–6 and continued to decline thereafter. Statistical work looking at the wage rate relative to the price of capital in each labour-intensive industry finds a clear link with a falling labour intensity of production (Das & Sen 2015).

WOMEN

India has one of the lowest rates of female labour force participation (FLFP) in the world. Only 30 per cent of women of working age participate in the labour market. By comparison in 2008 FLFP (age 15+) was 68 per cent in China and Vietnam, 21 per cent in Pakistan, 35 per cent in Sri Lanka, 63 per cent in Bangladesh, and 58 per cent in Nepal (Thomas 2012). FLFP in India has been declining since the 1990s and fell further after these figures were collected for 2008. The decline of FLFP among the age group 6–14 years (child workers) from about 20 per cent in 1982 to a negligible 1 per cent by 2011–12 is a good sign. Also reason for optimism is the fact that the FLFP of young girls has declined because of increasing enrolment in secondary and higher education. There are some positive developments for female employment. Growth of female employment in education is also due to programmes such as Sarva Shiksha Abhiyan which boosted employment of female teachers in efforts to universalize primary school enrolment. Improved education among young women has also created some well-paid employment in new service sectors such as IT, telecommunications, financial intermediation, and the hotel trade. Female employment in services increased from almost 14 million in 1994 to 22.5 million in 2012. The share of employed women in traditional female sectors such as textiles and food manufacturing has declined and more women have found employment in management and professional occupations (Kijima 2006: 100).

The dominant story, however, has been a low and declining level of FLFP. Much of the decline has been driven by the agricultural sector, where between 2004/05 and 2009/10 close to 22 million women left agricultural work. This decline was related to ongoing mechanization which occurred in those activities that women traditionally engaged in, such as threshing and winnowing. Women leaving agriculture have failed to find jobs in other economic sectors. In manufacturing, female employment has fluctuated, while almost 6 million found jobs between 1994 and 2005, more than 3 million lost jobs from 2005 to 2010. Female employees, particularly in manufacturing, tend to be hired as temporary workers so are the first to lose jobs when the economy slows down, as it did after the 2008 Global Financial Crisis (Thomas 2012).

The enduring low levels of FLFP can be explained in general by slow employment growth in India, and specifically, by patriarchal norms that restrict women to performing domestic activities and place restrictions on their ability to leave the home alone. This is particularly true of married women who are likely to have responsibilities for care of children and the elderly. The proportion of females who attend to domestic duties as a share of all females between 1993/4 and 2009/10 increased from 29.1 per cent to 34.7 per cent in rural areas and 41.7 per cent to 46.5 per cent in urban areas respectively (*ibid.*: 47). Education has surprisingly little impact on FLFP and it certainly doesn't appear to universally liberate and empower women to leave the household to find employment. In 2009/10 among urban females with graduate degrees 60 per cent of them were reported to be attending to domestic duties, which was twice that level for rural females with primary or middle-school education. In 2009/10 there were 12.7 million women with graduate degrees attending to domestic duties (*ibid.* 2012). Independently of other determinants, in urban areas of southern and north-eastern India FLFP participation rates are higher. This is partly because cultural norms in these areas are more amenable to women acquiring education and working outside the household (Mehrotra & Parida 2017).

"Missing" women is defined as "the additional number of females who would be alive if there had been equal treatment of the sexes among the cohorts that are alive today". Global estimates of missing women range from 60 to 101 million for the mid-1990s (Klasen & Wink 2003: 270). To illustrate the extent of the phenomenon of missing women, the total estimated figures for missing women are larger than the combined death tolls of both world wars (*ibid.*: 264).

The biological norm for the male to female ratio at birth is around 1.05. Since the 1901 census in India there has been a steady trend towards a greater percentage of males in the population. Between 1901 and 1991, the male to female ratio increased from 1.029 to 1.079 in India for the population as a whole (Dyson 2001: 342). The male to female ratio in India varies widely by state: from high figures in Haryana (1.161), Punjab (1.145) and Uttar Pradesh (1.109) in the north to low figures in Kerala (0.945) in the south. For India as a whole, the 2011 census showed some improvement in the sex ratio for the population as a whole. The life expectancy of women continued to increase and adult female mortality improved faster than for males (Visaria 2005: 42). The big problem was that the child sex ratio (children below the age of 6) dropped from 927 girls per 1,000 boys in 2001, to an all-time low of 914 in 2011 (John 2011).

The preference for sons prevalent in India cannot explain this trend alone. If families want more sons this will increase fertility rates as families will continue to have more children to ensure more sons. Some kind of deliberate intervention is needed to alter the gender balance. This trend is not a consequence of religion. Muslim Pakistan has as big a problem as India of missing women, while Muslim Bangladesh which has seen a transformation of the economic and social role of women in recent decades does not. In India the two states with the highest ratio of missing women are predominantly Hindu Haryana and Sikh Punjab (Kabeer & Mahmud 2004).

This book has discussed elsewhere how rising incomes are expected to generate improvements in wider measures of human development. In India a contrary trend is at work, which militates against the rising status of women. This process is called "Sanskritisation". Sanskritisation refers to the efforts of lower-caste households to adopt the higher status cultural practices of higher-caste households. These practices include refusing to permit the remarriage of widowed women, the adoption of a vegetarian diet, withdrawing women from the labour market (purdah), and payment of a dowry to the groom's family on marriage. As a household experiences rising incomes over time they find themselves able to afford to adopt these cultural norms. FLFP rates, for example, decline with rising household income. So as incomes rise and women are withdrawn from the labour force and require ever higher dowry payments on marriage, their culturally determined monetary burden to the household actually increases. There is good evidence for Sanskritisation in India. Over the course of the twentieth century male to female ratios among low-caste groups, previously normal, have steadily converged with the adverse ratios of higher-caste groups (Dreze & Sen 1995). Although dowry demands are illegal, the law is seldom enforced (Vaz & Kanekar 1990). Dowry payments are widely expected (Ulrich 1989), have increased in size, and spread into southern India where a bride-price (payment from the groom) used to be the norm (Heyer 1992; Rahman & Rao 2004). A more educated bride does not alleviate any demands for dowry payment from her family, instead she generally requires an even better educated husband (wives generally cannot be better educated than their husbands) so her family will have to pay an even higher dowry. So, educating a daughter incurs not only the cost of schooling but later in life a higher dowry payment, the payment of which can tip a household into absolute poverty.

The allocation of resources within the household, such as food and medical care, is subject to discrimination. In India, boys are more likely to be breastfed and later receive higher status foods such as milk and fats (Das Gupta 1987; Pebley & Amin 1991). Boys are more likely to be taken to a doctor (Alderman & Gertler 1997) and to be immunized (Arnold *et al.* 1998). The maximum differentials in the allocation of medical care occur in the first two years of life, the years of highest child mortality (Das Gupta 1987). Poverty may force some households to ration scarce resources and allocate them to sons who are more likely to stay with the family and earn a wage in later life. Poverty, however, is not enough to explain household discrimination. There has been steady economic growth in India since 1950 and declining national poverty, in rural and urban areas since *c.*1980. Despite this improvement the male to female ratio has been rising over time. By the early 2000s in elite areas of Delhi there were around 796 girls per 1000 boys (Manhoff 2005: 902). According to the 2001 census, the

Punjab had the most abnormal sex ratios of any state in India while also being among the most developed states (Kurian 2000), with near absent extreme poverty (Shergill & Singh 1995).

A mother's education is commonly held to be advantageous in various ways. Infant mortality for example is significantly lower for literate mothers (Beenstock & Sturdy 1990), girls' school attendance is higher (Unni 1998), and children are more likely to receive medical treatments such as vaccinations, vitamin-A supplements, and oral rehydration in the case of diarrhoea (Kravdal 2004). Rising female literacy in the context of a pre-existing culture of son preference can generate a perverse outcome. Abortions are more common among better educated and higher-income women who are better able to access healthcare (Unisa *et al.* 2007). Gender selective abortions are illegal but spread rapidly once they first became available in the large cities of India in the early-1980s and by the 1990s were readily available in rural India (Sudha & Rajan 1999). By 2000, interventions were being openly offered with the slogan "spend Rs500 ($10) now to avoid Rs500,000 (dowry) later". Despite a 1996 law that made it illegal for the sex of children to be divulged to parents, and a 2001 Supreme Court order for states to enforce the ban of the use of ultrasound to determine the sex of the foetus, estimates of sex-selective abortions range from 100,000 to 500,000 each year (Bhat 2006; Jha *et al.* 2006). A survey of Haryana showed that 18 per cent of women had an abortion and for a third of those the purpose was sex selection (Unisa *et al.* 2007).

Gender selective abortions are only part of the story. While sex ratios at birth are high the trend of excess female mortality continues until the age of 35 (Ravindran 1995). Most women who "disappear" do so after birth. Estimates for the 1980s showed that four times as many excess female deaths happened after birth than through abortions (Das Gupta *et al.* 1998: 90). There was a steady rise in the post-birth male to female ratio among the 0–6 age group during the 1990s (Dyson 2001). Except for Kerala in the south, the cohort of young children has become more male in every state according to the census of 2011. Female infanticide – the intentional killing of a female child – is widely prevalent in contemporary India (Gardner 2003). In the late-1980s, almost 10 per cent of female births in Tamil Nadu resulted in infanticide (George *et al.* 1992) and the practice continued into the 1990s (Chunkath & Athreye 1997; Sudha & Rajan 1999). In the Salem district of Tamil Nadu in 2000, 42 per cent of infant deaths were reported to be due to "social reasons" (Srinivasan & Bedi 2007: 859).

6

Making the Indian economy unique

This chapter deals with two key factors that are very specific to the Indian economy: the democratic paradox of public service delivery and the service-sector-led growth puzzle, and also discusses, briefly, the challenge of climate change.

THE DEMOCRATIC PARADOX OF PUBLIC SERVICE DELIVERY

Education is good for economic growth. Education will assist in the adoption of new technology, in attracting FDI and boosting the productivity of labour, as well as more generally in terms of improving the functioning of the democratic process and also of welfare indicators (such as child mortality, fertility and child literacy). In India (see chapter 5) enrolment rates have risen rapidly in recent years but quality measures of Indian schooling remain atrocious. The slow improvement in quantity and the longstanding poor quality of education represents a paradox. Both elites (being able to employ more productive workers and receiving more FDI) and the poor (higher incomes and better health) would benefit from better education. Education is unlike tax-based income redistribution, which imposes a cost on one group (often the richer) to raise the incomes of another group (often the poorer). India is also a democracy in which the poor, rural and illiterate vote more than the rich, urban and educated and where perhaps as many as 70 per cent of the population live on less than \$2 per day. So why are politicians not voted in and out of office according to their promise and performance in the delivery of public services, in particular education? Where is the democratic politics of public service delivery in contemporary India? Recall the survey which showed that parents did not view the dire state of education in their village as a pressing problem. In order to answer these questions, we first need to examine whether India's economic growth has delivered equivalent welfare gains.

Growth without development

The widely-held view is that three decades of rapid economic growth in India has not translated into equivalent welfare gains for all parts of the population, called here "growth without development".

There are dissenters to this view. Panagariya (2008) and Bhagwati and Panagariya (2013) highlight that while national poverty levels stagnated between the 1950s and 1970s there has been steady, even rapid decline ever since, and that "there is now irrefutable evidence that sustained growth alongside liberalising reforms has reduced poverty not just among the better off castes but across all broadly defined groups" (Bhagwati & Panagariya 2013: 37). Even though the gap in average incomes of the richest and poorest states has increased over the last three decades they note that even the poorest states (such as Bihar and Orissa) are now growing much faster than before. Panagariya (2008) argues that social and human development indicators have improved consistently for the poorest, including those related to child labour, infant mortality, and primary school (especially girl) enrolment. Evidence does support the contention that the poor have shared, to some extent, in economic growth since the 1980s. Chapter 3 showed that poverty rates have declined across India in recent decades. But, as Dreze and Sen argued, when they refered to the country as resembling "islands of California in a sea of Sub-Saharan Africa" (2013: ix), there is clear evidence of rising inequality. The most spectacular gains occurred at the top end of the corporate sector. The corporate profit share in GDP doubled between the late-1980s and 2009 and wealthy owners reaped the benefits. By the early 2010s Indian billionaire wealth as a share of GDP had risen to levels above Mexico, Brazil, Colombia and the United States, and was similar to those in Russia and Saudi Arabia (Walton 2011). The share of national income earned by the top 1 per cent of the population declined between the 1950s and the 1970s and incomes of the bottom 50 per cent and middle 40 per cent grew faster than the average. But, the trend changed thereafter and today the top 1 per cent income share (22%) is at its highest since at least 1922 (the earliest time data available) (Chancel & Piketty 2017).

The "sea of Sub-Saharan Africa" becomes even more evident when looking at the wider measures of human development discussed throughout this book. The rising literacy rate after 1980 hides depressing concerns about the quality of Indian education for the mass of the population, as shown in Chapter 5. Despite repeated governmental aspirations to raise public health spending to 3 per cent of GDP; spending has languished at 1 per cent of GDP for more than two decades, lower than all but ten countries in the world. In India 70 per cent of total healthcare expenditure is financed through out-of-pocket expenditure rather than pre-paid health insurance. Such often unexpected expenditure causes around 30 million people every year to fall into absolute poverty (Krishna 2010). There are striking inequalities in immunisation coverage by rural/urban areas, by caste and between states (Baru *et al.* 2010). The proportion of underweight children in India by the mid-2000s (43%) was higher than in Sub-Saharan Africa (20%), or the least developed countries as a whole (25%) and much higher than China (4%) (Dreze & Sen 2013: 160). Almost half of women between 15 and 49 in India suffered from malnutrition in some form in 2005/6 (Jose & Navaneethan 2008).

The following sections introduces four explanations for the phenomenon of growth without development: the pattern of economic growth, an elite revolt, discrimination, and the state and liberalization.

The pattern of economic growth

The first explanation is that economic growth has not created employment for the poorest. From the 1990s onwards output growth in agriculture has been associated with declining employment and employment crea-tion in other sectors, which was not sufficient to compensate (see Chapter 5). During the 2000s output growth in the service sector reached nearly 10 per cent per annum, much of which came from business services, communications and trade, which created a few well-paid jobs but not mass employment (Singh 2006: 83; Mukherjee 2013: 3). Even those few well-paid jobs that were created were geographically very concentrated. Between 2004/05 to 2009/10 Maharashtra, Karnataka, Delhi, Gujarat, Kerala and Andhra Pradesh accounted for 91 per cent of the 2.3 million new jobs generated in India in finance and business services (including software services) (Thomas 2012).

An elite revolt

As we have seen in our earlier discussion of the Bardhan thesis in Chap-ter 4, at the time of independence it has been argued that the middle class shared "an attitude towards the nation and the society, a sense of ideal-ism and high minded purpose transcending purely individual concerns" (Varma 1998: 27) but that by the 1990s, economic liberalization had been supported by and contributed to a more insular and selfish lifestyle, moti-vated by material gain and manifest in the middle classes paying little in taxation and arranging for the private provision of previously public wel-fare such as wells for water, private schools and gated communities.

Kohli argues that the power and influence of Indian business has grown enormously in recent decades; reflected in their dominant share of total investment, increasing control over the media and financing of elections. Indian business is well organized through politically influential pro-business lobby groups such as the Confederation of Indian Industry (CII). This, argues Kohli, has created a "pro-business political economy" and an economic policy that is less concerned with creating open markets, vigorous competition and the free entry of new firms, and more about boosting the profits of politically influential incumbents. Evidence of help to incumbents includes official sanction of the flouting of labour laws, casualization of the labour force and the striking shift in distribution from wages to profits at the all-India level that started in the late 1980s and then increased after the 1990s (Walton 2011: 42). A specific manifestation of this alliance are the nearly 600 special economic zones (SEZs) created by the government between 2005 and 2010, which involved the use of state authority to seize the property of (mainly) small farmers and hand it over cheaply to private companies. Subsequent employment in SEZs for local people were confined to poorly paid and insecure positions as gardeners, drivers, guards or cleaners (Levien 2011).

Discrimination

Caste based and other forms of inequalities remain widely prevalent in contemporary India. In the Uttar Pradesh press club, university faculty, bar association, top ranks of the police and trade unions, NGOs, media and other public institutions, for example, the share of upper castes is around 75 per cent compared to their 20 per cent share in the population. In Delhi there is no evidence of any significant backward caste presence in any of these same institutions, with the partial exception of students who have entered elite universities through the quota system. A survey of 315 editors and other leading members of the print and electronic media in Delhi found that not one of them was from the STs or SCs (Dreze & Sen 2013: 220–1). Similar patterns exist by gender. Women face abnormally high levels of mortality, access less health care, are less likely to participate in the labour force, to inherit, to have freedom of movement and to remain free of domestic and other forms of violence (*ibid.*). In 2004/05 only 12.9 per cent of women in urban areas who had completed higher secondary schooling were participating in the labour force (less than half the rate for illiterate women). Labour force participation among university educated women was higher but more than 70 per cent of women who were "graduates and above" were not employed (Unni & Raveendran 2007: 198).

There is little evidence for the rapid social mobility that could progressively dissolve these inequalities. The occupational background of successive generations shows that there is a "great deal of class continuity in

India" (Kumar *et al.* 2002a: 2985). Men born into business families themselves tend to become businessmen and men born into unskilled manual families tend to stay as unskilled manual workers. Only 5 per cent of lower agriculturalists experience any form of upward mobility. This limited upward mobility is almost exclusively driven by the contraction of the agricultural sector which has forced people into other low-paid occupations. Once this change has been accounted for there is little statistical evidence of any weakening of the links between fathers' and sons' class; positions and jobs at the top remain relatively closed (Kumar *et al.* 2002b). Inequality and discrimination are not the same thing. Lower castes could be poorer because they remain in rural areas or choose to acquire less education for their children, and not because of the active constraints of discrimination. There is, however, evidence for a "discrimination effect". Lower-caste people earn lower wages for any given level of education (Barooah 2005). Experimental evidence has shown that low caste, or Muslim job applicants, were less likely to be called to job interviews than identically qualified higher caste or Hindu applicants (Thorat & Attewell 2007). In a study of urban call-centres, it was found that lower caste are less likely to be called for interview than higher caste applicants (Banerjee *et al.* 2009).

The state and liberalization

Many scholars have doubts about the capacity of the Indian state to implement any form of effective welfare to more tightly link economic growth and development. Herring argued that India's state was "too democratic, soft and embedded, to govern the market" (1999: 1). There is even good evidence that the capacity of the state in India has been declining. Recall Table 2.4 which showed data collected by the World Economic Forum and used to compile indices to measure various aspects of governance. Comparing the reports from 2006/07 and 2014/15 revealed a widespread deterioration in state capacity in India, across the quality of institutions, judicial independence, favouritism in government decision-making, wastefulness in government spending, and an improving, if poor, measure of the reliability of the police.

Key to the weak state is the decline of the civil service of which Appu says, the "once superb administrative structure lies in ruins, reduced to a shambles" (2005: 826). The civil service has long been subordinate to the short-term demands of politicians. Civil servants face the destructive uncertainty of rapid and often arbitrary transfers. During the 1980s, for example, over 60 per cent of IAS officers in Haryana, Andhra Pradesh and Rajasthan served in their post for less than one year. The power to transfer is a tool used by politicians to extract obedience and compliance and enable pliant civil servants to be placed in key positions. Officers are expected to demonstrate loyalty by focusing resources on schemes of benefit to supporters and potential supporters of the ruling party (Banik 2001). The "head" of the state body comprising elite institutions at the national and sometimes state level, Pritchett (2009) argues, is functional and has even been rejuvenated in recent years. The Election Commission since the 1980s, for example, has increased its independence and pre-sided over many difficult elections (Subramanian 2007) but the head is no longer reliably connected to its own limbs. Pritchett (2009) has noted that in government services like police, tax collection, education, health, power and water supply there is rampant absenteeism, indifference and incompetence. The civil service from top to bottom has been personalized, politicized and corrupted. Among teachers, nurses, and police officers, the significant deviation of daily practices from desirable professional norms has become institutionalized. Pritchett characterizes India thus as a "flail-ing state".

Compounding this declining capacity of the state, argue many, is an inexorable logic of liberalization. Ongoing trade liberalization has under-mined efforts to mobilize tax revenue in India, which barely exceeds 10 per cent of GDP (see Chapter 2). International trade is easier to tax than thousands of businessmen, or millions of consumers. In a typical develop-ing country trade taxes have accounted for one-third of government tax revenues. There is strong evidence that developing countries have lost rev-enue as a result of trade liberalization (Khattry & Rao 2002). Tanzi (2001) argues globalization has created "fiscal termites" that will undermine tax revenue in India over the longer term. These fiscal termites include electronic commerce that make it harder to monitor and tax financial transactions, growth in world trade within multinational corporations (MNCs) that is easier to hide through various forms of transfer pricing, the growth of offshore tax havens, and the creation of new financial instruments, such as derivatives, that are hard to register by transaction or jurisdiction. Globalization can also put pressure on government tax revenue and expenditure through more indirect means. The exit option of mobile asset holders is strengthened by liberalization (especially financial) and so encourages policy-makers to compete for international investment by reducing taxes (and as a consequence social expenditures) (Swank 2003). In 2005 Nokia agreed to invest in Tamil Nadu. Other states, including Maharashtra and Haryana, had been interested in hosting the FDI and there was tough bidding competition between them. Nokia used this competition to extract huge benefits from Tamil Nadu. As well as the benefits of being located in a SEZ, Nokia received extra tax incentives, control over the labour force and land at concessional rates (Dutta 2009).

Towards more inclusive growth

There is good evidence to suggest that economic growth in India became more inclusive after the mid-2000s. This change has been missed in many studies which tend to focus on the decades since liberalization in the early 1990s. Across India there was a sharp acceleration in the rate of poverty decline. Total poverty declined at an annual average rate of 0.74 per cent between 1993/4 and 2004/05 and almost three times faster, by 2.18 per cent, between 2004/05 and 2011/12 (Ghatak *et al.* 2014: 40). This poverty decline was not just a consequence of rapid economic growth but there were clear signs of greater inclusivity. At the all-India level between 2004/05 and 2009/10 poverty among the most disadvantaged groups, in urban areas among casual labourers and in rural areas poverty among wage labourers, fell more rapidly than among other occupational groups (Thorat & Dubey 2012). In Uttar Pradesh between 2004/05 and 2011/12 poverty reduction was faster in rural areas than in urban areas, which reduced the gap between urban and rural poverty. The rate of poverty decline among SCs was more rapid than among upper castes (Arora & Singh 2015). This inclusivity extended to education where the overall gaps between SC/ST and other caste groups in education were declining from the mid-2000s (Hnatkovska & Lahiri 2013).

The following section seeks to explain the shift to growth with (more) development after *c.*2004 and examines in turn ideas related to improved information, a revolt of the activists, and changing politics.

To increase their chances of election and re-election, politicians must credibly communicate to voters that they were personally responsible for any successes of public policy. It is generally much harder for politicians to take credit for "health status" or "teaching quality" than for more clearly observable inputs such as opening a new hospital or school. A newly employed teacher will be well aware of their political patron who gave them the job, but parent-voters will have less information about whether the teacher is qualified and motivated. Were that teacher compelled to put in the necessary time and effort to raise standards of education, parent-voters would then find it difficult to assign this improvement to the efforts of a particular politician (Keefer & Khemani 2004). Even the elites in urban areas suffer from lack of information regarding public service delivery. One study directly observed doctors in clinical practice in middle-class Delhi. Only 52 per cent of practitioners held the necessary qualification and in observation only 10 per cent of public-sector doctors asked the appropriate questions to gauge a medical condition from the symptoms declared by a patient (Das & Hammer 2007). Better information can help a community to demand and so increase the incentives to supply better public services.

An improvement in information available to voters and activists is part of the answer to the puzzle outlined in this chapter. Literacy, which Amartya Sen has argued to be essential for the functioning of democracy, to allow public debate and information exchange over the quality of public services, increased from 48 per cent of the adult population in 1991 to 74.04 per cent in 2011 (World Bank 2018). From one national television channel in the 1980s (the government owned Doordarshan) by 2012 there were over 800 private channels, of which more than 400 were showing news on a regular basis. By 2012 there were more than 86,000 newspapers with a daily circulation of over 370 million. *The Times of India* increased its national circulation from 1 million in 1996 to more than 3 million in 2007 becoming the world's most read daily. The link between newspaper circulation in India and government responsiveness to economic shocks, such as floods, has been shown to be significant (Besley & Burgess 2000). The Right to Information Act of 2005 has improved the transparency and accessibility of information and so made governmental affairs more open. The Act guarantees unrestricted access to virtually any government document or to information more generally which has to be given to any citizen who applies for it. There are fines for civil servants failing to comply within thirty days. There are around one million applications for information annually. In a sample of households in Andhra Pradesh, Maharashtra and Rajasthan, Shankar *et al* (2011) find a positive link between attendance at public meetings (a proxy for information) and participation in the NREGA by SCs and STs. Jeffrey and Doron (2012) found that mobile phones in Uttar Pradesh were able to undermine structures of privilege and social discrimination by linking grassroots organizations representing low-caste people with the capacity of the mobile phone to "connect, motivate and organize", which "nibbled away" at the isolation and subservience of low-caste villagers.

Better information is only part of the explanation. There is more media but less diversity in ownership. Media in India is owned by and tends to reflect the interests of the corporate sector. This bias is reinforced by the fact that media professionals (as noted earlier) tend to come disproportionately from privileged backgrounds in terms of caste and class. Even "enough" information on the failing of public services is not sufficient to elicit pressure for change. All too often fieldwork has shown that there is often only a weak link between better information and better public services. Ban *et al* (2010) found that although people were well informed about the responsibility of local governments to keep villages clean across four southern Indian states this information did not result in cleaner villages. Better information may not help when households have long-established low expectations about public service provision. Households may then have little desire to invest time and energy in efforts to improve public services and instead households are likely to choose to opt out of public provision. The Delhi elite's investment in private wells, cisterns, and roof-top storage tanks have enabled middle-class households to get 24-hour water, and so reduced their concerns with poor-quality public water supply (Pritchett 2009). Recall the case study of nurses in Udaipur, Rajasthan where the NGO Seva Mandir monitored their attendance at rural health clinics. The information led to only a temporary improvement in nurse attendance. The study showed that ensuring nurses come to work was a low priority for the local health administration and incentive systems can be quickly distorted where supportive political will is lacking. There was no countervailing pressure working through the political system to utilize the available information regarding absent nurses to actually deliver better-functioning primary health care (Banerjee *at al.* 2008).

Better information is not enough if elites are able to capture the benefits associated with public services. The 2000s witnessed passionate social activism that has challenged the elite capture of public service delivery. Employment guarantee was mentioned in the 2004 Congress election manifesto. The initial draft of the Employment Guarantee bill brought before parliament was subject to fierce criticism from activists, which motivated the formation of the NGO, People's Action for Employment Guarantee. The bill went back for redrafting. Unusually the welfare aspects of the bill were strengthened over time rather than being compromised in response to pressures from powerful employers who opposed welfare. Employment guarantee was strengthened through the extension to anyone requesting work (not just households below the poverty line), through the greater role accorded to village government (*panchayats*) in its implementation and also through the extended central government financing of the scheme (Hasan 2012). Similarly, the impetus for educational reform came from the National Alliance for Fundamental Right to Education, which eventually came to encompass more than 2,000 voluntary organizations. In 2010 the Right to Education Act came into force providing for free education for all children up to the age of 14 (Corbridge *et al.* 2013). Hnatkovska and Lahiri (2013: 248) argue that the declining overall caste gaps in education in Uttar Pradesh after 1993 were related to the low-caste Bahujan Samaj Party (BSP) becoming part of the state governing coalition in that same year and vigorously promoting the employment and representation of low-caste people in public employment and public life.

While civil society activism has been important it is not enough to explain the tightening of the link between economic growth and development. Many government initiatives failed to influence actual policy or inspire civil society mobilization on their behalf. The 2006 Sachar Committee Report reflected on the deprivation of Muslims. The recommendations of the report were opposed by the BJP and also by other groups including Congress Dalit MPs who feared any reallocation of resources away from their own (also deprived) constituents. Implementation of the committee's recommendations was passed on to the newly created Ministry for Minority Affairs (MMA), no assessment or monitoring system was set up, expenditure allocations were minimal, and even the minister in charge called it "powerless and redundant" (Hasan 2012: 171). Another example is the failure to act upon the 2007 recommendations of the National Commission for Enterprises in the Unorganised Sector (NCEUS), which sought to spread entitlements to unorganized sector workers. More generally, activists and interest groups have long influenced policy reform in India, whether mobilizations based on language in the 1950s, unionized labour in the 1960s, farmer movements in the 1980s, or caste organizations in the 1990s. In all cases the government responded by advancing subsidies to particular groups and other benefits to buy off that mobilization. The fuller question is why an ongoing (if increasing) tradition of activism only after 2004 managed to convince the state to implement a programme of welfare that helped promote wider inclusive growth.

The argument that broad-based welfare intervention is an obedient response by the state to the various rulings by the Supreme Court in recent years, labelled "judicial activism", is also insufficient (D'Costa & Chakraborty 2019). The state has long been able to subvert and undermine the law and constitution for political ends. Among the many examples are watering down the legal provisions of land reform and labour laws to benefit particular groups. Corbridge *et al* (2013) labelled the civil society drive for rights to education, food and work as, "one of middle class activism" (2013: 117). Again, this is not a sufficient explanation. The middle class often seeks self-serving policy changes, such as income tax cuts or privileged urban land zoning for middle-class amenities such as shops, schools and housing. A fuller answer needs to engage with why that particular fraction of the middle classes – the pro-poor activists – had such a disproportionate influence on the state to successfully press for the provision of broad-based welfare.

The final argument in this chapter is that there was a change in the nature of the political system in the 1990s, and especially so after 2004. There is good evidence that the provision of welfare and some public services became more rules-based and pro-poor after 2004 and that this is central to explaining why growth became more inclusive.

A good example of better functioning social policy after the mid-2000s is the National Rural Employment Guarantee Act (NREGA). Since 2008 the NREGA provides rural households with a legally mandated minimum of 100 days work at minimum wages. Total employment generated is much larger than earlier programmes. The Sampoorna Grameen Rozgar Yojana (SGRY) and National Food for Work Programme (NFFWP) together generated 856 million person days in 2003/04. In 2012/13 NREGA generated 2.3 billion person days of employment for 80 million people. In 2010/11 the scheme cost the central government 0.5 per cent of GDP (around $7 billion), which was significant when compared to central government tax revenues of only 10 per cent of GDP and existing spending on health of 1.3 per cent and education of 3 per cent of GDP.

By insisting that participants do physically demanding work at a low-wage rate NREGA has been created so the non-poor will not have any incentive to participate. Participation rates are striking among the entire bottom half of the consumption distribution (Dutta *et al* 2012; Liu & Barrett 2013). This is not poor targeting, but evidence of the success of the programme in reaching the needy poor. The official poverty line in India is a "destitution line" (Dreze & Sen 2013: 189) that allows for income enough to purchase a barely adequate quantity of cheap calories and, for example, Rs10 per month for footwear and Rs40 for medical care. A more realistic poverty line that encompasses those likely to benefit from working on NREGA is the $2 a day poverty line. Those living on less than $2 a day in India declined from 76 per cent of the population in 2005 to 69 per cent in 2010 (World Development Indicators 2014). That this group would benefit from NREGA can be seen by a comparison of NREGA wages, which are very similar to average wages that can be earned undertaking casual labour in the rural economy (Dutta *et al* 2012: 61). NREGA has benefited women in particular. In random visits to worksites across six northern states in 2008 the proportion of women workers on the scheme was 32 per cent (Khera & Nayak 2009). Although lower than it would be with equal employment opportunities for women this share is much higher than the shares of women otherwise working in casual wage labour in those same rural areas (Dutta *et al* 2012). There is ample evidence of inefficiency and corruption in the operation of the NREGA, such as wage payments being siphoned away by contractors, government and bank officials (Adhikari 2010; Government of India 2013). There is nothing surprising about such problems which reflect longstanding weaknesses in welfare provision in India. But, general surveys have found NREGA does have positive impacts, that these impacts are improving over time and NREGA is operating as a large-scale programme of rules-based welfare (McCartney & Roy 2016). By the late-2000s payments to workers were increasingly made directly to bank accounts which seems to have reduced corruption (Vanaik & Siddhartha 2008), and surveys show that this change was popular among the scheme's beneficiaries (Adhikari & Bhatia 2010).

The success of another set of pro-poor interventions was demonstrated by Jodhka (2008) who undertook a survey of 321 Dalit entrepreneurs in 2008 in Haryana and western Uttar Pradesh. These Dalit entrepreneurs came from disadvantaged backgrounds, for example 90 per cent of their mothers and 68 per cent of their fathers were illiterate. These entrepreneurs were beneficiaries of targeted government interventions. Among the Balmiki Dalits 30 per cent had college (degree and above) and 31 per cent had school education up to Grade 10–12 (16–18 yrs). While two-thirds relied mainly on help with start-up capital from family and extended kin, almost one-fifth of the sample reported receiving a loan from a formal institution like a bank and half of the sample were aware of special government schemes to help Dalits. Another example is the Public Distribution System (PDS) (see Chapter 5). A nine state village-level survey of the PDS in 2011 shows that reforms led to a widespread trend towards widening coverage. Andhra Pradesh and Chhattisgarh have achieved 80 per cent coverage from low levels, while Rajasthan, Bihar and Jharkhand have significantly expanded coverage (Khera 2011a). This increased coverage has benefited the poorest, "the expansion has covered those who are most vulnerable and live at the margins, such as SCs and STs. Also, a greater number of households in the lower income classes now not only have greater access to the PDS, but are also consuming larger quantities from the PDS" (Rahman 2014: 68).

Public policy became more oriented to the long term from the early-2000s. The share of infrastructure spending in GDP increased and much of this went into long-gestation projects such as power supply which offered only limited short-term political benefits. Electricity consumption in kWh per capita grew by 2.5 per cent between 1999 and 2004 and 6.4 per cent per annum between 2004 and 2011. There have long existed private markets in stolen electricity in India, often organized by mafia-like groups, and the tolerance or connivance of the state in this process represented clientelistic-based "welfare". The deeper explanation for these improvements in public policy is that politics changed, especially after 2004, in such a way as to give politicians more incentive to build bigger coalitions and to think more long term.

The number of competitors a party faces in a "first-past-the-post"-system influences the size of the constituency a politician needs to appeal to in order to get a majority. With only two effective parties each needs a majority to win the seat, hence each has to build alliances across broad social groups. As the number of competitive parties increases, a party will need an ever smaller coalition to win the seat. In Lok Sabha elections in India between 1957 and 1991, a winning party needed 55 per cent of the vote in districts where there were two, and 38 per cent in districts with three or more, effective parties. The argument in this chapter is that the structure of politics in India changed from the 1990s onwards in a way that saw the political fragmentation dating from the late-1960s being partially reversed. This was discussed in some detail in Chapter 2. The decline of Congress during the 1990s saw the emergence of a relatively stable two-party (alliance) system. The combined share of votes won by the two main parties (the BJP and Congress) remained very stable over the 1990s and 2000s. The choice for 2014 was frequently presented as being a national choice between Narendra Modi and Rahul Gandhi and their regional allies. The result saw a small (less than 3%) increase in their combined share of the votes and a negligible increase (0.73%) in their combined seat share. It was telling that Modi kept his alliance together in 2014 even though the BJP had itself won an absolute majority. The strengthening of a two-party alliance system in India gave politicians more incentive to target bigger electoral coalitions, and so shift from narrowly targeted to more broad- and rules-based welfare provision. When three-quarters of the population live on less than $2 a day electoral success in a two-party alliance system comes from broadly targeting anti-poverty programmes in a rules-based system.

Unlike the provision of government jobs or the construction of school buildings, efforts to improve service delivery such as ensuring better quality teaching does not yield quick results. From the late 1990s and especially after 2004 there was a decline in political instability that gave politicians and political parties a greater incentive to consider the longer term. The BJP went into the 2004 election reasonably convinced it would win, as did the Congress in 2009; both headed relatively stable coalitions largely constructed before the elections. This was in sharp contrast to the 1990s when unstable coalitions put together largely after the elections were faced with the constant threat (and reality) of collapse. As referred to in Chapter 2 we can characterize this gradual stabilization of Indian politics as a shift from "roving" to "settled" bandits (Olson 1993). Politicians facing a high probability of losing office in the near future ("roving bandits"), whether democratic or authoritarian, face an incentive to maximize predation in the short run. A leader with a monopoly of power and a reasonable expectation of surviving in office and winning subsequent elections ("stationary bandits") will have an incentive to promote long-run economic growth. A stationary bandit will conduct "theft" through predictable taxes or bribes leaving producers with an incentive to generate incomes. The stationary bandit also has an incentive to provide public goods such as, in this case, broad-based welfare (Olson 1993). The dynastic nature of the Congress party gave the government led by Sonia Gandhi after 2004 an incentive to invest in the pro-poor reputation of Congress through schemes like NREGA in order to benefit a subsequent generation, her son Rahul Gandhi as the next party leader.

There are also interesting wider questions. Why did economic growth after 2004 seem more tightly linked to poverty reduction and employment creation for the poorest, but not for example to nutrition (as discussed in the previous chapter) where India became an international outlier? (Walton 2009: 17). While the government managed to look more to the long term in the case of infrastructure provision including electricity generation, credit to the corporate sector remained locked into the short term. Over the 1990s and 2000s the reform of the long-term oriented Development Finance Institutions (DFIs) kept 80 per cent of bank liabilities as short term and so firms remained constrained in their access to long-term lending (Bhattacharjee & Chakrabarti 2013; Ray 2015).

SERVICES AS A NEW PARADIGM OF INDIAN DEVELOPMENT

There is a well-established and expected "normal" path of structural change during the process of economic growth and development. Historical data from today's developed countries suggests that economic growth and development would be associated with a sharp decline in the share of GDP generated by the primary (agricultural) sector, a significant rise in the share of industry, and at very high levels of GDP per capita a decline in the share of industry and rise of the service sector. For India from 1950 to the mid-1980s the fit is quite close. The share of agriculture in GDP declined by 25 per cent and industry (and services) gained. Then things turned unusual. The share of industry stabilized after 1990 and the continuing decline of agriculture was picked up entirely by the rising service sector. In 1990 the share of India's service sector in GDP was very close to what we would predict given India's level of GDP per capita. Service-led growth after 1990 saw India becoming an outlier in terms of the share of services in GDP. By 2010 India had a share of the service sector equivalent to an upper-middle-income country (Kochhar *et al* 2006; Gordon & Gupta 2010: 7).

There is a second strand to this thinking which talks about consequences rather than just statistical regularities. This view sees manufacturing as an "engine of growth" and argues that a large manufacturing base is required to promote and sustain rapid economic growth. In modern economics Kaldor (1967) has been the leading exponent of this "structural theory" of economic growth. This view was discussed at length in Chapter 1. The Kaldorian analysis takes account of both demand and supply factors. Agriculture is characterized by lower income elasticity of demand for its output compared with manufacturing products. This means that as incomes rise over time demand may switch to better brands of coffee or consumers may drink coffee in nice coffee shops rather than at home, but there won't be much extra total consumption of coffee (hence demand for coffee beans). By contrast people's capacity to consume more manufactured goods such as electronics, cars, computers, and clothing seems unlimited. These differences in the income elasticity of demand imply that the relative demand for manufactured goods and hence output of industry will rise over time relative to agricultural products. As a consequence of these demand differentials those regions or countries with an industrial base should experience faster economic growth. Again India is odd. India has experienced nearly four decades of rapid service-sector-led economic growth.

The growth of the service sector

There is a basic problem with all of this discussion. It is very hard to define and measure service output. Services have traditionally been defined in terms of the shared physical location of the producer and consumer to realize a transaction; a teacher and pupil together in the classroom for example. However in recent decades advances in digital technology have reduced the need for physical proximity and led to rapid international trade in knowledge-based services, such as data processing, or software development (Bhagwati 1984), or technological advances in financial services (such as credit cards) (Gordon & Gupta 2004). It is now possible to watch university lectures online. It is also often hard to identify the output or productivity of service-sector activity. A manufacturing plant or farm may find it easy to pay workers piece rates based on the physical output of cars or potatoes for example. But what is the output or productivity of a teacher? The number of students taught? The exam scores reached by the average student? The amount of the curriculum completed in a particular term? The improvement among students in memorizing for an exam or in their ability to think independently?

Another problem is that the growth of the service sector globally over the last few decades has certainly been overstated. There has been a global trend towards industrial firms using specialist subcontractors to provide services previously provided in-house, such as legal, accounting, and security. Bhagwati (1984) calls this process "splintering". There certainly is good evidence in India of both agriculture and industry using more service-sector inputs since 1980. But the data suggests splintering does not change the broad contours of the service-led growth story in India. At most, splintering would have added about 0.25–0.50 per cent to annual growth in the 1990s (Gordon & Gupta 2004) and even less thereafter (Singh 2006). Table 6.1 shows that the growth of service-sector output has shown a steady acceleration since the 1950s, becoming the fastest growing sector of the Indian economy after 1991.

Table 6.1   Sectoral growth rates (annual %), 1951–2000

	1951–80	1981–90	1991–2000
Agriculture	2.1	4.4	3.1
Industry	5.3	6.8	5.8
Services	4.5	6.6	7.5
GDP	3.5	5.8	5.8

Source: Gordon & Gupta 2004: 29.

The nature of service-sector growth in India has also changed over time. In the 1950s and 1960s, transport, storage, communication and trade, hotels and restaurant services grew faster than the overall sector. In the 1970s and 1980s, financing and business services started growing rapidly, in the 1990s education and health and after 2000, telecommunications was the fastest growing, followed by financing and business services (Gordon & Gupta 2004; Mukherjee 2013). The most dramatic recent dimension of service growth has been software and IT enabled services. This category includes call centres, software design, and business process outsourcing. Business services including IT was the fastest growing sector in the 1990s with annual growth averaging nearly 20 per cent (Gordon & Gupta 2004). Despite this rapid growth business services comprised only about 1.75 per cent of GDP and accounted for just 3 per cent of total services output by the early 2000s (*ibid.*). By 2010/11 the IT business process outsourcing (BPO) sector contributed 6.4 per cent of India's GDP, 14 per cent of exports and 10 per cent of all service-sector revenues (Aggarwal 2012).

A global service sector phenomenon that showcases India is Bollywood. In 2016 India made 2,336 feature films and the Indian market grew by 10 per cent. There are many regional cinema industries in India and

Bollywood, based in Mumbai, accounts for around 20 per cent of the films produced but more than 40 per cent of box office takings. Hollywood has only a 10 per cent share of the $2 billion Indian market. Exports tend to follow the Indian diaspora with 55 per cent of exports going to the US, UK and Canada. Despite the lack of a large diaspora, Russia is also a large market. The growth of Hindi television channels has seen an integration with television companies which now often finance and distribute cinema. Most Bollywood films are produced by small firms and the industry has little vertical integration. With costs still low and mass audiences at cinemas combined with growth in satellite broadcasting, means that successful films have a much higher profit margin that Hollywood movies. Until the 1990s literacy rates were 50 per cent and the ownership of televisions was very limited, so cinema had a mass reach. India still sells more cinema tickets than any other country and earns domestic revenue second only to the US. Scholars have argued that Indian cinema has closely reflected economic change: before 1980 its films portrayed private profit as being anti-social and now they celebrate business and commerce. Bollywood has begun going overseas and in 2009 despite the global economic crisis, the Indian media company, Reliance Entertainment acquired the majority of shares in Steven Spielberg's company Dreamworks (Bouka *et al* 2015).

Table 6.2 Percentage share of GDP by sector (decade average), 1950s–2000s

Sector	1950s	1960s	1970s	1980s	1990s	2000s
Agriculture	55.3	47.6	42.8	37.3	30.9	21.8
Industry	14.8	19.6	21.3	22.3	23.3	24.5
Services	29.8	32.8	35.9	40.3	45.7	53.7

Source: Mukherjee 2013: 3.

As a consequence of these patterns of growth Table 6.2 shows that since 1950 there has only been a slow growth in the share of manufacturing

215

output in GDP, a steady decline in the share of agriculture and a continuous rise in the share of services.

This pattern of structural change is unusual in a comparative international context. In India the share of industry in GDP was little changed between the 1970s and 2000s. Other countries were much more successful in boosting the share of industry. By 2000 industry's share of GDP reached 40+ per cent in South Korea and Indonesia, 30+ per cent in China, Malaysia and Thailand, and in Bolivia, Brazil, Chile, Peru and Venezuela (Dasgupta & Singh 2005: 1039). By the 1990s services constituted 60 per cent of GDP growth in India compared to 34 per cent in China and 43 per cent across all developing countries (Banga 2005; Aggarwal 2012).

Government policy and services

The growth of the software industry is a puzzle within a puzzle. The efforts of the government to promote the growth of other technology-intensive sectors (with the possible exception of pharmaceuticals) have not been notably successful. As software started growing rapidly in the 1990s India ranked poorly when measured by indicators such as the quality of the telecommunications network, the number of internet subscribers, telephone connections, the number of scientists and engineers per million population and access to personal computers. The Indian government did try to encourage investment in these areas but India even in 2001 was only ranked sixty-third in the UNDPs new Technology Achievement Index (TAI) (Kapur 2007). One view explains the success of the sector in reference to the absence of government intervention, or of "benign neglect". The IT sector was not subject to the attentions of the lower levels of the Indian bureaucracy through laws like the Factories Act which permitted intrusive regulations and inspections on health and safety laws and employment conditions. The non-material nature of IT output also helped constrain state agencies from regulation and taxation of the sector (Joseph & Harilal 2001).

"Benign neglect" is an exaggeration. The state constructed dedicated software technology parks (STPs) from the late-1980s, which offered high-speed data communication, easy access to tax and export incentives and imported inputs (such as hardware). Exports from STPs accounted for more than 60 per cent of overall software exports by the late-1990s (Kapur 2007). State investment in R & D labs was important in creating human capital. The six key IT clusters in India – Bangalore, Chennai, Hyderabad, Mumbai, New Delhi, Pune – had the highest concentration of public-sector R & D establishments (especially defence-related) as well as publicly-funded science and engineering institutions. These institutions provided little direct link with new software firms, but did provide a ready-made pool of skilled labour (*ibid.*). When Texas Instruments invested in Bangalore in 1985 with the latest satellite telecommunication infrastructure, it was attracted by an existing R & D research cluster. In Bangalore already, were various public sector enterprises, including Bharat Electronics Ltd, Hindustan Aeronautics Ltd, Hindustan Machine Tools, Indian Telephone Industries and various Defence Research and Development Organisations including Centre for Artificial Intelligence and Robotics, Aeronautical Development Agency, and the Defence Avionics Research Establishment (Balakrishnan 2006: 3870). By the late-1990s India was producing about 65,000 engineers and 95,000 diploma-holders annually in engineering and technology through a network of public and private colleges. In Karnataka (home of Bangalore) by the early-2000s there were 132 engineering colleges with capacity for 25,000 students and 200 diploma institutes (Kapur 2007). Partly as a result of this vast labour supply the average annual wage of software professionals in India in the early 2000s was about 10–20 per cent of comparable wages in the United States (*ibid.*: 391). Much of this state intervention was organized through collective private-sector lobbying and representation. The role of the National Association of Software and Services Companies (NASSCOM) is noteworthy here. NASSCOM represents almost all firms in the sector both domestic and foreign (2,200+ firms representing more than 90 per cent of industry revenues according to their website in early 2019) which gives the industry a unified voice in engaging with the state to promote its own interests (*ibid.*).

It is worth making the point that some of the factors enabling faster growth of software exports after 1991 had little to do with government reforms. These included the dramatic decline in telecommunications costs, the commercialization of the internet and the Y2K bug which generated global demand for Indian software engineers to fix the problem (Kumar 2001).

Services and spill-overs

Some early discussion focused on whether service-sector growth could be sustained without serious implications for inflation. By the mid-1980s 80 per cent of consumer expenditure went on consumer goods and only 20 per cent on services. So, while service-led growth was generating higher incomes it wasn't providing the supply of consumer goods to fulfil the resulting consumer demand. The impact was predicted to be either upward pressure on prices as demand outstripped supply of consumer goods, or else more imports and hence growing balance of payments problems and debt (Bhattacharya & Mitra 1990). This early discussion broadened out into a general discussion of linkages between services and the rest of the economy. Later arguments suggested that as the workforce of the IT sector is largely drawn from the English-speaking, educated, urban class and that rising incomes among such a group would boost demand for cars, real estate, tourism, air travel, and other imported goods, which would create little employment in India (Aggarwal 2012). Others have suggested that technological upgrading remains slow (D'Costa 2006) and that much of the service sector exists to serve the manufacturing sector (marketing, retail and accounting) so that it is difficult to sustain service-sector growth without first having a manufacturing base (Chang 2010: 100).

More detailed and disaggregated data for India shows that there are close production linkages between services and other sectors. Between 1968/9 and 1993/4 for example the amount of service-sector inputs to produce one unit of agriculture grew three-fold, those required to produce one unit of industry output increased by 50 per cent, and to produce one unit of service output doubled (Sastry *et al* 2003: 2391). Using an even more disaggregated input–output approach to the level of 115 activities across ten broad economic sectors using data for 1993–4 shows the Indian economy to be service-intensive. Indices of backward and forward linkages show that the service sector by the early-1990s had more linkages with other sectors than either industry or agriculture. The implication of this was that output growth in the service sector could induce growth elsewhere through forward linkages, and that the growth of the service sector is not just driven by external factors (Banga 2005). Updating this data to 1998–9 showed that sectors like transport, communications, financing, insurance and real estate all became even more service intensive (Singh 2006). The adoption of modern manufacturing processes in the 1990s such as just-in-time production (JIT), build-to-order and increasing export orientation made it necessary for industrial firms to use high-quality services of various kinds that had to be procured from specialized service providers (Banga & Goldar 2004). From almost no contribution to manufacturing growth in the 1980s, more than 2 per cent annual growth of manufacturing was explained through the use of services as an input during the 1990s (*ibid.*: 13).

There was also some evidence of negative linkages from the service sector in the form of labour movement. According to one study, between 1964 and 1986 58.5 per cent of graduates from the Indian Institute of Technology, Madras migrated abroad (Kumar 2001: 4284). By 2000 Indian IT professionals dominated the highly-skilled US H-1B visas and numbered about half of the 400,000 global total in the US. Shortages of IT workers in Western Europe led to the expansion of working visas in Germany, Japan, Ireland, France, Italy and South Korea, which facilitated the migration of software engineers. The British government enacted a fast-track work permit system to allow IT workforce into the country to meet an estimated demand for about 150,000 professionals (Kumar 2001). The software sector was facilitating the migration of highly skilled professionals from a country desperately short of skills, which had expended much effort and cost in training them. Much-needed skilled workers in sectors such as medicine and civil engineering were repackaging their skills to work in the better paid IT sector (Kapur 2007). Business process outsourcing (BPO) grew by 70 per cent in 2001–02 and by the early-2000s already employed 170,000 workers. These call centres deal mainly with international customers providing customer care, support and help desks, with about 90 per cent of them engaged in voice-based work; 97 per cent are aged between 20 and 30, they are English speaking, and 97 per cent were educated to degree level. Indian call centres are about 40 per cent cheaper to run that US ones. They rely on unsocial hours and operate 24 hours a day, 365 days a year, so employees are not eligible for national holidays and often have to work night shifts. The technology requires employees to submit to an intensively monitored work environment via specially designed software, so BPOs operate more like a production line than an office. There are no opportunities to learn new skills after the 4–8 hours of initial training. The sector has very high levels of staff turnover and the workers have been labelled by some as "cyber-coolies" (Ramesh 2004).

Over time the growth of the domestic industry helped to stem the outflow of manpower from India. According to a partial database from the IIT Delhi Alumni Association (IITDAA) the rate of "brain-drain" declined gradually over the 1990s (Kumar 2001: 4285). The Indian diaspora, especially the IT sector in the US, has served as a means of building the reputation of India through its diaspora of software engineers. Companies like Yahoo, Hewlett Packard, and General Electric opened subsidiaries in India largely because of the confidence engendered by the presence of Indians working in their US operations. Many of these subsidiaries were headed by returning Indians. One estimate shows that 71 of 75 MNCs in Bangalore's software technology park were headed by Indians who had lived and worked overseas. The IndUS Entrepreneur (TIE) is a group of US-based Indian IT entrepreneurs and network professionals founded in 1992. In less than ten years the group emerged as a successful and politically powerful networking organization. The core of this network is a group of angel investors who began recycling both their wealth, knowledge and expertise, some of it to start-ups in India. Also important is the role members of the group played in advising (and pressuring) the Indian government to change the regulatory framework for venture capital in India. These reforms helped the venture capital industry grow rapidly by the late-1990s (Kapur 2007).

In 2004–05 total exports of IT services and software was $12.2 billion which then showed annual growth of 32.3 per cent. While 64 per cent of the sector's output had been exported in 1999–2000, this had increased to 74 per cent by 2004–05 (Balakrishnan 2006). This export dependency was in sharp contrast to the patterns of growth elsewhere. The domestic share of software revenue was 56 per cent in Japan, 90 per cent in Western Europe, and 75 per cent in the US (Chakraborty & Jayachandran 2001: 3257). This export orientation means that software firms are more likely to operate as enclaves within the domestic economy. Computer hardware is imported, well-paid employees are likely to spend their incomes on imported consumer goods, the software produced is almost entirely exported, and the bulk of this work is highly customized, of use to the final customer oversees but of little relevance to the Indian economy (Kumar 2001: 4286). This pattern changed after *c*.2005 when domestic sales started increasing rapidly (Kite 2013). Domestic firms in India started using IT to improve their internal processes. After 2005 the major private domestic sector purchasers of software included communications, finance, manufacturing and retail and logistics (*ibid*). State governments in India contributed to the domestic adoption of IT technology through initiatives such as e-governance and e-education for the rural sector. The Gyandooot intranet system commenced operations in Madhya Pradesh in 2000 and quickly reached half a million people across 800 villages. Farmers use the system to gain access to government services such as getting a caste certificate, land ownership certificates, or to find out twice-daily crop prices (Kapur 2007).

Services and employment

The growth of the service sector has been characterized as "jobless growth". India has an exceptionally low share of employment in services when compared to other countries (Gordon & Gupta 2004; Ghose 2016).

In 1993 around 63 per cent of the population was engaged in agriculture while 22 per cent worked in services (in both formal and informal sectors), by 2009–10 these figures had changed to 53 per cent and 25.3 per cent (Mukherjee 2013: 6). There are perhaps 3 million workers in the software sector, compared to 25 million in the auto and auto-components sectors.

The growth of the service sector has helped women enter and remain in the labour force. Between 1993 and 2000 the share of women employees in the software sector increased from 10 to 19 per cent and in IT-enabled services women accounted for 37 per cent of jobs (Kumar 2001: 4284). But, 80 per cent of service-sector employment is in the unorganized/informal sector. Retail and wholesale trade, for example, mainly provide unorganized employment. Neither is the formal service sector predominantly private. In 2009 75 per cent of organized employment in services was in the public sector (Mukherjee 2013). The bulk of the service-sector workforce is trapped in low-wage and low-productivity sectors while the booming sectors only employ a tiny fraction of the workforce (Aggarwal 2012). Much of the service economy in India has operated like a subsistence sector to absorb migrant workers moving to urban areas and working in construction or petty retail trade (Dehejia & Panagariya 2013).

Exports

In recent years the WTO has promoted the liberalization of trade in services and started to tackle the numerous restrictions on services trade. These have included the non-recognition of foreign professional qualifications (in medicine or accountancy for example), local procurement in government construction contracts, and licence or visa requirements on the entry of foreign service providers (Banga 2005). Technical progress including the IT revolution and trade liberalization has made it easier to trade in services as in the case of outsourcing, call-centres, back-office business services. The service sector has been the largest and fastest growing sector of the world economy since *c*.1980 and now constitutes 60 per cent of global output (*ibid.*).

Between 1980 and 2010 India's service exports grew annually by 13.2 per cent, nearly double that of the world average. Indian exports of services increased from $25 billion in 2002 (including $7.5 billion of software) to $160 billion in 2017 ($125 billion of software) (Bosworth & Collins 2008; Mukherjee 2013). By 2011 India was the eighth largest service exporter. Indian service exports go mainly to the US, followed by the UK and other European countries and English-speaking developed countries, such as Canada. In 2010 computer and IT services were 45.8 per cent of India's total service exports, other business services 23.4 per cent, travel 11.4 per cent, transportation 10.7 per cent, and financial services 4.9 per cent (Mukherjee 2013). Exports of sofware are a poor guide to the amount of actual foreign exchange earned as the sector is also very import intensive. India is the world's seventh largest importer of services. The sector relies for example on imported finished software and hardware. One survey of a representative sample of 58 firms shows that the proportion of net exports in total exports increased from 38 per cent to 52 per cent of total exports over the 1990s. This was a good sign as it suggested that the proportion of domestic value added was rising in Indian software exports, reflecting our earlier discussion about the strengthening of domestic linkages (Kumar 2001).

Foreign direct investment

There has been a substantial increase in FDI since the 1990s. In 1980 India received $80 million in FDI, rising to $3–4 billion per year in the 1990s, and with a surge after 2003 to $42.5 billion in 2008. India's share of global FDI increased from 0.15 per cent in 1980 to 2.44 per cent in 2009 and 1.98 per cent in 2010 (Mukherjee 2013). There has also been a shift of FDI from manufacturing to the services sector. The share of services in total FDI stock increased from less than 25 per cent in the 1970s, to around 50 per cent in 1990, to 60 per cent after 2002 (Banga 2005). Outward FDI has also become significant. In 2011 62.1 per cent of India's outward investments were in services. Financial, insurance, real estate, and business services accounted for 29 per cent of total outward investments followed by transport, communications and storage (15.3%), and wholesale and retail trade, restaurants and hotels (11.5%). Major destinations included Mauritius, the Netherlands, Singapore and the United States (Mukherjee 2013). By the late 1990s 212 Indian software companies had set up 509 overseas offices or subsidiaries, more than half of them in the US (Kumar 2001).

FDI has not been crucial over the long term to the success of the software industry in India. Although all the major software firms have a base in India, their overall share in India's exports of software is marginal. Foreign corporations are mainly engaged in low-skill call-centre work and higher-end software services work exported from India is almost exclusively from local firms (Saraswati 2012). By the late-1990s among the top 20 companies only six were MNCs or joint ventures, and only 79 from 572 NASSCOM members were reported as foreign subsidiaries. Even some of these were actually subsidiaries of companies promoted by NRIs in the US such as Mastech, CBSI, IMR, and Syntel rather than those associated with US MNCs (Kumar 2001: 4280). Successful software firms did not generally emerge from existing large Indian businesses. Of the 12 largest software firms (annual sales exceeding $100 million) only one by the late 1990s was linked to a large industrial house. This was Tata Consulting Services (TCS) of the Tata Group and only one was an MNC (IBM Global Services India Ltd). The rest were new firms, often started by individuals who left other software firms, and had no links with the old industrial economy of India (Kapur 2007).

Financial services, telecommunications and computer software have received the bulk of inward FDI. By the late 2000s there remained various constraints to inward FDI in other service sectors. Various sectors such as real estate, railway transport services, legal professional services, multi-brand retailing, and insurance had a cap on FDI ranging between 20 and 74 per cent. Broadcasting services, air transport services, and satellite and telecommunications continued to ban or restrict foreign ownership (Mukherjee 2013). There has been a passionate debate about whether FDI should be permitted into the retail sector. The distribution sector includes wholesale and retail, accounts for 16 per cent of GDP and employs 40 million people. Retail is dominated by the informal and small scale, which constitutes around 95 per cent of retail sales and around 99 per cent of food sales (Kohli & Bhagwati 2013; Lakatos & Fukui 2014). The global retail phenomenon of the 1990s that included the growth of very large retailers such as Wal-Mart, Costco, Tesco, Carrefour, Aldi, and Metro has spread across eastern Europe, east Asia and Latin America, but made less impression on India (Kalhan & Franz 2009).

Since 1991 barriers to FDI in retail have been relaxed and 100 per cent foreign ownership in some sectors has been granted. Firms in "cash and carry" and wholesale trading have been permitted to have 100 per cent foreign ownership since 1997. Single brand retailing was opened up to FDI in 2006, although the rate of foreign participation was capped at 51 per cent. Firms entering under this route have included Next, The Body Shop, and Marks & Spencer. International firms cannot sell multiple brands in a retail outlet but can own 100 per cent equity in wholesale stores. Between 2000 and 2010 MNCs like Wal-mart and Metro invested $1.8 billion in such "cash and carry" stores that are confined to selling to small retailers, cooperatives, hotels and restaurants (Kohli & Bhagwati 2013). In 2011 the central government approved measures to allow majority ownership in multi-brand retail firms and 100 per cent ownership in single brand retail. There was opposition from both traders and politicians, which forced a suspension of the policy change a few weeks later (Lakatos & Fukui 2014). The fear was that permitting the entry of foreign retailers would threaten the livelihoods of the millions of small traditional stores and street vendors who dominate the Indian retailing industry (*ibid.* 2014).

Change is happening but is driven by large domestic firms such as Reliance, Tata, Birla and others who have entered the supermarket sector. The annual growth of this organized food and grocery retail sector reached 35–40 per cent by the mid-2000s (Kalhan & Franz 2009). Demand is growing, spurred by the consumption of an expanding urban middle class. In 2010, management consultants McKinsey predicted that India's urban population would increase by 250 million between 2008 and 2020 (Kohli & Bhagwati 2013). The global experience of supermarkets in building efficient farm to supermarket shelf supply chains is highly relevant for India. At present an estimated $10 billion worth of farm produce is estimated to be lost in the supply chain between farm and consumer through inadequate cold-storage and transportation. This amounts to about 35–40 per cent of fruits and vegetables and about 10 per cent of foodgrains. The attention to quality in supermarkets would also be crucial in tackling problems such as the estimated 25 per cent of pharmaceutical sales that are counterfeit drugs, and the many food-borne illnesses common in India (Lakatos & Fukui 2014). Improved quality in the distribution supply chain would also help India export (Kohli & Bhagwati 2013).

Kohli and Bhagwati (2013) argue that any expansion of large retailers will not be at the expense of small informal retail as each sector offers consumers distinct advantages, so the two sectors can co-exist. The advantages of the unorganized sector include lower fixed and operating costs through, for example, the ability to convert homes into shops, the use of low-cost labour, and less loss due to theft. Most small shops give credit to customers with whom they have a long-term relationship, and offer the intimacy of local shopping, haggling and combining with a visit to the chai stall. Most Indian consumers make small but frequent purchases. As 75 per cent of the population lives on less than $2 a day, consumers are often constrained to purchase single sachets of shampoo, creams, detergents, edible oils and spices. In addition, less than 20 per cent of Indian homes have a fridge, which in turn limits the purchases of perishable goods, or have homes with limited storage space for wheat, rice, and lentils.

Productivity

Traditionally manufacturing has been seen as the source of dynamic productivity gains (see Chapter 1). This traditional view also sees that there are inherent constraints on boosting productivity growth within the service sector. Many services like haircuts or teaching, for example, cannot be mechanised or replaced by technology, so output is limited by the labour-intensity of production. This traditional view of services is increasingly seen to be mistaken. Econometric evidence shows that during the 1990s the use of services as an input into manufacturing had a positive and statistically significant impact on productivity in manufacturing (Banda & Goldar 2004). Technological change has increased the capacity of the service sector to promote productivity growth. The use of ICTs has made some services more routinized and hence more like manufacturing, and a large-scale call centre is now run more like a productive (and exploitative) factory. ICTs may also help to reduce transaction costs by reducing the cost and time of making an economic exchange, think Amazon or Flipkart rather than a traditional shopping mall (Singh 2006).

Services are not just useful as an input into other sectors, but services themselves have shown rapid growth in productivity. Between 1993 and 2004 India experienced productivity (TFP) growth in services of 3.9 per cent per annum compared to 1.1 per cent in industry and 0.5 per cent in agriculture (Bosworth & Collins 2008: 54). There is evidence going back to 1980 that productivity has been growing fastest in services (Mukherjee 2013: 7). However, this sort of all-India data should be viewed with some suspicion. The service sector comprises a wide spectrum of low productivity activities in the informal sector like repair and maintenance, transport, shoe-shine, hawkers, personal services. Services also include high productivity professional, legal and technology activities (Joshi 2004). More disaggregated data, however does confirm the widespread and rapid growth of productivity across many different service sectors such as financial intermediation, computer services, business services, communications and legal and technical services. Other sectors, typically those that are less amendable to technological change, have experienced slower productivity growth, such as education, healthcare and social work, hotels and restaurants and other community, social and personal services (Mukherjee 2013). We should remember that it is difficult to measure productivity in sectors such as finance. As dramatically demonstrated by the 2008 Global Financial Crisis productivity growth in those activities was not due to a real rise in their productivity, such as a reduction in trading costs due to financial innovation, but such innovations had obscured (rather then genuinely reduced) the riskiness of financial assets so allowing the global financial sector to grow at an unsustainable rate (Chang 2010).

The productivity story can be seen more clearly in a case study of the software sector in India. Despite rapid growth of output and exports there was some pessimism about software by the 1990s. The provision of labour services to overseas clients on their premises through onsite consultancy started in the late-1970s. This became known as "body shopping" and comprised about 70 per cent of service exports by the 1990s. On-site consultancy was a low value added activity with Indian engineers charged for on an hourly basis, who undertook low-end programming services such as coding and testing. This under-utilized the skills of well-trained Indian engineers (Kumar 2001; Chakraborty & Jayachandran 2001). The 1990s and afterwards became a story of productivity-led growth in software contrary to the pessimistic expectations. Indian companies moved away from body shopping and demonstrated their technological and project management skills by successfully completing turnkey projects for large companies. The proportion of on-site exports declined from 90 per cent in 1988 to 56 per cent in 2000/01. Indian companies made a conscious effort to increase exports of high-end consulting and packaged software. By the late 1990s they had managed to develop and launch a number of proprietary software products and gained a particular niche in banking, financial and accounting software. These include for example I-Flex which has been used by over 240 financial institutions in 69 countries. Banking solutions from Infosys such as Financle, Bankaway and Payaway were adopted by 22 domestic and 16 overseas banks across 12 countries. TCS launched packaged software for banking, insurance, securities, health care and accounting (Kumar 2001: 4280). An important measure of this upgrading was acquisition of quality certification. By 2001, 250 Indian companies had obtained the International Standards Organisation 9000 (ISO 9000) certificate, 38 Indian companies had received SEI-CMM (Software Engineering Institute, USA Capability Maturity Model) certificate at Level 3 or above, and of the 31 companies certified at Level 5 worldwide 16 were in India (Kumar 2001). NASSCOM assisted the sector in diffusing US best practice, pushed the state to invest in technical institutions, infrastructure and to help the international visa mobility (and hence skill acquisition) of software professionals. The software sector engaged in a dynamic process of learning-by-doing which was facilitated by engagement with the state (D'Costa 2016: 34).

The service sector represents a contemporary paradox which this section has briefly tried to explain in terms of India-specific economic and social factors. The sustainability of rapid-service-led economic growth has been called into question, but this section has been cautiously optimistic regarding spill-overs, exports, FDI and productivity, if less so about sustained employment growth. This "sustainability" question is of particular importance when discussing the so-called "middle-income trap" which is noted in the conclusion to the book.

CLIMATE CHANGE

Carbon dioxide parts per million in the atmosphere have increased from 280 in 1800 to 370 in 2001 and to 408 in 2018. A safe limit is estimated to be 450, which gives a 50 per cent chance of a 2°C rise in average temperature. While most of the safe limit is composed of carbon dioxide, other greenhouse gases include methane, nitrous oxide, and CFCs. We can also think in terms of a carbon budget. There is an available 1 trillion tonnes of global safe emissions. The first half of this budget was used up over a period of 250 years but at the current rate of emissions the rest of the budget will be used up in 40 years. It is forecast that by 2050 140% of the safe carbon space will have been used up by developed countries (80%), China (40%) and India (20%) and more by the rest of the developing world. So, even though developed countries are historically responsible it is imperative that developing countries including India must adjust. Even at the "safe" level of 2 per cent average global warming, the impact is estimated to lead to the global loss of coral from the oceans, and in Sub-Saharan Africa alone the extinction of 20 per cent of species. Were global temperatures to rise by 5 per cent, then London, Shanghai, New

York, Tokyo, and Hong Kong would be at risk from rising sea levels, and Sub-Saharan Africa would experience a one-third decline in agricultural yields (Billet 2009).

India is predicted to be the world's most populated country by 2030 with an estimated population of 1.5 billion. India has long had a heavy reliance on the use of fossil fuels. One interesting aspect of the climate change debate in India is that there is a near consensus in the media and resulting commitment as to the reality of man-made global warming (Billet 2009). In 1990 India used 578 million tonnes of oil equivalent in energy, by 2003 this had increased to 1,023 and by 2025 is forecast to reach 2,200. Of this increase 27 per cent will be driven by population growth, with the balance driven by economic growth, despite improvements in energy efficiency and a shift away from energy intensive sectors (manufacturing to services). In China the impact of population will be even less, at 8.5 per cent. Without intervention India will not make any significant reduction in carbon emissions. Since the 1990s India has liberalized its economy and increasingly relied on market prices and private profit incentives to guide the allocation of resources and investment decisions. Coal in India is cheap and plentiful and prices fell sharply after 2014. India is also locked into the use of carbon-intensive energy as heavy industry dating from the 1950s and 1960s and existing infrastructure was built to use coal and oil. Falling poverty will rapidly reduce the 40 per cent of India's population currently without electricity and add to demands for carbon-intensive energy use.

Intervention is necessary but taxing or regulating the use of fossil fuels will be problematic. Taxation could raise the marginal cost of fossil fuel use, encourage non-carbon alternatives, raise revenue for the government to invest in other energy sources and compensate those losing from the higher taxes. But there are problems. Any effort to tax coal energy would likely induce a shift to wood and other biomass fuels which would be impossible to tax. Much of India's infrastructure is locked into the use of coal and oil and would not be able to adjust in the face of higher taxes. The informal sector, which is very hard to tax, constitutes 95 per cent of employment in India. Tax revenue in India is little over 10 per cent of GDP and only 3 million people pay income tax.

Technological change, particularly if backed up by assistance from developed countries, could offer a solution. Japan, for example, has boosted energy efficiency in steel production by 30 per cent in 30 years and achieved 100 per cent diffusion of the relevant technology. India's coal reserves are particularly prevalent in a form of dirty coal with a high ash content. This could be cleaned with appropriate technology but it would raise costs of energy production. There are some concerns that the 97 per cent of patents held in developed countries would hinder the diffusion of technology or impose significant costs through royalty payments. However, much of the useful technology is generic and not patent protected. Simple changes to Indian rural cooking stoves, for example, can dramatically increase energy efficiency. There are potential changes to boost energy efficiency among small and medium-sized enterprises. The Energy and Resources Institute (TERI) worked with British Gas to design a new furnace for use by the Molten Glass industry in Firozabad, which employs 150,000 people to make glass bangles for the Indian market. The new furnace reduced energy consumption by 60 per cent and if used nationally could have saved 400,000 tonnes of carbon dioxide emissions annually. These efforts at intervention remain marginal and resources available to support international efforts at technological change remain grossly inadequate. The United Nations Framework Convention on Climate Change (UNFCCC) was ratified in 1992 with the promise to aid technology transfer to LDCs to help combat climate change. The World Bank established the Clean Energy Fund in 2008 with only a few hundred million dollars. Commitment to expenditure on technology transfer declined with the Global Financial Crisis in 2008.

India has made an impressive domestic effort in some areas. It has raised taxes on petroleum products rather than passing on global price declines to consumers as have many other countries, taxes on coal have increased, afforestation has been promoted and investments in public transport infrastructure have been boosted (Subramanian 2018: 145).

Solar technology is estimated to have the potential to produce 94 per cent of India's energy needs to 2030 although currently only accounts for 1 per cent of India's energy use. The Jawaharlal Nehru National Solar Mission (JNSM) was launched by the prime minister in 2010 seeking to provide 20GW of solar energy by 2022. The scheme aimed to provide 20 million solar lighting systems as a cost effective replacement to kerosene in rural areas. Solar technology can be used off-grid in isolated areas which makes it suitable for India's rural economy. Incentives to promote the use of renewables has been difficult in India. Agreements to allow producers to charge high tariffs and commit government electricity providers to purchase renewable energy are undermined by the gross financial problems of India's State Electricity Boards and past history of reneging on similar agreements. There have been, however, successes in the private sector. The Indian company Suzlon started life in the 1990s as a textile manufacturer before becoming the world's fifth largest producer of wind power technology. After 2003 the company started exporting to the US and purchased firms in Germany and Belgium to access new technology. In 2012 the company was near bankruptcy, a few difficult years followed but Suzlon seemed to pull through and by 2017 had achieved the milestone of having installed 10,000 MW of wind energy plant in India.

Conclusion:
prospects for the Indian economy

By 2017 India had a GDP per capita (adjusted for PPP) of almost $2,000 and had graduated to the status of a lower-middle-income nation. Although many people in India remained in poverty, India was no longer, officially a poor country. India could begin thinking of the next stage of its quest to become a developed country or, as many of its political leaders aspire, a Great Power. The quest would seem straightforward if India continues to grow at 7–8 per cent annually. But will it?

POST-2008 ECONOMIC SLOWDOWN

Growth has been sustained in recent years despite the lingering effects of the Global Financial Crisis of 2008. Annual growth averaged 7.7 per cent between 2008 and 2012, slowing to 4.6 per cent between 2012–14, but then gradually revived to 6.6 per cent in 2017. This slowdown was led by the manufacturing sector where growth slowed from 8 per cent to only 0.2 per cent, service-sector annual growth continued steadily at more than 6 per cent between 2008 and 2012 (Mohan & Kapur 2015: 3). Total investment declined modestly from 35.7 per cent of GDP between 2008–12 and 34.8 per cent between 2012–14. This was caused by a steady decline in private corporate sector investment, 11.6 to 9.2 per cent of GDP while public investment was steady, 8.7 to 8.1 per cent of GDP (*ibid.*: 6). In late 2016 Prime Minister Modi announced that the two largest notes in India (Rs500 and Rs1000) would cease to be legal tender from the next day. This demonetization was announced as a means of tackling the black economy, corruption and terrorism. It was assumed (wrongly) that black money was mainly held in cash and that black marketeers would find their black wealth and livelihoods lost. In practice almost 100 per cent of the existing notes in circulation were eventually exchanged in banks for newly printed notes. The sudden demonetization of over 85 per cent of India's cash had a devastating impact on the predominantly cash-using informal economy. Small enterprises closed and workers went unpaid. The loss of production and demand in the informal economy pulled down growth in the formal economy and contributed to slower economic growth in 2017 (Kumar 2017).

The gross fiscal deficit increased from 2.5 per cent of GDP in 2007–08 to 6.0 per cent in 2008–09, due to a combination of a 1.1 per cent fall of GDP in tax revenue and a 2.2 per cent of GDP increase in general expenditures and a 0.9 per cent of GDP increase in subsidies. The increase in subsidies was mainly due to increased fuel subsidies to kerosene, diesel and liquid petroleum gas (Mohan & Kapur 2015: 19). Subramanian (2018: xlii) labelled the fertilizer subsidy, which costs 0.6 per cent of GDP as "one of the worst policies imaginable" as it mostly goes to large farmers and has "devastating environmental impacts". While global oil prices were rising they were held down for domestic consumers in India by higher subsidies which in turn increased both imports and subsidies. This shift in the fiscal stance (monetary policy also helped) boosted demand which was able to sustain economic growth through the global financial crisis. However, the expansion continued too long and contributed to subsequent inflation, and by 2012–13 the current account deficit had widened to 4 per cent of GDP. Large capital inflows during these years caused the real exchange rate to appreciate which added further to current account problems. In contrast to previous episodes of large capital flows there was little effort by the Reserve Bank of India (RBI) to sell rupees and add to foreign exchange reserves to slow the appreciation (Mohan & Kapur 2015).

SUSTAINING RAPID ECONOMIC GROWTH
OVER THE LONG TERM

Figure 7.1 below shows how both Brazil and South Korea experienced rapid and comparable economic growth in the 1960s and 1970s when they were both labelled "miracle economies". In the late-1970s both experienced the negative impact of a global economic recession and higher world oil prices. After a brief hiatus, growth in South Korea resumed (pausing briefly during the 1997 Asian Crisis and 2008 Global Financial Crisis). By 2014 South Korea was a high-income country with a GDP per capita of around $25,000. In Brazil growth never resumed after being buffeted in the late-1970s. By 2014 GDP per capita in Brazil at $5,000 was no more than 20 per cent of that in South Korea. This comparison has more

Figure 7.1 GDP per capita in Brazil and South Korea, 1960–2014 (constant 2005 US$)

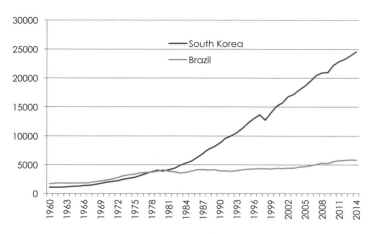

Source: World Bank Development Indicators 2018.

general relevance and has been labelled by scholars as the "middle-income trap". The argument runs along the lines that it is relatively easy to initiate economic growth (recall from our earlier discussion how many countries have experience spells of rapid economic growth). Growth in a very poor country can be boosted by the spread of a modern banking system and tax system that mobilizes savings and tax revenue, which can be funnelled into private and public investment, simple medical interventions (such as sanitation and vaccination) that reduce mortality and generate rapid population growth (and so of the labour force), social changes that permit women to leave the household and enter the labour force and structural changes that shifts resources from low productivity agriculture to higher productivity manufacturing. The problem comes when a country hits middle-income status – roughly where India is today or where Brazil was in the late-1970s – to sustain growth after that point, argue scholars, is harder.

There are limits to squeezing consumption in order to raise more savings and tax revenue. At some point women will have entered the labour force en masse and peasants will be working in factories. This process has yet to be completed in India, where a large fraction of the labour force remains in agriculture and women continue in the household. India is currently experiencing a demographic dividend – an increasing share of India's population are young and of working age. Such demographic dividends have contributed to economic growth in the past in China, South Korea and elsewhere. The effect in India is likely to be more muted. Young people provide a potential for economic growth that the Indian economy is failing to exploit by not creating enough jobs to absorb this labour into productive employment (Subramanian 2018: 230). To sustain rapid economic growth will require shifting to growth based on increased productivity. Productivity-led growth is harder to attain and rather than just accumulating ever more factors of production requires that an economy become more efficient, more innovative and more dynamic. It requires that the quality of education be improved, that labour becomes more adept at using new technology, that social mores change to become more hospitable to foreign ideas, technology and expertise, that scientists and universities develop a closer relationship with industry and high-technology services. These ideas have been discussed at length throughout this book. The big idea that brings them all together is that of *sustainable* economic growth. Can India sustain the rapid economic growth it has achieved since *c*.2003 and eventually attain the status of a high-income or developed economy? This book has provided evidence for India's shift to productivity-led growth after *c*.2003. A second question is whether India can continue to redistribute the resources of that growth to ensure wider improvements in measures of human development as it has been doing much better since *c*.2003, or will those benefits be captured by a well-connected elite?

The contemporary productivity-led growth story in India has some impressive elements. Economic growth after 2003 was not just investment-led, it was matched by impressive growth of productivity. As we have seen, the story of the software sector in India, after pessimistic forecasts in the 1990s, was one of productivity, moving up the value chain to produce turnkey projects and software solutions that were sold both domestically and globally. And India has long outpaced China in its ability to produce brand names with global resonance, which have included Infosys and Wipro (software), Ranbaxy and Dr Reddy (pharmaceuticals), and Bollywood (films). This difference has been explained by the greater emphasis on the private sector, better protection of intellectual property rights, and an Indian model of individual entrepreneurship and innovation versus the state-led investment model of China. The implications for long-term catch-up by India are today less evident as China has begun producing its own global brands, WeChat, Ali Baba and Huawei among others. And what relevance are global brands for the consumption of Indians, of which 80 per cent are simple products produced locally and bought in tiny sachets by the 70 per cent of the population who live on $2 a day or less? India has shown an impressive ability to acquire and utilize technology beyond the confines suggested by its low GDP per capita. Indeed, India has a space programme and in services and manufacturing its exports have shown an impressive ability to upgrade. But this techno-logical dynamism is embedded in an economy in which 60 per cent of the population work in low productivity, rain-dependent agriculture, and learn in one of the world's most unequal education systems that is renowned for producing a small number of world-class scientists and a mass of semi-literate people.

We can think of this discussion in terms of the deeper determinants of economic growth with which we opened the book. Instead of looking at the opportunities and constraints that existed in 1947 we think of them in relation to 2017. In terms of geography, the legacy at independence of rail-ways has been added to in recent years with the construction of improved highways (the Golden Quadrilateral), interventions that have drastically reduced the prevalence of malaria, investments to boost growth in trop-ical agriculture, an expansion of air-travel facilities and of technologies such as mobile phones that can overcome the costs of distance and being landlocked. Challenges remain, however, regarding constraints on the ability of people to migrate at distance in India for economic reasons. In terms of institutions, we noted that there is a lot of concern about the gradual decay and corruption of formal institutions relating to the courts, political parties, and property rights, but the economy has been shielded from any resulting negative effects as politics has become more stable and investors have been able to construct informal deals with politicians and civil servants to give long-term security to their investment. We also noted how easy it is for such inside and informal deals to turn into a more exploitative relationship where insiders seek to protect their own position against dynamic newcomers and disruptive technological change and so stifle economic growth and innovation. In terms of the state, while pock-ets of excellence remain in the Reserve Bank of India (RBI), the Election Commission (EC) and elsewhere, state capacity and independence has long been declining. In terms of economic structure India is doing some-thing unusual and has been experiencing service-led growth over the last few decades. Contrary to traditional views that emphasize the centrality of manufacturing as the engine of growth, this book has made a cautiously optimistic case in terms of spill-overs, exports, FDI and productivity that services in India can remain an engine of growth even if challenges remain respecting generating employment in, and mobilizing tax revenue from, the sector. For any productivity story the continuing problems respecting both the quality and inequalities of education in contemporary India are crucial. Regarding technology (an important input into much productivity growth), India has proved adept at utilizing new technology in both software and pharmaceuticals, but in 2005 only registered 384 patents in the US, which was better than Brazil, Russia or South Africa, but a long way behind countries such as South Korea and Hong Kong (3–4,000). In terms of culture, the passion with which India, from top to bottom of the income scale, has embraced the desire for consumption made possible in a liberalized economy, has cleared any concern that India is too frugal and too aesthetic to sustain rapid economic growth. Rising wages and falling poverty among STs and SCs and the rise of Dalit-based entrepreneurs even indicates caste-based restrictions on employment labour mobility are declining. Concerns remain, particularly about how culture can undermine the ability of women to participate in economic growth. The problem of missing women and low FLFP remain constraints on the ability of women to participate fully and contribute to sustaining rapid economic growth. The enduring organization of the family-based firm has clearly been a useful means to promote economic growth in the past, but may now be increasingly a drag on corporate success in contemporary India.

There is no clear answer to the question. The possibilities of India becoming stuck in a middle-income trap are very real, as demonstrated by the case of Brazil. But, for each of the deeper determinants there are reasons to be both optimistic and pessimistic. On balance perhaps the analysis in this book and particularly so since 2003 is that economic growth looks both sustainable and, despite widening measures of inequality, more inclusive in terms of public service delivery and improvements in social indicators.

References

Adhikari, A. & K. Bhatia (2010). "NREGA wage payments: can we bank on the banks", *Economic and Political Weekly*, 2 January, 30–7.

Aggarwal, A. (2012). "India's service sector: gateway to development?", *Economic and Political Weekly*, 30 June, 119–23.

Ahluwalia, I. (1985). *Industrial Growth in India: Stagnation Since the Mid-Sixties*. New Delhi: Oxford University Press.

Ahluwalia, M. (1978). "Rural poverty and agricultural performance in India", *Journal of Development Studies* 14:3, 298–323.

Ahsan, A. & C. Pages (2005). *Helping or Hurting Workers? Assessing the Effects of De Jure and De Facto Labour Regulation in India*. Washington, DC: World Bank.

Ahsan, A. and C. Pages (2008). "Are all labour regulations equal? Evidence from Indian manufacturing", IZA Discussion Paper No. 3394. Bonn: IZA.

Alesina, A., R. Baqir & W. Easterly (1999). "Public goods and ethnic divisions", *Quarterly Journal of Economics* 114:4, 1243–84.

Alderman, H. & P. Gertler (1997). "Family resources and gender differences in human capital investments: the demand for children's medical care", in L. Haddad, J. Hoddinott & H. Alderman (eds), *Intrahousehold Resource Allocation in Developing Countries: Models, Methods and Policy*. Baltimore, MD: John Hopkins University Press.

Alfaro, L. & A. Chari (2009). "India transformed? Insights from the firm level 1988–2005", NBER Working Paper No. 15448. Cambridge, MA: NBER.

Alfaro, L & A. Chari (2012). "Deregulation, misalloction, and size: evidence from India", NBER Working Paper No. 18650. Cambridge, MA: NBER.

Ali, I. (2003). *The Punjab under Imperialism, 1885–1947*. Karachi: Oxford University Press.

Anand, R. & V. Tulin (2014). "Disentangling India's investment slowdown", IMF Working Paper WP/14/47. Washington, DC: IMF.

Anand, R., K. Kochhar & S. Mishra (2015). "Make in India: which exports can drive the next wave of growth", IMF Working Paper WP/15/19. Washington, DC: IMF.

Appu, P. (2005). "The all India services: decline, debasement and destruction", *Economic and Political Weekly*, 26 February, 826–32.

Arnold, F., A. Choe & T. Roy (1998). "Son preference, the family-building process and child mortality in India", *Population Studies* 52:3, 301–15.

Aslam, M. & G. Kingdon (2012). "Parental education and child health: understanding the pathways of impact in Pakistan", *World Development* 40:10, 2014–32.

Baddeley, M., K. McNay & R. Cassen (2006). "Divergence in India: income differentials at the state level, 1970–97", *Journal of Development Studies* 42:6, 1000–922.

Balakrishnan, P. (2006). "Benign neglect or stategic intent? Contested lineage of Indian software industry", *Economic and Political Weekly*, 9 September, 3865–72.

Balakrishnan, P. (2014). "The great reversal: a macro story", *Economic and Political Weekly*, 24 May, 29–34.

Balakrishnan, P. & M. Parameswaran (2007). "Understanding economic growth in India: a prerequisite", *Economic and Political Weekly*, 14 July, 2915–22.

Banerjee, A. *et al.* (2007). "Can information campaigns raise awareness and local participation in primary education?", *Economic and Political Weekly*, 14 April, 1365–72.

Banerjee, A. *et al.* (2009). "Labour market discrimination in Delhi: evidence from a field experiment", *Journal of Comparative Economics* 37, 14–27.

Banerjee, A., A. Deaton & E. Duflo (2004). "Health care delivery in rural Rajasthan", *Economic and Political Weekly*, 28 February, 944–9.

Banerjee, A. & E. Duflo (2006). "Addressing Absence", *Journal of Economic Perspectives* 20:1, 117–32.

Banerjee, A. & L. Iyer (2005). "History, institutions, and economic performance: the legacy of colonial land tenure systems in India", *American Economic Review* 95:4, 1190–213.

Banerji, R. (2011). "Challenging Bihar on Primary Education", *Economic and Political Weekly*, 12 March, 33–9.

Banga, R. (2005). "Critical issues in India's service-led growth", ICRIER Working Paper No. 171, October.

Banga, R. & B. Goldar (2004). "Contribution of services to output growth and productivity in Indian manufacturing: pre and post reforms", ICRIER Working Paper No. 139. New Delhi.

Banik, D. (2001). "The transfer Raj: Indian civil servants on the move", *European Journal of Development Research* 13:1, 106–34.

Bardhan, P. (1984). *The Political Economy of Development in India*. New Delhi: Oxford University Press.

Barnes, T. *et al.* (2015). "Labour contractors and global production networks: the case of India's auto supply chain", *Journal of Development Studies* 51:4, 355–69.

Barooah, V. (2005). "Caste, inequality, and poverty in India", *Review of Development Economics* 9:3, 399–414.

Baru, R. *et al.* (2010). "Inequities in access to health services in India: caste, class and region", *Economic and Political Weekly*, 18 September, 49–58.

Basu, S. (2000). "Economic policy and the development of capitalism in India: the role of regional capitalists and political parties", in F. Frankel *et al.* (eds) *Transforming India: Social and Political Dynamics of Democracy*. New Delhi: Oxford University Press.

Bates, R. (2000). "Ethnicity and development in Africa: a reappraisal", *American Economic Review* 90:2, 131–4.

Beenstock, M. & P. Sturdy (1990). "The determinants of infant mortality in regional India", *World Development* 18:3, 443–53.

Behrman, J. & A. Deolalikar (1987). "Will developing country nutrition improve with income? A case study from rural south India", *Journal of Political Economy* 95:3, 492–507.

Bertrand, M. & A. Schoar (2006). "The role of the family in family firms", *Journal of Economic Perspectives* 20:2, 73–96.

Besley, T. & R. Burgess (2000). "The political economy of government responsiveness: theory and evidence from India", STICERD 28. London: LSE.

Besley, T. & R. Burgess (2002). "Can labour market hinder economic performance? Evidence from India", STICERD 33. London: LSE.

Bhagwati, J. (1984). "Splintering and the disembodiment of services and developing countries", *World Economy* 7:2, 133–44.

Bhagwati, J. (1993). *India in Transition: Freeing the Economy*. Oxford: Clarendon Press.

Bhagwati, J. & P. Desai (1970). *India: Planning for Industrialization*. Oxford: Oxford University Press.

Bhagwati, J. & A. Panagariya (2013). *Why Growth Matters: How Economic Growth in India Reduced Poverty and the Lessons for Other Developing Countries*. New York: Public Affairs.

Bhagwati, J. & T. Srinivasan (1975). *Foreign Trade Regimes and Economic Development: India*. New York: Columbia University Press.

Bhalla, G. & G. Singh (2009). "Economic liberalisation and Indian agriculture: a statewise analysis", *Economic and Political Weekly*, 26 December, 34–44.

Bhalotra, S. (1998). "The puzzle of jobless growth in Indian manufacturing", *Oxford Bulletin of Economics and Statistics* 60:1, 5–32.

Bhat, P. (2002). "Returning a favour: reciprocity between female education and fertility in India", *World Development* 30:10, 1791–803.

Bhat, P. (2006). "Sex ratio in India", *The Lancet* 367:9524, 1725–6.

Bhattacharjea, A. (2006). "Labour market regulation and industrial performance in India: a critical review of the empirical evidence", *Indian Journal of Labour Economics* 49:2, 211–32.

Bhattacharjea, A. (2009). "The effects of employment protection legislation on Indian manufacturing", *Economic and Political Weekly*, 30 May, 55–62.

Bhattacharjee, S. & D. Chakrabarti (2013). "Financial liberalisation, financing constraint and India's manufacturing sector", *Economic and Political Weekly*, 9 February, 61–7.

Bhattacharya, B. & A. Mitra (1990). "Excess growth of tertiary sector in Indian economy: issues and implications", *Economic and Political Weekly*, 3 November, 2445–50.

Bhattacharya, B. & A. Mitra (1991). "Excess growth of tertiary sector", *Economic and Political Weekly*, 1 June, 1423–4.

Billett, S. (2009). "Dividing climate change: global warming in the Indian mass media", *Climate Change*, 5 June, 1–16.

Bloom, D. *et al.* (1998). "Geography, demography, and economic growth in Africa", *Brookings Papers on Economic Growth in Africa* 2, 207–95.

Bosworth, B. & S. Collins (2008). "Accounting for growth: comparing China and India", *Journal of Economic Perspectives* 22:1, 45–66.

Bouka, E., M. Merkouri & T. Metaxas (2005). "Identifying Bollywood as a crucial factor of India's economic development: a review analysis", MPRA Paper No. 64658. Berlin.

Bramall, C. (2009). *Chinese Economic Development*. Abingdon: Routledge.

Broadberry, S. & B. Gupta (2010). "The historical roots of India's service-led development: a sectoral analysis of Anglo-Indian productivity differences, 1870–2000", *Explorations in Economic History* 47, 264–78.

Brown, J. (2003). *Nehru: A Political Life*. New Haven, CT: Yale University Press.

Byres, T. 1981. "The new technology, class formation and class action in the Indian countryside", *Journal of Peasant Studies* 8:4, 405–54.

Cashin, P. & R. Sahay (1996). "Internal migration, center-state grants, and economic growth in the states of India", IMF Staff Papers 43:1, 123–71.

Cassen, R. & K. McNay (2005). "The condition of the people", in T. Dyson, R. Cassen & L. Visaria (eds), *Twenty-First Century India: Population, Economy, Human Development, and the Environment.* Oxford: Oxford University Press.

Cerra, V., A. Rivera & S. Saxena (2005). "Crouching tiger, hidden dragon: what are the consequences of China's WTO entry for India's trade", IMF Working Paper WP/05/01.

Chakrabarty, B. (2006). *Forging Power: Coalition Politics in India.* Oxford: Oxford University Press.

Chakraborty, C. & C. Jayachandran (2001). "Software sector: trends and constraints", *Economic and Political Weekly*, 25 August, 3255–61.

Chakravarty, S. (1979). "On the question of home market and prospects for Indian growth", *Economic and Political Weekly*, special issue, August, 1229–42.

Chakravarty, S. (1987). *Development Planning: The Indian Experience.* Oxford: Clarendon Press.

Chambers, R. & G. Von Medazza (2013). "Sanitation and stunting in India: undernutrition's blind spot", *Economic and Political Weekly*, 22 June, 15–18.

Chancel, L. & T. Piketty (2017). "Indian income inequality, 1922–2014: from British Raj to billionaire Raj", Wealth and Income Database Working Paper Series No. 2017/11. Paris.

Chand, R., S. Raju & L. Pandey (2007). "Growth crisis in agriculture: severity and options at national and state levels", *Economic and Political Weekly*, 30 June, 2528–33.

Chandra, B., A. Mukherjee & M. Mukherjee (2008). *India Since Independence.* New Delhi: Penguin.

Chandrasekhar, C. (1988). "Aspects of growth and structural change in Indian industry", *Economic and Political Weekly*, special issue, November, 2359–70.

Chandrasekhar, S. & A. Mukhopadhyay (2006). "Primary education as a fundamental right: cost implications", *Economic and Political Weekly*, 2 September, 3797–804.

Chang, H.-J. (1993). "The political economy of industrial policy in Korea", *Cambridge Journal of Economics* 17, 131–57.

Chang, H.-J. (2007). *Bad Samaritans: Rich Nations, Poor Policies and the Threat to the Developing World.* London: Random House.

Chang, H.-J. (2010). *23 Things They Don't Tell You About Capitalism.* London: Penguin.

Chatterjee, E. (2019). "'All shook up'? State professionals in the reform era", in

E. Chatterjee & M. McCartney (eds), *Class and Conflict: Revisiting Pranab Bardhan's Political Economy of India*. New Delhi: Oxford University Press.

Chatterjee, P. (1997). "Development planning and the Indian state", in T. J. Byers (ed.), *The State, Development Planning and Liberalisation in India*. New Delhi: Oxford University Press

Chaudhury, N. *et al.* (2006). "Missing in action: teacher and health workers in developing countries", *Journal of Economic Perspectives* 20:1, 91–116.

Chen, L., E. Huq & S. Souza (1981). "Sex bias in the family allocation of food and health care in rural Bangladesh", *Population and Development Review* 7:1, 55–70.

Chibber, V. (1999). "Building a developmental state: the Korean case reconsidered", *Politics and Society* 27:3, 309–46.

Chibber, V. (2003). *Locked in Place: State-Building and Late Industrialisation in India*. Princeton, NJ: Princeton University Press.

Chima, R., C. Goodwin & A. Mills (2003). "The economic impact of malaria in Africa: a critical review of the evidence", *Health Policy* 63, 17–36.

Chaudhuri, S. (2002). "Economic reforms and industrial structure in India", *Economic and Political Weekly*, 12 January, 155–62.

Chunkath, S. & V. Athreya (1997). "Female infanticide in Tamil Nadu: some evidence", *Economic and Political Weekly*, 26 April, 21–8.

Coffey, D. *et al.* (2014). "Revealed preference for open defecation: evidence from a new survey in rural north India", *Economic and Political Weekly*, 20 September, 43–55.

Collier, P. 2007. *The Bottom Billion: Why the Poorest Countries Are Failing and What Can Be Done About It*. Oxford: Oxford University Press.

Collins, W. (1999). "Labor mobility, market integration, and wage convergence in late nineteenth-century India", *Explorations in Economic History* 36, 246–77.

Corbridge, S. & J. Harriss (2000). *Reinventing India: Liberalisation, Hindu Nationalism and Popular Democracy*. Cambridge: Polity.

Corbridge, S., J. Harriss & C. Jeffrey (2013). *India Today: Economy, Politics and Society*. Cambridge: Polity.

Cotton, J. (1991). "The limits to liberalization in industrializing Asia: three views of the state", *Pacific Affairs* 64:3, 311–27.

Crabtree, J. (2018). *The Billionaire Raj: A Journey Through India's New Gilded Age*. New York: Tim Duggan Books.

Cuberes, D. & M. Jerzmanowski (2009). "Democracy, diversification and growth reversals", *Economic Journal* 119, 1270–302.

Cutler, D. *et al.* (2010). "Early-life malaria exposure and adult outcomes: evidence from malaria eradication in India", *American Economic Journal: Applied Economics* 2, 72–94.

Damodaran, H. (2008). *India's New Capitalists: Caste, Business, and Industry in a Modern Nation*. London: Palgrave Macmillan.

Das, J. & J. Hammer (2007). "Money for nothing: the dire straits of medical practise in Delhi, India", *Journal of Development Economics* 83, 1–36.

Das, J. & T. Zajonc (2010). "India shining and Bharat drowning: comparing two Indian states to the worldwide distribution in mathematics achievement", *Journal of Development Economics* 92:2, 175–87.

Das Gupta, M. (1987). "Selective discrimination against female children in rural Punjab, India", *Population and Development Review* 13:1, 77–100.

Dasgupta, S. & A. Singh (2006). "Manufacturing, services and premature deindustrialisation in developing countries", UNU-WIDER Research Paper No. 2006/49.

Datt, G., V. Kozel & M. Ravallion (2003). "A model-based assessment of India's progress in reducing poverty in the 1990s", *Economic and Political Weekly*, 25 January, 355–61.

Datt, G. & M. Ravallion (2002). "Is India's economic growth leaving the poor behind?", *Journal of Economic Perspectives* 16:3, 89–108.

Datt, G. & M. Ravallion (2010). "Shining for the poor too?", *Economic and Political Weekly*, 13 February, 55–60.

D'Costa, A. (2003). "Uneven and combined development: understanding India's software exports", *World Development* 31:1, 211–26.

D'Costa, A. (2005). *The Long March to Capitalism: Embourgeoisment, Internationalization and Industrial Transformation in India*. London: Palgrave Macmillan.

D'Costa, A. (2006). "ICTs and decoupled development: theories, trajectories and transitions", in G. Parayil (ed.), *Political Economy and Information Capitalism in India: Digital Divide, Development Divide and Equity*. Basingstoke: Palgrave Macmillan.

D'Costa, A. (2011). "Geography, uneven development and distributive justice: the political economy of IT growth in India", *Cambridge Journal of Regions, Economy and Society* 4:2, 237–51.

D'Costa, A. (2016). *International Mobility, Global Capitalism, and Changing Structures of Accumulation: Transforming the Japan–India IT Relationship*. Abingdon: Routledge.

D'Costa, A. (2018). "Why does an impoverished India produce a globally mobile wealthy class?", Dialogue of Civilizations Research Institute, Berlin. Available at: https://doc-research.org/2018/10/why-does-an-impoverished-india-produc e-a-globally-mobile-wealthy-class/ (accessed 25 March 2019).

D. Costa, A. & A. Chakraborty (eds) (2017). *The Land Question in India: State, Dispossession, and Capitalist Transition*. Oxford: Oxford University Press.

De Long, J. & L. Summers (1991). "Equipment investment and economic growth", *Quarterly Journal of Economics* 106:2, 445–502.

Deokar, B. & S. Shetty (2014). "Growth in Indian agriculture: responding to policy initiative since 2004–05", *Economic and Political Weekly*, 28 June, 101–104.

Deaton, A. (2003). "Adjusted Indian poverty estimates for 1999–2000", *Economic and Political Weekly* 38:4, 25 January, 322–6.

Deaton, A. (2007). "Height, health, and development", *Proceedings of the National Academy of Sciences* 104:33, 13232–7.

Deaton, A. (2008). "Height, health and inequality: the distribution of adult heights in India", *American Economic Review* 98:2, 468–74.

Deaton, A. & J. Dreze (2009). "Food and nutrition in India: facts and interpretations", *Economic and Political Weekly*, 14 February, 42–65.

Deaton, A. & V. Kozel (2005). "Data and dogma: the great Indian poverty debate", *The World Bank Research Observer* 20:2, 177–99.

Dehejia, R. & A. Panagariya (2013). "Services growth in India: a look inside the black box", in J. Bhagwati & A. Panagariya (eds), *Reforms and Economic Transformation in India*. New Delhi: Oxford University Press.

Derbyshire, I. (1987). "Economic change and the railways in north India, 1860–1914", *Modern Asian Studies* 21:3, 521–45.

Desai, A. (1981). "Factors underlying the slow growth of Indian industry", *Economic and Political Weekly*, annual issue, March, 381–92.

Desai, S. & A. Thorat (2013). "Beyond the great Indian nutrition debate", *Economic and Political Weekly*, 16 November, 18–22.

Dhawan, B. (1996). "Relationship between public and private investments in Indian agriculture with special reference to public canals", *Indian Journal of Agricultural Economics* 51:1/2, 209–19.

Dixit, A. (2009). "Agriculture in a high growth state: case of Gujarat (1960 to 2006)", *Economic and Political Weekly*, 12 December, 64–71.

Donaldson, D. (2010). "Railroads of the Raj: estimating the impact of transportation infrastructure", LSE Asia Research Centre Working Paper No. 41. London: LSE.

Doner, R., B. Ritchie & D. Slater (2005). "Systematic vulnerability and the origins of developmental states: northeast and southeast Asia in comparative perspective", *International Organisation* 59, 327–61.

Dreze, J. (2004). "Mid-day meals and children's rights", *Economic and Political Weekly*, 8 May, 1937–8.

Dreze, J. & H. Gazdar (1996). "Uttar Pradesh: the burden of inertia", in J. Dreze &

A. Sen (eds), *Indian Development: Selected Regional Perspective*. New Delhi: Oxford University Press.

Dreze, J. & A. Goyal (2003). "Future of mid-day meals", *Economic and Political Weekly*, 1 November, 4673–83.

Dreze, J. & A. Sen (1995). *India: Economic Development and Social Opportunity*. New Delhi: Oxford University Press.

Dreze, J. & A. Sen (2013). *An Uncertain Glory: India and its Contradictions*. London: Allen Lane.

Dutta, M. (2009). "Nokia SEZ: price of success", *Economic and Political Weekly*, 3 October, 23–5.

Dutta, P. (2006). "Returns to education: new evidence for India, 1983–99", *Education Economics* 14:4, 431—51.

Dutta, P. *et al.* (2012). "Does India's employment guarantee scheme guarantee employment?", *Economic and Political Weekly*, 21 April, 55–64.

Dyson, Y. (2001). "The preliminary demography of the 2001 census", *Population and Development Review* 2:2, 341—56.

Dyson, T. & M. Moore (1983). "On kinship structure, female autonomy, and demographic behaviour in India", *Population and Development Review* 9:1, 35–60.

Easterly, W. & R. Levine (1997). "Africa's growth tragedy: policies and ethnic divisions", *Quarterly Journal of Economics* 112:4, 1203–50.

Evans, P. (1995). *Embedded Autonomy: States and Industrial Transformation*. Princeton, NJ: Princeton University Press.

Fallon, P. & R. Lucas (1993). "Job security regulations and the dynamic demand for industrial labour in India and Zimbabwe", *Journal of Development Economics* 40:2, 241–75.

Fan, V. & A. Mahal (2011). "What prevents child diarrhoea? The impact of water supply, toilets, and hand-washing in rural India", *Journal of Development Effectiveness* 3:3, 340–70.

Fernandes, A. & A. Pakes (2009). "Evidence of underemployment of labour and capital in Indian manufacturing", in E. Ghani & S. Ahmed (eds), *Accelerating Growth and Job Creation in South Asia*. New Delhi: Oxford University Press.

Fernandes, L. (2006). *India's New Middle Class: Democratic Politics in an Era of Economic Reform*. Minneapolis, MN: Minnesota University Press.

Frankel, F. (1969). "Democracy and political development: perspectives from the Indian experience", *World Politics* 21:3, 448–68.

Fulford, S. (2014). "Returns to education in India", *World Development* 59, 434–50.

Gadgil, S. & S. Gadgil (2006). "The Indian monsoon, GDP and agriculture", *Economic and Political Weekly*, 25 November, 4887–95.

Gallup, J. & J. Sachs (1999). "Geography and economic development", Centre for International Development, Working Paper No. 1, Harvard University.

Gallup, J. & J. Sachs (2000). "The economic burden of malaria", Centre for International Development, Working Paper No. 2, Harvard University.

Gandhi, A. & M. Walton (2012). "Where do India's billionaires get their wealth?", *Economic and Political Weekly*, 6 October, 10–14.

Ganguly, S. (1991). "From the defence of the nation to aid to the civil: the army in contemporary India", *Journal of Asian and African Studies* 26:1, 11–26.

Garg, M. & K. Mandal (2013). "Mid-day meal for the poor, privatised education for the non-poor", *Economic and Political Weekly*, 27 July, 155–63.

George S., R. Abel & B. Miller (1992). "Female infanticide in rural south India", *Economic and Political Weekly*, 30 May, 1153–6.

Geruso, M. & D. Spears (2014). *Sanitation and Health Externalities: Resolving the Muslim Mortality Paradox*. University of Texas at Austin working paper .

Ghatak, M. & P. Ghosh (2011). "The land acquisition bill: a critique and a proposal", *Economic and Political Weekly*, 8 October, 65–72.

Ghatak, M., P. Ghosh & A. Kotwal (2014). "Growth in the time of UPA: myths and realities", *Economic and Political Weekly*, 19 April, 34–43.

Ghemawat, P. & M. Patibandla (1999). "India's exports since the reforms: three analytic industry studies", in J. Sachs, A. Varshney & N. Bajpai (eds), *India in the Era of Economic Reforms*. New Delhi: Oxford University Press.

Ghose, A. (2016). *India Employment Report 2016: Challenges and the Imperative of Manufacturing-Led Growth*. New Delhi: Oxford University Press.

Gillespie, S. (2013). "Myths and realities of child nutrition", *Economic and Political Weekly*, 24 August, 64–7.

Goldar, B. (2011). "Growth in organised manufacturing employment in recent years", *Economic and Political Weekly*, 12 February, 20–23.

Gordon, J. & P. Gupta (2004). "Understanding India's service revolution", IMF Working Paper WP/04/171. Washington: IMF.

Government of India (2013). *Report of the Comptroller and Auditor General of India on Performance Audit of the Mahahtma Gandhi National Rural Employment Guarantee Scheme*. New Delhi: Ministry of Rural Development.

Government of India (1961). *Second Five-Year Plan*. New Delhi.

Goyal, S. & P. Pandey (2012). "How do government and private schools differ?", *Economic and Political Weekly*, 2 June, 67–76.

Grabowski, R. (1994). "The successful developmental state: where does it come from?", *World Development* 22:3, 413–22.

Guiso, L., P. Sapienza & L. Zingales (2006). "Does culture affect economic outcomes", *Journal of Economic Perspectives* 20:2, 23–48.

Gulati, A. & S. Bathla (2001). "Capital formation in India agriculture: re-visiting the debate", *Economic and Political Weekly*, 19 May, 1697–708.

Habib, I. (2006). *Indian Economy, 1858–1914*. New Delhi: Tulika Books.

Hammer, J., Y. Aiyar & S. Samji (2007). "Understanding government failure in public health services", *Economic and Political Weekly*, 6 October, 4049–57.

Hanchate, A. & T. Dyson (2005). "Prospects for food demand and supply", in T. Dyson, R. Cassen & L. Visaria (eds), *Twenty-First Century India: Population, Economy, Human Development, and the Environment*. Oxford: Oxford University Press.

Hanson, A. (1966). *The Process of Planning: A Study of India's Five-Year Plans, 1950–1964*. Oxford: Oxford University Press.

Harilal, K. & J. Joseph (2003). "Stagnation and revival of Kerala economy: an open economy perspective", *Economic and Political Weekly*, 7 June, 2286–94.

Harriss, J. (1992). "Does the 'depressor' still work? Agrarian structure and development in India: a review of the evidence and argument", *Journal of Peasant Studies* 19:2, 189–227.

Harriss, J. (1993). "What is happening in rural west Bengal? Agrarian reform, growth and distribution", *Economic and Political Weekly*, 12 June, 1237–47.

Harriss, J. & N. Kohli (2009). "Notes on the differing 'states' of child undernutrition in rural India", IDS Bulletin 40:4, 9–15.

Harriss, J. & P. de Renzio (1997). "Missing link or analytically missing? The concept of social capital (An introductory bibliographical essay)", *Journal of International Development* 9:7, 919–37.

Harriss-White, B. (2003). *India Working: Essays on Society and Economy*. Cambridge: Cambridge University Press.

Hasan, R. & K. Jandoc (2010). "The distribution of firm size in India: what can survey data tell us?", Asian Development Bank Working Paper Series No. 213. Manila, Philippines.

Hasan, Z. (2012). *Congress after Indira: Policy, Power, Political Change, 1984–2009*. New Delhi: Oxford University Press.

Hatekar, N. & A. Dongre (2005). "Structural breaks in India's growth: revisiting the debate with a longer perspective", *Economic and Political Weekly*, 2 April, 1432–5.

Hausmann, R., L. Pritchett & D. Rodrik (2004). *Growth Accelerations*, Kennedy School of Government, Harvard University.

Herring, R. (1999). "Embedded particularism: India's failed developmental state", in M. Woo-Cumings (ed.) *The Developmental State in Historical Perspective*. Ithaca, NY: Cornell University Press.

Heyer, J. (1992). "The roles of dowries and daughters' marriages in the

251

accumulation and distribution of capital in a south Indian community", *Journal of International Development* 4:4, 419–36.

Himanshu & A. Sen (2013). "In-kind food transfers I: impact on poverty", *Economic and Political Weekly*, 16 November, 46–54.

The Hindu, 17 February 2015.

Hirway, I. & N. Shah (2011). "Labour and employment under globalisation: the case of Gujarat", *Economic and Political Weekly*, 28 May, 57–65.

Hnatkovska, V. & A. Lahiri (2013). "The post-reform narrowing of inequality across castes", in J. Bhagwati & A. Panagariya (eds), *Reforms and Economic Transformation in India*. New Delhi: Oxford University Press.

Huff, W., G. Dewit & C. Oughton (2001). "Building the developmental state: achieving economic growth through cooperative solutions: a comment on bringing politics back in", *Journal of Development Studies* 38:1, 147–51.

Huntingdon, S. (1968). *Political Order in Changing Societies*. New Haven, CT: Yale University Press.

Hurd, J. (1975). "Railways and the expansion of markets in India, 1861–1921", *Explorations in Economic History* 12:3, 263–88.

Husain, Z. (2011). "Health of the national rural health mission", *Economic and Political Weekly*, 22 January, 53–60.

Irudaya Rajan, S. & K. James (2008). "Third national family health survey in India: issues, problems and prospects", *Economic and Political Weekly*, 29 November, 33–8.

Isham, J. *et al.* (2005). "The varieties of resource experience: natural resource export structures and the political economy of economic growth", *World Bank Economic Review* 19:2, 141–74.

Jaffrelot, C. (2003). *India's Silent Revolution: The Rise of the Lower Castes in North India*. London: Hurst.

Jayachandran, S. & R. Pande (2013). "Choice not genes: probable cause for the India-Africa child height gap", *Economic and Political Weekly*, 24 August, 77–9.

Jeffrey, R. & A. Doron (2012). "Mobile-izing: democracy, organization and India's first 'mass mobile phone' elections", *Journal of Asian Studies* 71:1, 63–80.

Jeffrey, C., P. Jeffrey & R. Jeffrey (2005). "Reproducing difference? Schooling, jobs, and empowerment in Uttar Pradesh, India", *World Development* 33:12, 2085–101.

Jenkins, R. (2019). "Business interests and state autonomy in India", in E. Chatterjee & M. McCartney (eds), *Class and Conflict: Revisiting Pranab Bardhan's Political Economy of India*. New Delhi: Oxford University Press.

Jha, P. *et al.* (2006). "Low male-to-female sex ratio of children born in India: national survey of 1.1 million households", *The Lancet*, 367:9506, 185–6.

Jodhka, S. (2008). "Caste and the corporate sector", *Indian Journal of Industrial Relations* 44:1, 185–93.

John, M. (2011). "Census 2011: governing populations and the girl child", *Economic and Political Weekly*, 16 April, 10–12.

Johnson, C. & M. Bowles (2010). "Making the grade? Private education in northern India", *Journal of Development Studies* 46:3, 485–505.

Jones, B. & B. Olken (2008). "The anatomy of start-stop growth", *Review of Economics and Statistics*, 90:3, 582–87.

Jong-a-Pin, R. & J. De Haan (2011). "Political regime change, economic liberalization and growth accelerations", *Public Choice* 146, 93–115.

Jose, S. (2011). "Adult undernutrition in India: is there a huge gender gap?", *Economic and Political Weekly*, 16 July, 95–102.

Jose, S. & K. Kavaneetham (2008). "A factsheet on women's malnutrition in India", *Economic and Political Weekly*, 16 August, 61–7.

Jose, S. & K. Navanaatham (2010). "Social infrastructure and women's malnutrition", *Economic and Political Weekly*, 27 March, 83–9.

Joseph, K. & K. Harilal (2001). "Structure and growth of India's IT exports: implications of an export-orientated growth strategy", *Economic and Political Weekly*, 25 August, 3263–70.

Joseph, R. (2011). "The R&D scenario in Indian pharmaceutical industry", RIS Discussion Paper No. 176, New Delhi.

Joshi, S. (2004). "Tertiary sector-driven growth in India: impact on employment and poverty", *Economic and Political Weekly*, 11 September, 4175–8.

Joshi, V. (2016). *India's Long Road: The Search for Prosperity*. Gurgaon: Penguin.

Joshi, V. & I. Little (1994). *India: Macroeconomics and Political Economy, 1964–1991*. New Delhi: Oxford University Press.

Kabeer, N. & S. Mahmud (2004). "Globalisation, gender and poverty: Bangladesh women workers in export and local markets", *Journal of International Development* 16:1, 93–109.

Kaldor, N. (1967). *Strategic Factors in Economic Development*. Ithaca, NY: Cornell University Press.

Kalhan, A. & M. Franz (2009). "Regulation of retail: comparative experience", *Economic and Political Weekly*, 8 August, 56–64.

Kannan, K. & G. Raveendran (2009). "Growth sans employment: a quarter century of jobless growth in India's organised manufacturing", *Economic and Political Weekly*, 7 March, 80–91.

Kapur, D. (2007). "The causes and consequences of India's IT boom", in B. Nayar (ed.), *Globalization and Politics in India*. New Delhi: Oxford University Press.

Kaur, P. (2007). "Growth acceleration in India", *Economic and Political Weekly*, 14 April, 1380–6.

Kaviraj, S. (1988). "A critique of the passive revolution", *Economic and Political Weekly*, special issue, 2429–44.

Keefer, P. & S. Khemani (2004). "Why do the poor receive poor services?", *Economic and Political Weekly*, 28 February, 935–43.

Khattry, B. & J. Rao (2002). "Fiscal faux pas? An analysis of the revenue implications of trade liberalisation", *World Development* 30:8, 1431–44.

Khera, R. (2011a). "Revival of the public distribution system: evidence and explanations", *Economic and Political Weekly*, 5 November, 36–50.

Khera, R. (2011b). "India's public distribution system: utilisation and impact", *Journal of Development Studies* 47:7, 1038–60.

Knack, S. & P. Keefer (1997). "Does social capital have an economic payoff: a cross-country investigation", *Quarterly Journal of Economics* 112, 1251–88.

Khan, M. (2010). *Governance Capabilities and the Property Rights Transition in Developing Countries.* Department of Economics, SOAS, London.

Khera, R. & N. Nayak (2009). "Women workers and perceptions of the national rural employment guarantee act", *Economic and Political Weekly*, 24 October, 49–57.

Kidron, M. (1965). *Foreign Investments in India.* Oxford: Oxford University Press.

Kijima, Y. (2006). "Why did wage inequality increase? Evidence from urban India, 1983–99", *Journal of Development Economics* 81:1, 97–117.

Kingdon, G. (1996a). "The quality and efficiency of private and public education: a case-study of urban India", *Oxford Bulletin of Economics and Statistics* 58:1, 57–82.

Kingdon, G. (1996b). "Private schooling in India: size, nature and equity effects", *Economic and Political Weekly*, 21 December, 3306–14.

Kingdon, G. (2007). "The progress of school education in India", *Oxford Review of Economic Policy* 23:2, 168–95.

Kingdon, G. *et al.* (2005). "Education and literacy", in T. Dyson, R. Cassen & L. Visaria (eds), *Twenty-First Century India: Population, Economy, Human Development, and the Environment.* Oxford: Oxford University Press.

Kingdon, G. & M. Muzammil (2013). "The school governance environment in Uttar Pradesh, India: implications for teacher accountability and effort", *Journal of Development Studies* 49:2, 251–69.

Kingdon, G. & V. Sipahimalani-Rao (2010). "Para-teachers in India: status and impact", *Economic and Political Weekly*, 20 March, 59–67.

Kite, G. (2013). "India's software and IT services revolution: a teacher to treasure", *Economic and Political Weekly*, 27 July, 164–72.

Klasen, S. & C. Wink (2003). "'Missing Women': Revisiting the Debate", *Feminist Economics* 9:2/3, 263–99.

Kochhar, K. *et al.* (2006). "India's pattern of development: what happened, what follows?", IMF Working Paper, WP/06/22. Washington, DC: IMF.

Kohli, A. (1990). *Democracy and Discontent: India's Growing Crisis of Governability*. Cambridge: Cambridge University Press.

Kohli, A. (2004). *State-Directed Development: Political Power and Industrialisation in the Global Periphery*. Cambridge: Cambridge University Press.

Kohli, A. (2006). "Politics of economic growth in India, Part I: the 1980s", *Economic and Political Weekly*, 1 April, 1251–9.

Kohli, A. (2012). *Poverty Amid Plenty in the New India*. Cambridge: Cambridge University Press.

Kohli, R. & J. Bhagwati (2013). "Organised retailing in India: issues and outlook", in J. Bhagwati & A. Panagariya (eds), *Reforms and Economic Transformation in India*. New Delhi: Oxford University Press.

Kothari, B. & T. Bandyopadhyay (2010). "Can India's 'literate' read?", *International Review of Education* 56:5/6, 705–28.

Kotwal, A., B. Ramaswami & W. Wadhwa (2011). "Economic liberalisation and Indian economic growth: what's the evidence", *Journal of Economic Literature* 49:4, 1152–99.

Kravdal, O. (2004). "Child mortality in India: the community-level effect of education", *Population Studies* 58:2, 177–92.

Kremer, M. *et al.* (2005). "Teacher absence in India: a snapshot", *Journal of the European Economic Association* 3:2/3, 658–67.

Krishna, A. & V. Brihmadesam (2006). "What does it take to become a software professional?", *Economic and Political Weekly*, 29 July, 3307–14.

Krishna, A. (2010). *One Illness Away: Why People Become Poor and How They Escape Poverty*. Oxford: Oxford University Press.

Kumar, N. (2001). "Indian software industry development: international and national perspective", *Economic and Political Weekly*, 10 November, 4278–90.

Kurian, N. (2000). "Widening regional disparities in India: some indicators", *Economic and Political Weekly*, 12 February, 539–50.

Kumar, A. (2017). *Demonetisation and the Black Economy*. New Delhi: Penguin Random House.

Kumar, N. (2000). "Mergers and acquisitions by MNEs: patterns and implications", *Economic and Political Weekly*, 5 August, 2851–8.

Kumar, S., A. Heath & O. Heath (2002a). "Determinants of social mobility in India", *Economic and Political Weekly*, 20 July, 2983–7.

Kumar, S., A. Heath & O. Heath (2002b). "Changing patterns of social mobility: some trends over time", *Economic and Political Weekly*, 5 October, 4091–6.

Kurian, N. (2000). "Widening regional disparities in India: some indicators", *Economic and Political Weekly*, 12 February, 539–50.

Kurosaki, T. (1999). "Agriculture in India and Pakistan, 1900–95: productivity and crop mix", *Economic and Political Weekly*, A160–8.

Kuznets, S. (1955). "Economic growth and income inequality", *American Economic Review* 45:1, 1–28.

Lakatos, C. & T. Fukui (2014). "The liberalization of retail services in India", *World Development* 59, 327–40.

Lal, D. (1998). *Unintended Consequences: The Impact of Factor Endowments, Culture, and Politics on Long-Run Economic Performance*. Cambridge, MA: MIT Press.

Lall, S. (1999). "India's manufacturing exports: comparative structure and prospects", *World Development* 27:10, 1769–86.

Leftwich, A. (1995). "Bringing politics back in: towards a model of the developmental state", *Journal of Development Studies* 31:3, 400–27.

Leftwich, A. (2000). *States of Development: On the Primacy of Politics in Development*. Cambridge: Polity.

Lerche, J. (2014). "Regional patterns of agrarian accumulation in India", paper presented at the Foundation for Agrarian Studies, Tenth Anniversary Conference, Kochi, 9–12 January.

Levien, M. (2011). "Special economic zones and accumulation by dispossession in India", *Journal of Agrarian Change* 11:4, 454–83.

Little, I., D. Mazumdar & J. Page (1987). *Small Manufacturing Enterprises: A Comparative Analysis of India and Other Economies*. New York: Oxford University Press.

Loriaux, M. (1999). "The French developmental state as myth and moral ambition", in M. Woo-Cumings (ed.), *The Developmental State in Historical Perspective*. New York: Cornell University Press.

Manhoff, A. (2005). "Banned and enforced: the immediate answer to a problem without an immediate solution: how India can prevent another generation of missing girls", *Vanderbilt Journal of Transnational Law* 38, 889–920.

Marjit, S. & S. Kar (2009). "A contemporary perspective on the informal labour market: theory, policy and the Indian experience", *Economic and Political Weekly*, 4 April, 60–71.

Mascarenhas, R. (1982). *Technology Transfer and Development: India's Hindustan Machine Tools Company*. Boulder, CO: Westview.

Mathur, A., S. Das & S. Sircar (2006). "Status of agriculture in India: trends and prospects", *Economic and Political Weekly*, 30 December, 5327–36.

Mazumdar, D. & S. Sarkar (2004). "Reforms and employment elasticity in organised manufacturing", *Economic and Political Weekly*, 3 July, 3017–29.

McCartney, M. (2009). *India: The Political Economy of Growth, Stagnation and the State, 1951–2007*. Abingdon: Routledge.

McCartney, M. (2015). *Economic Growth and Development: A Comparative Introduction*. London: Palgrave Macmillan.

McCartney, M. & I. Roy (2016). "A consensus unravels: NREGA and the paradox of rules-based welfare in India", *European Journal of Development Research* 28:4, 588–604.

Mehrotra, S. (1990). *India and the Soviet Union: Trade and Technology Transfer*. New Delhi: Oxford University Press.

Mehrotra, S. *et al.* (2013). "Turnaround in India's employment story: silver lining amidst joblessness and informalisation?", *Economic and Political Weekly*, 31 August, 87–96.

Mehrotra, S. & J. Parida (2017). "Why is the labour force participation of women declining in India?", *World Development* 98, 360–80.

Mehta, B. & S. Sarkar (2010). "Income inequality in India: Pre- and post-reform periods", *Economic and Political Weekly*, 11 September, 45–55.

Menon, P., K. Raabe & A. Bhaskar (2009). "Biological, programmatic and sociopolitical dimensions of child undernutrition in three states in India", *IDS Bulletin* 40:4, 60–9.

Ministry of Finance (Government of India) (2016). Available at: https://www.india budget.gov.in/budget2013-2014/es2012-13/estat1.pdf (accessed 28 May 2019).

Mishra, S. (2006). "Farmers suicides in Maharashtra", *Economic and Political Weekly*, 22 April, 1538–45.

Mishra, P. (2013). "Has India's growth story withered?", *Economic and Political Weekly*, 13 April, 51–9.

Misra, A.-M. (2000). "Business culture and entrepreneurship in British India, 1860–1950", *Modern Asian Studies* 34:2, 333–48.

Mitra, A. (2005). *Terms of Trade and Class Relations: An Essay in Political Economy*. New Delhi: Chronicle Books.

Mody, A., A. Nath & M. Walton (2011). "Sources of corporate profits in India: business dynamism or advantages of entrenchment?", IMF Working Paper WP/11/8. Washington, DC: IMF.

Mohan, R. (2002). "Small scale industry policy in India: a critical evaluation", in A. Krueger (ed.), *Economic Policy Reforms and the Indian Economy*. New Delhi: Oxford University Press.

Mohan, R. & M. Kapur (2015). "Pressing the Indian growth accelerator: policy imperatives", IMF Working Paper WP/15/53. Washington, DC: IMF.

Mohanty, M. (2007). "Political economy of agrarian transformation: another view of Singur", *Economic and Political Weekly*, 3 March, 737–41.

Mooij, J. (1998). "Food policy and politics: the political economy of the public distribution system in India", *Journal of Peasant Studies* 25:2, 77–101.

Mooij, J. (1999). "Food policy in India: the importance of electoral politics in policy implementation", *Journal of International Development* 11, 625–36.

Morris, M. (1967). "Values as an obstacle to economic growth in South Asia: an historical survey", *Journal of Economic History* 27:4, 588–607.

Morris, M. (1979). "South Asian entrepreneurship and the Rashomon effect, 1800–1947", *Explorations in Modern Economic History* 16, 341–61.

Mukherjee, A. (2007). "The return of the colonial in Indian economic history: the last phase of colonialism in India", presidential address to the Indian History Congress, December, New Delhi.

Mukherjee, A. (2013). "The service sector in India", ADB Economics Working Paper Series No. 352. Manila, Philippines.

Mundle, S. & M. Govinda Rao (1991). "Volume and composition of government subsidies in India, 1987–88", *Economic and Political Weekly*, 4 May, 1157–72.

Munshi, K. (2004). "Social learning in a heterogeneous population: technology diffusion in the Indian Green Revolution", *Journal of Development Economics* 73, 185–213.

Munshi, K. & M. Rosenzweig (2005). "Why is mobility in India so low? Social insurance, inequality and growth", CID Working Paper No. 121, Harvard University.

Muralidharan, K. & V. Sundararaman (2011). "Teacher performance: experimental evidence from India", *Journal of Political Economy* 119:1, 39–77.

Nagaraj, R. (1990). "Industrial growth: further evidence and towards an explanation and issues", *Economic and Political Weekly*, 13 October, 2313–32.

Nagaraj, R. (2000a). "Indian economy since 1980: virtuous growth or polarisation?", *Economic and Political Weekly*, 5 August, 2831–3.

Nagaraj, N. (2000b). "Organised manufacturing employment", *Economic and Political Weekly*, 16 September, 3445–8.

Nagaraj, R. (2006). "Public sector performance since 1950: a fresh look", *Economic and Political Weekly*, 24 June, 2551–7.

Nagaraj, R. (2008). "India's recent economic growth: a closer look", *Economic and Political Weekly*, 12 April, 55–61.

Nagaraj, R. (2011). "Growth in organised manufacturing employment: a comment", *Economic and Political Weekly*, 19 March, 83–4.

Nambissan, G. (2012). "Private schools for the poor: business as usual?", *Economic and Political Weekly*, 13 October, 51–8.

Narayanamoorthy, A. (2007). "Deceleration in agricultural growth: technology fatigue of policy fatigue", *Economic and Political Weekly*, 23 June, 2375–9.

Naude, W. (2007). "Geography and development in Africa: overview and implications for regional cooperation", WIDER Discussion Paper No. 2007/03. Helsinki.

Nayyar, D. (1978). "Industrial development in India: some reflections on growth and stagnation", *Economic and Political Weekly*, special issue, 1265–78.

Nayyar, D. (2006). "Economic growth in independent India: lumbering elephant or running tiger", *Economic and Political Weekly*, 15 April, 1451–8.

Narayana, D., E. Mridul & M. Chandan (1992). "Growth, technical dynamism and policy change in the Indian motor vehicle industry", in A. Ghosh *et al.* (eds), *Indian Industrialization: Structure and Policy Issues*. New Delhi: Oxford University Press.

Neetha, N. (2002). "Flexible production, feminisation and disorganisation: evidence from the Tiruppur knitwear industry", *Economic and Political Weekly*, 25 May, 2045–52.

Nordhaus, W. (2006). "Geography and macroeconomics: new data and new findings", *Proceedings of the National Academy of Sciences* 103:10, 3510–17.

North, D. (1990). *Institutions, Institutional Change and Economic Performance*. Cambridge: Cambridge University Press.

North, D. (1994). "Economic performance through time", *American Economic Review* 84:3, 359–68.

North, D. (1995). "The new institutional economics and third world development", in J. Harriss, J. Hunter & C. Lewis (eds), *The New Institutional Economics and Third World Development*. London: Routledge.

Okada, A. (2004). "Skills development and interfirm learning linkages under globalisation: lessons from the Indian automobile industry", *World Development* 32:7, 1265–88.

Olson, M. (1993). "Dictatorship, democracy and development", *American Political Science Review* 87:3, 567–76.

Olson, M. (2000). *Power and Prosperity: Outgrowing Communist and Capitalist Dictatorships*. New York: Basic Books.

Pal, R. (2013). "Out-of-pocket health expenditure: impact on the consumption of Indian households", *Oxford Development Studies* 41:2, 258–79.

Panagariya, A. (2004). "India in the 1980s and 1990s: a triumph of reforms", IMF Working Paper, WP/04/43.

Panagariya, A. (2008). *India: The Emerging Giant*. New York: Oxford University Press.

Panagariya, A. (2013). "Does India really suffer from worse child malnutrition that sub-Saharan Africa?", *Economic and Political Weekly*, 4 May, 98–111.

Pandey, P., S. Goyal & V. Sundararman (2008). "Community participation in public schools: the impact of information campaigns in three Indian states", Policy Research Working Paper No. 4776. Washington, DC: World Bank.

Pardesi, M. & S. Ganguly (2010). "India and Pakistan: the origins of their different politico-military trajectories", *India Review* 9:1, 38–67.

Patibandla, M. & B. Petersen (2002). "Role of transnational corporations in the revolution of a high-tech industry: the case of India's software industry", *World Development* 30:9, 1561–77.

Patnaik, U. (2007). "Neoliberalism and rural poverty in India", *Economic and Political Weekly*, 28 July, 3132–50.

Pattnaik, I. & A. Shah (2010). "Is there a glimpse of dynamism in Orissa's agriculture", *Economic and Political Weekly*, 26 June, 756–9.

Pebley, A. & A. Amin (1991). "The impact of a public-health intervention on sex differentials in childhood mortality in rural Punjab, India", *Health Transition Review* 1:2, 143–67.

Perlitz, U. (2008). "India's pharmaceutical industry on course for globalisation", Deutsche Bank Research, Asia Current Issues, 9 April. Frankfurt.

Piketty, T. (2014). *Capital in the Twenty-First Century*. Cambridge, MA: Harvard University Press.

Pritchett, L. (2009). "Is India a flailing state? Detours on the four lane highway to modernisation", HKS Faculty Research Working Paper Series RWP09-013, Kennedy School of Government, Harvard University.

PROBE (1999). *Public Report on Basic Education*. Oxford: Oxford University Press.

Purfield, C. (2006). "Mind the gap: is economic growth in India leaving some states behind?", IMF Working Paper WP/06/103. Washington, DC: IMF.

Radhakrishna, R. (2005). "Food and nutrition security of the poor: emerging perspectives and policy issues", *Economic and Political Weekly*, 30 April, 1817–21.

Radhakrishna R. (2009). "Food consumption and nutritional status in India: emerging trends and perspectives", Working Papers id:2210, eSocialSciences.

Rahman, L. & V. Rao (2004). "The determinants of gender equity in India: examining Dyson and Moore's thesis with new data", *Population and Development Review* 30:2, 239–68.

Rahman, (2014). "Revival of rural public distribution system expansion and outreach", *Economic and Political Weekly*, 17 May, 62–8.

Ramachandran, V. & V. Rawal (2009). "The impact of liberalization and globalization on India's agrarian economy", *Global Labour Journal* 1:1, 56–91.

Ramesh, B. (2004). "Cyber coolies in BPO: insecurities and vulnerabilities of non-standard work", *Economic and Political Weekly*, 31 January, 492–7.

Rangarajan, C. (1982). "Industrial growth: another look", *Economic and Political Weekly*, annual Number April, 589–604.

Rangaraju, B., J. Tooley & P. Dixon (2012). "The private school revolution in Bihar: findings from a survey in Patna Urban", India Institute Study, New Delhi.

Rao, C. (2000). "Declining demand for food grains in rural India: causes and implications", *Economic and Political Weekly* 35:4, 201–06.

Ravindran, T. (1995). "Women's health in a rural poor population in Tamil Nadu", in M. Das Gupta, L. Chen & T. Krishnan (eds), *Women's Health in India: Risk and Vulnerability*. New Delhi: Open University Press.

Ray, P. (2015). "Rise and fall of industrial finance in India", *Economic and Political Weekly*, 31 January, 61–8.

Rodrik, D. (1995). "Getting interventions right: how South Korea and Taiwan grew rich", *Economic Policy* 10:20, 55–107.

Rodrik, D. (2006). "Industrial development: stylised facts and policies", Harvard University.

Rodrik, D. (2013). "Unconditional convergence in manufacturing", *Quarterly Journal of Economics* 128:1, 165–204.

Rodrik, D. & A. Subramanian (2004). "From Hindu growth to productivity surge: the mystery of the Indian growth transition", Harvard University.

Ross, M. (1999). "The political economy of the resource curse", *World Politics* 51:2, 297–322.

Rothermund, D. (1993). *An Economic History of India: From Pre-Colonial Times to 1991*, second edition. London: Routledge.

Roy, S. (2016). "Faltering manufacturing growth and employment: is 'making' the answer?", *Economic and Political Weekly*, 26 March, 35–42.

Roy, T. (2002). "Economic history and modern India: redefining the link", *Journal of Economic Perspectives* 16:3, 109–30.

Rudolph, L. & S. Rudolph (1987). *In Pursuit of Lakshmi: The Political Economy of the Indian State*. Chicago, IL: University of Chicago Press.

Sachs, J. *et al.* (2004). "Ending Africa's poverty trap", Brookings Papers on Economic Activity 1, 117–240.

Sahn, D. & D. Stifel (2003). "Progress towards the millenium development goals in Africa", *World Development* 31:1, 23–50.

Sapsford, D. & V. Balasubramanyan (1999). "Trend and volatility in the net barter terms of trade, 1900–92: new results from the application of a (not so) new method", *Journal of International Development* 11:6, 851–7.

Sarangapani, P. (2009). "Quality, feasibility and desirability of low cost private schooling", *Economic and Political Weekly*, 24 October, 67–9.

Sarangapani, P. & C. Winch (2010). "Tooley, Dixon and Gomathi on private education in Hyderabad: a reply", *Oxford Review of Education* 36:4, 499–515.

Saraswati, J. (2012). *Dot.compradors: Power and Policy in the Development of the Indian Software Industry*. London: Pluto Press.

Saraswati, J. (2013). "The IT industry and interventionist policy in India", in B. Fine, J. Saraswati & D. Tavasci (eds), *Beyond the Developmental State: Industrial Policy into the Twenty-First Century*. London: Pluto Press.

Sarkar, A. (2007). "Development and displacement: land acquisition in west Bengal", *Economic and Political Weekly*, 21 April, 1435–42.

Sastry, D. *et al.* (2003). "Sectoral linkages and growth prospects: reflections on the Indian economy", *Economic and Political Weekly*, 14 June, 2390–97.

Selvaraj, S. & A. Karan (2009). "Deepening health insecurity in India: evidence from national sample surveys since 1980s", *Economic and Political Weekly*, 3 October, 55–60.

Sen, K. & D. Das (2015). "Where have all the workers gone? Puzzle of declining labour intensity in organised Indian manufacturing", *Economic and Political Weekly*, 6 June, 108–15.

Sen, A. & Himanshu (2004). "Poverty and inequality in India – I", *Economic and Political Weekly*, 18 September, 4247–63.

Sen, K. (2007). "Why did the elephant start to trot? India's growth acceleration re-examined", *Economic and Political Weekly*, 27 October, 37–47.

Sen, K. (2009). "What a long strange trip it's been: reflections on the causes of India's growth miracle", *Contemporary South Asia* 17:4, 363–77.

Sen, K. & S. Kar (2014). "Boom and bust? A political economy reading of India's growth experience, 1993–2013", IEG Working Paper No. 342. New Delhi.

Shah, A. (2014). *The Army and Democracy: Military Politics in Pakistan*. Cambridge, MA: Harvard University Press.

Sharma, A. (2006). "Flexibility, employment and labour market reforms in India", *Economic and Political Weekly*, 27 May, 2078–85.

Shergill, H. & G.Singh (1995). "Poverty in Rural Punjab: trend over green revolution decades", *Economic and Political Weekly*, 24 June.

Sheth, D. (1999). "Secularisation of caste and making of new middle class", *Economic and Political Weekly*, 21 August, 2503–10.

Shetty, S. (1978). "Structural retrogression in the Indian economy since the mid-sixties", *Economic and Political Weekly*, annual number, February, 185–244.

Shukla, S. (2014). "Mid-day meal: nutrition on paper, poor food on the plate", *Economic and Political Weekly*, 15 February, 51–7.

Sidhu, H. (2002). "Crisis in agrarian economy in Punjab: some urgent steps", *Economic and Political Weekly*, 27 July, 3132–8.

Siddiqa, A. (2007). *Military Inc: Inside Pakistan's Military Economy*. London: Pluto Press.

Singh, S. (2004). "Future of mid-day meals", *Economic and Political Weekly*, 28 February, 998–1000.

Singh, N. (2005). "The idea of South Asia and the role of the middle class". Stanford Centre for International Development, Working Paper No. 243.

Singh, N. (2006). "Services-led industrialisation in India: assessment and lessons", Department of Economics, University of Santa Cruz.

Sinha, A. (2007). "The changing political economy of federalism in India: a historical-institutionalist approach", in B. Nayar (ed.), *Globalization and Politics in India*. New Delhi: Oxford University Press.

Sivasubramonian, A. (2004). *The Sources of Economic Growth in India, 1950/51 to 1999/00*. New Delhi: Oxford University Press.

Sood, A., P. Nath & S. Ghosh (2014). "Deregulating capital, regulating labour: the dynamics in the manufacturing sector in India", *Economic and Political Weekly*, 28 June, 58–68.

Spears, D. (2012). "Increasing average exposure to open defecation in India, 2001–2011", Centre for Development Economics, Delhi School of Economics.

Spears, D. (2013). "The nutritional value of toilets: how much international variation in child height can sanitation explain?", Centre for Development Economics, Delhi School of Economics.

Sridharan, E. (2004). "The growth and sectoral composition of India's middle class: its impact on the politics of liberalisation", *India Review* 3:4, 405–28.

Srinivasan, S. & A. Bedi (2007). "Domestic violence and dowry: evidence from a south Indian village", *World Development* 35:5, 857–80.

Stiglitz, J. (2013). *The Price of Inequality*. New York: Norton.

Strauss, J. & D. Thomas (1998). "Health, nutrition and economic development", *Journal of Economic Literature* 36:2, 766–817.

Studer, R. (2008). "India and the great divergence: assessing the efficiency of grain markets in eighteenth and nineteenth century India", *Journal of Economic History* 68:2, 393–437.

Subramanian, A. (2007). "The evolution of institutions in India and its relationship with economic growth", *Oxford Review of Economic Policy* 23:2, 196–220.

Subramanian, A. (2018). *Of Counsel: The Challenges of the Modi-Jaitley Economy*. New Delhi: Penguin Viking.

Sudha, S. & S. Rajan (1999). "Female demographic disadvantage in India 1981–1991: sex selective abortions and female infanticide", *Development and Change* 30:3, 585–618.

Sundar, K. (2004). "Lockouts in India, 1961–2001", *Economic and Political Weekly*, 25 September, 4377–85.

Sundaram, K., L. Jain & S. Tendulkar (1988). "Dimensions of rural poverty: an inter-regional profile", *Economic and Political Weekly*, 19 November, 2395–408.

Sundaram, K. & S. Tendulkar (2003). "Poverty among social and economic groups in India in 1990s", *Economic and Political Weekly*, 13 December, 5263–76.

Tanzi, V. (2001). "Globalisation and the work of fiscal termites", *Finance and Development* 38:1, 34–7.

Teitelbaum, E. (2006). "Was the Indian labor movement ever co-opted", *Critical Asian Studies* 38:4, 389–417.

Thamarajakshi, R. (1990). "Intersectoral terms of trade revisited", *Economic and Political Weekly*, 31 March, A-48-52.

Thomas, J. (2012). "India's labour market during the 2000s: surveying the changes", *Economic and Political Weekly*, 22 December, 39–51.

Thorat, S. & P. Attewell (2007). "The legacy of social exclusion: a correspondence study of job discrimination in India", *Economic and Political Weekly*, 13 October, 4141–5.

Thorat, S. & A. Dubey (2012). "Has growth been socially inclusive during 1993–94 – 2009–10?", *Economic and Political Weekly*, 10 March, 43–54.

Thorat, S. & K. Newman (2007). "Caste and economic discrimination: causes, consequences and remedies", *Economic and Political Weekly*, 13 October, 4121–4.

Thorat, S. & N. Sadana (2009). "Discrimination and children's nutritional status in India", *IDS Bulletin* 40:4, 25–9.

Tilak, J. (2008). "Education in 2008-09 Union Budget", *Economic and Political Weekly*, 17 May, 49–56.

Timberg, T. (1971). "A study of a great Marwari firm: 1860–1914", *Indian Economic and Social History Review* 8:3, 264–83.

Tooley, J. & P. Dixon (2006). "'De facto' privatisation of education and the poor: implications of a study from sub-Saharan Africa and India", *Compare* 36:4, 443–62.

Tooley, J. & P. Dixon (2007). "Private schooling for low-income families: a census and comparative survey in East Delhi, India", *International Journal of Educational Development* 27:2, 205–19.

Tooley, J., P. Dixon & S. Gomathi (2007). "Private schools and the millennium development goal of universal primary education: a census and comparative survey in Hyderabad, India", *Oxford Review of Education* 33:5, 539–60.

Topalova, P. (2004). "Overview of the Indian corporate sector: 1989–2002", IMF Working Paper 04/64.

Tripathi, D. & J. Jumani (2007). *The Concise Oxford History of Indian Business*. New Delhi: Oxford University Press.

Tudor, M. (2013). *The Promise of Power: The Origins of Democracy in India and Autocracy in Pakistan*. New Delhi: Cambridge University Press.

Ulrich, Y. (1989). "Cross-cultural perspectives on violence against women", *Response Nursing Network on Violence Against Women* 12, 21–3.

Unisa, S., S. Pujari & R. Usha (2007). "Sex selective abortion in Haryana: evidence from pregnancy and antenatal care", *Economic and Political Weekly*, 6 January, 60–66.

Unni, J. (1998). "Gender differentials in schooling in gender, population and development", in M. Krishnaraj, R. Subarshan & A. Shariff (eds), *Gender, Population and Development*. New Delhi: Oxford University Press.

Unni, J. & G. Raveendran (2007). "Growth of employment 1993/04 to 2004/05: illusion of exclusiveness?", *Economic and Political Weekly*, 20 January, 196–9.

Vaidyanathan, A. (1977). "Constraints on growth and policy options", *Economic and Political Weekly*, 17 September, 1643–50.

Vakulabharanam, V. (2010). "Does class matter? Class structure and worsening inequality", *Economic and Political Weekly*, 17 July, 67–76.

Vakulabharanam, V. & S. Motiram (2011). "Political economy of agrarian distress in India since the 1990s", in S. Ruparelia *et al.* (eds), *Understanding India's New Political Economy: A Great Transformation*. Abingdon: Routledge.

van de Walle, D. (1985). "Population growth and poverty: another look at the Indian time series data", *Journal of Development Studies* 21:3, 429–39.

Vanaik, A. (1990). *The Painful Transition: Bourgeois Democracy in India*. London: Verso.

Vanaik, A. & Siddhartha (2008). "Bank payments: end of corruption in NREGA", *Economic and Political Weekly*, 26 April, 33–9.

Varma, P. (1998). *The Great Indian Middle Class*. New Delhi: Viking.

Varshney, A. (1998). *Democracy, Development and the Countryside: Urban-Rural Struggles in India*. Cambridge: Cambridge University Press.

Vaz, L. & S. Kanekar (1990). "Predicted and recommended behaviour of a woman as a function of her inferred helplessness in the dowry and wife-beating predicaments", *Journal of Applied Psychology* 20, 751–70.

Veeramani, C. (2007). "Sources of India's export growth in pre- and post-reform periods", *Economic and Political Weekly*, 23 June, 2419–27.

Virmani, A. (2004a). "India's economic growth from socialist rate of growth to Bharatiya rate of growth", ICRIER Working Paper No. 122, New Delhi.

Virmani, A. (2004b). "Sources of India's economic growth: trends in total factor productivity", ICRIER Working Paper No. 131, New Delhi.

Virmani, A. & D. Hashim (2011). "J-curve of productivity and growth: Indian manufacturing post-liberalization", IMF Working Paper, WP/11/163, Washington.

Visaria, L. (2005). "Mortality trends and the health transition", in T. Dyson, R. Cassen & L. Visaria (eds), *Twenty-First Century India: Population, Economy, Human Development, and the Environment*. Oxford: Oxford University Press.

Wallack, J. (2003). "Structural breaks in Indian macroeconomic data", *Economic and Political Weekly*, 11 October, 4312–15.

Walton, M. (2009). "The political economy of India's malnutrition puzzle", *IDS Bulletin* 40:4, 16–24.

Walton, M. (2011). "Inequality, rents and the long-run transformation of India", Kennedy School of Government, Harvard University.

Weil, D. (2005). *Economic Growth*. London: Addison-Wesley.

Swank, D. (2003). "Withering welfare? Globalisation, political economic institutions, and contemporary welfare states", in L. Weiss (ed.), *States in the Global Economy: Bringing Domestic Institutions Back In*. Cambridge: Cambridge University Press.

Wolpert, S. (1996). *Nehru: A Tryst with Destiny*. New Delhi: Oxford University Press.

Woods, D. (2004). "Latitude or rectitude: geographical or institutional determinants of development", *Third World Quarterly* 25:8, 1401–14.

World Bank (2009). *World Development Report 2009: Reshaping Economic Geography*. Washington, DC: World Bank.

World Bank (2018). *World Development Indicators*. Available at: https://datacatalog.worldbank.org/dataset/world-development-indicators (accessed 28 May 2019).

World Economic Forum (2006). *The Global Competitiveness Report, 2006–07*. Geneva.

World Economic Forum (2014). *The Global Competitiveness Report, 2014–15*. Geneva.

World Health Organisation (2008). *World Malaria Report 2008*. Geneva.

Wu, Y. (2004). "Rethinking the Taiwanese developmental state", *The China Quarterly* 177:91, 91–114.

Zagha, R. (1999). "Labour and India's economic reforms", in J. Sachs, A. Varshney & N. Bajpai (eds), *India in the Era of Economic Reforms*. New Delhi: Oxford University Press.

Index